PAPER TRAILS

Paper Trails

A GUIDE TO PUBLIC RECORDS IN CALIFORNIA

SECOND EDITION

by Stephen Levine
and Barbara T. Newcombe

Center for Investigative Reporting
SAN FRANCISCO

California Newspaper Publishers Association
SACRAMENTO

Paper Trails
A Guide to Public Records in California
second edition

Book design and production: Peter Ivey
Cover illustration: Robert Arnold

ISBN: 0-9621793-2-9
Library of Congress Card Catalog Number: 95-70276

Center for Investigative Reporting
500 Howard St., Suite 206
San Francisco, CA 94105

California Newspaper Publishers Association
1225 8th Street, Suite 260
Sacramento, CA 95814

10 9 8 7 6 5 4 3 2 1

Printed in the United States of America

Contents

Acknowledgments

As recently as 1987, the makings of this book were contained on hundreds of individual pieces of paper in dozens of file folders in two cardboard boxes at the Center for Investigative Reporting. A guide of this type can only graduate from such a state and come into being through the collaboration and efforts of many individuals. David Kaplan at the Center for Investigative Reporting realized the potential for a resource like *Paper Trails* and guided the project through difficult times and contributed the editing expertise that shapes much of the book.

The California Newspaper Publishers Association, thanks in large part to the vision of Terry Francke, decided to underwrite the publishing cost of the first edition. Jack Bates and Thomas Newton at CNPA saw the need to keep this project alive when they stepped forward and, with the help of Dan Noyes, Rick Tulsky and Becky Clark at CIR, made the production of a second edition possible. CIR has over the years provided a steady and stable home for the project, contributed editorial resources, a lot of advice, the services of many exceptional interns, and other invaluable intangible support.

A great deal of credit goes to Dan Noyes of the Center, who saw the need for this type of guide many years ago and somehow preserved the research until time could bring it to pass, and who provided continuous encouragement toward completion of the second edition. Mae Churchill at the Urban Policy Research Institute in Los Angeles agreed to contribute the original 1970s research conducted by Michael Miller.

This edition has benefited greatly from the research, reporting, and writing skills of two exceptional CIR interns: Caitlin Babb and Alethea Yip. CIR staff member Maria Sison provided truly invaluable assistance and support at crucial times. CIR interns Josh Romonek and Amy McCabe Heibel also contributed to this project. Their intelligence, sincerity, and dedication will take them far in whatever areas they choose.

CIR staff member James Curtiss played a key role in the emergence of both editions with the contribution of his copy editing experience, production knowledge and encouraging words. San Francisco city librarian Laura Lent is responsible for most of the research in education. Peter Ivey is the designer whose visual acumen makes this book easier for the rest of us to use.

Many officials patiently explained the intricacies of government to us. We would like to thank Gerald de Maria, Alex Kline, Ellie Kimbrough, Bernice Peterson, Rick Castro, Richard Iglehard, and William Mehrwein, all of whom contributed their knowledge of local government. At the state level assistance came from Lisa Buetler, Caren Daniels-Meade, Carrie Cornwell, Geeta Patel, Justin Keay, Joe Samora, and Melissa Warren. A special word of thanks goes to the staff at the Institute of Governmental Studies at the University of California

Berkeley. Thanks also go to Chris Mays and Ray Kiddy for contributing their knowledge of the California government Internet system.

The John D. and Catherine T. MacArthur Foundation, LEXIS-NEXIS, and Pillsbury Madison & Sutro provided support for this project through general assistance to CIR. Attorneys Judy Alexander and Ed Davis also assisted by contributing their time to CIR.

The authors and publishers also appreciate the assistance of Randy Fleming, Cathy Vanick, Nicole O'Hay and everyone at Publishers Group West for helping produce and distribute this guide.

For their help and encouragement thanks also go to present and former CIR staff and associates: Diana Hembree, Sarah Henry, Ricardo Sandoval, Sharon Tiller, Holly Ziemer, Sarah Bailey, George Clyde, Richard H. P. Sia, Eileen Siegel, Loren Stein, Steve Talbot, Meredith Thouron, Wendy Wank, Rick Young, Juan Avila-Hernandez, Rocky Kistner, Constance Matthiessen, Sue Ellen McCann, Eve Pell, Raul Ramirez, and David Weir.

Special thanks also go to Paul Downs, Melissa Crabbe, Adam Crocker, Patty Felkner, Brian Hill, Kemala Karmen, Susan LaCroix, Mike Mahoney, Margaret Phillips, Rosanne Spector, and our families.

—Stephen Levine and Barbara T. Newcombe

Introduction

"...access to information concerning the conduct of the people's business is a fundamental and necessary right of every person in this state."

—The California Public Records Act

Knowledge of the activities of government is essential for an informed citizenry to engage in a representative democracy. Information access through public records is the key to that knowledge. And while the authors of the California Public Records Act recognized the importance of citizen access to public information, they made no provisions for locating relevant records amid the ocean of information maintained by government agencies.

For many, the first edition of *Paper Trails* filled the gap between the right of access and the ability to obtain public records in California by serving as a road map to existing records. *Paper Trails* is not a "how-to" book. This has been better done elsewhere (see Bibliography). It is a "where-to" book—a guide to where to get started finding critical government information in the nation's most populous state.

Much has changed in the area of public records in the six years since the first edition of this book was published. While the number of California government agencies has grown during this time, the budgets and staff sizes of these agencies have shrunk significantly. This has led to an increase in the average workload of government employees which, in turn, has made it more difficult for public records researchers to gain help from beleaguered civil servants in identifying and locating information collected and stored by their agencies. An even more adverse condition has also taken shape: many records are no longer considered in the public sphere due to the actions of legislators, the courts, and agency officials. Also, in response to reduced budgets and staff sizes, many reporting requirements for state agencies have been eliminated, thereby eliminating whole categories of records.

In a more positive light, government agencies are increasingly storing public records in electronic format and moving toward making these records readily available to the public, either on computer disk or tape, through electronic bulletin boards or on the Internet. This is occurring at a slow pace, however, and largely as a result of the efforts of public records and open-government advocates.

This edition of *Paper Trails* addresses and reflects all these developments and changes. The entire book has been revised and updated to reflect records that have been either added or eliminated by any given agency, to indicate which records have changed in terms of public accessibility, which are available in computerized format, and to include all applicable changes in public records access. Telephone numbers for offices and divisions of state agencies have been added in this edition. Three appendices are now included: the first contains the full text of the California Public Records Act; the second has a sample public records request letter that may be used when writing to public agencies for records; the third contains a guide for connecting to electronic bulletin boards and Internet sites operated by California government agencies.

We have also expanded the state agency listings in this book to include twenty more agencies. This includes newly created agencies such as the California Environmental Protection Agency, the Department of Pesticide Regulation, and the Managed Risk Medical Insurance Board. Expanded listings are also given for records related to alcohol and drug treatment programs and facilities, education, emergency medical services, fair employment and housing, the State Bar, state government information service providers, the State Lottery, social services, and business and corporate listings, to name a few.

All these changes reflect important modifications in the way public records are stored, maintained, and made available to the public. We hope this guide will remain a useful and practical tool for journalists, academics, private investigators, attorneys, research professionals, activists, and lawmakers who tapped into the first edition, as well as for those encountering it for the first time.

How to Use this Guide

WHERE TO BEGIN

A001   *Paper Trails* contains descriptions of public records kept by government agencies. For each record identified, a title, description, and the contents of the record are given.

Each entry in this guide is accompanied by a number in the margin. These entry numbers are used to help identify records here, in the body of this text, and correspond to entry numbers used in the index of this guide. They do not correspond to any indexing or document record numbers used by any public agency.

Entry numbers that are preceded by an "A" indicate introductory material or descriptions of routine records common to most agencies; those preceded by a "C" indicate city or county records; by an "E," education records; by an "R," special district or regional government records; numbers that begin with an "S" are for state records. Information contained in appendices is not indexed.

Use the Index. The key to using this guide is the index. Specific agencies are listed both in the index and the text by the key word in the title. For example, see "Banking Department, State," not "State Banking Department." If you want information on a particular person, check the index entries under "names" or "names and addresses." For information on a corporation, look under "corporate information." For records on real estate ownership, check "real property ownership."

The focus is on records that contain primary information—that is, records not duplicated elsewhere. Many of these exist as a result of a law or regulation. Press releases, newsletters, and other publications are not included, except in isolated cases. Where information is confidential, publicly available summaries of that information are given. Because it has proved impossible to provide researchers with a complete guide to all state, regional, and local public records, this guide is an attempt to assist public records researchers uncover the most important documents and suggest what else remains.

Records listed in this guide are organized into four main sections as summarized in A002–A005. A separate section describing records routine to most agencies begins at A014.

A002   ***City and County Records.*** Virtually all types of city and county government offices are covered. Both the content and means of record-keeping varies from place to place. Entries are grouped by purpose or function (Health Services, Fire, Recorder, etc.), rather than department title, since titles are not standardized. These records are the keys to finding information on local real estate, local businesses, vital statistics (births, deaths, marriages), and government operations. Every local listing is coded with the letter "C" and a number.

A003   ***Education Records.*** Because of their number and complexity, records related to education are listed in a separate section. Sources of records range from local schools and school districts, through vocational and special schools, to the University of California. Each education listing is coded with an "E" and a number.

A004   ***Special District and Regional Records.*** The state Controller's office lists more than 5,000 "special districts" in California government, from mosquito abatement to mass transit. An overview of special districts is followed by a brief discussion of what kinds of records are available and how to research them further. Each district listing is coded with the letter "R" and a number.

A005   ***State Records.*** The state telephone book shows more than 150 entries for separate agencies ranging from the Governor's Office to the Colorado River Board. A recent study revealed more than 400 state boards and commissions. To include all of them would have made this book too heavy to lift. Instead, the number of offices covered has been pared down to 73 key agencies. For clues on how to research the others, refer to the Routine Records section (A014-A023). A more comprehensive list of state agencies can be found at the end of the state section (S720). Every state listing is coded with the letter "S" and a number.

A006   ***Federal Records.*** Thousands of federal records pertain to California. Although not covered here, several worthwhile guides are available through the federal government (see Bibliography).

A007   ***What a Record Is.*** The state Records Management Act of 1963 defines records as "all papers, maps, exhibits, magnetic or paper tapes, microfilm, photographic films and prints, digitized document images, punched cards, and other documents produced, received, owned or used by an agency, regardless of physical form or characteristics." Specifically excluded are "library and museum materials made or acquired and preserved solely for reference or exhibition purposes, and stocks of publications and printed (blank) forms…" The status of electronic mail messages is currently in dispute.

A008   ***How Records Are Arranged and Indexed.*** How the state's varied records are arranged and indexed is not standardized. State law may mandate that a record be kept, but not how it is kept. The maintenance and preservation of public records in California vary wildly. Names and categories of records change from office to office. Records kept by the county assessor, courts, recorder, and tax collector are exceptions for which arrangement and indexing systems are well organized and somewhat standardized. They are included here. "Arranged by" means how the individual records within a group or series are filed. "Indexed by" means how a separate finding or retrieval system is organized. As an example, criminal case files are arranged by the case number and indexed by the defendant's name. Property deeds are arranged by the recorder's book and page number (a sequential means of entering them as they are received) and indexed by the names of the grantor and grantee (seller and buyer).

A009   **_Computerization of Public Records._** There is an important difference between records maintained and stored in electronic format and those made available on-line via telephone line and computer modem. The first group includes all computerized records kept on magnetic disk or tape. Public records access laws cover information stored in this manner. It is rare to find a government department not in the throes of transferring records to electronic storage. Public records on-line include those records government agencies have made available for access through the Internet or electronic bulletin boards (BBS). Unfortunately, while many government agencies are moving to establish an on-line presence, most are not making public records available at these sites. A notable exception is the State Legislature, which maintains a multiservice Internet access point. Where, as this guide goes to press, records are stored in electronic format or made available by an agency on-line, it is noted within the record's descriptive entry in this guide. Information on how to find and connect to agencies on-line is provided in Appendix C. Commercial vendors (LEXIS-NEXIS, Dataquick, and others) buy entire groups of records, such as UCC, tax lien, and real property records, and resell them after making them accessible electronically. For a list of vendors see _A Public Records Primer_ (full citation in Bibliography).

PUBLIC ACCESS IS THE LAW

A010   **_The California Public Records Act._** In 1968, California legislators enacted the Public Records Act (Cal. Govt. Code 6250-6268), spelling out what many taxpayers had long argued: that state and local records, with certain exceptions, must be open to the public. A number of records are specifically exempted by state law. The withholding of other records, however, must be justified by government officials, who have to show that the public interest in not disclosing the information outweighs the public interest in disclosing it. This means that the burden of proof rests with the government, and that officials need to show good reason why they are unwilling to show you a particular record.

   The Public Records Act covers virtually all non-federal government offices in the state, including counties, cities, school districts, municipal corporations, special districts, political subdivisions, boards, and commissions. The act requires these agencies to adopt written guidelines for public access to records that "shall be posted in a conspicuous public place at the offices of such bodies."

   The California Public Records Act specifically provides the public the right to inspect and obtain a copy of a public record. The Act also imposes a duty on a public agency to segregate or take out exempted portions of a public record and make the remainder of the document available for public inspection and copying.

   There are important exceptions to the Public Records Act. Records of the courts and State Legislature are exempt from the provisions of the Act. However, the California State and U.S. constitutions have been interpreted to guarantee access to court records. Access to records of the State Legislature is covered by the Legislative Open Records Act (Cal. Gov. Code, Section 9070 *et seq.*). Also, any special provision for confidentiality or privilege found in any state law takes precedence over the act. This includes, for example, the attorney-client privilege in the Evidence Code and adoption records in the Civil Code. In addition, the Act itself specifically exempts certain records from public disclosure. These are listed in Section 6254 of the Act (see Appendix A).

Officials may adopt policies to minimize the disruption of normal office routine or exposure of the record to theft, change, or defacement. Unfortunately, this can result in rules that effectively restrict access. Also, search fees, while not authorized by the Act—which refers only to charges covering "direct costs of duplication"—can also be daunting and should be resisted if burdensome. The full text of the Public Records Act is included in Appendix A, and a sample records request letter is included in Appendix B. For a careful assessment of the Public Records Act, and your legal rights to see court and legislative records as well, consult the *Reporter's Handbook on Media Law* (see Bibliography).

Bear in mind that the uncooperative attitudes of some officials may not be due to a compulsive wish to hoard their precious files. Clerks and managers across the state complain, some with good reason, that their offices are under-staffed and that they have little time for taxpayers often unsure about what they're looking for. While enacting into law the right to see public records, state officials made no allowance for helping taxpayers find those records.

A011   In general, it is best not to accept the first "no" from a public official as an answer to a request for public records. You have the right to a written state-ment within 10 days, formally notifying you of the denial, citing the law that requires or justifies it, and signed by the person responsible for the decision. If you are skeptical of the legal justification for a denial, you may wish to consult an attorney familiar with the state Public Records Act.

A012   ***The Information Practices Act of 1977*** (Cal. Civil Code 1798-1798.76). The IPA gives anyone the right to see otherwise confidential personal information in records concerning his or her own person. The State Personnel Board publishes a guide to this Act (see Bibliography). To determine an individual's right to records containing personal information not held by a government agency, such as medical records held by a physician (covered under Cal. Health and Safety Code, Section 1795), consult the index to California Codes available in county law libraries.

PRESERVATION OF RECORDS

A013   Current or active records are usually maintained in public offices. Records that are inactive, obsolete, or otherwise unneeded may be destroyed, put into temporary storage and then destroyed, or saved indefinitely, usually in some sort of archive (see State Archives, S616). The "keep or destroy" rules for state records are quite carefully spelled out. Department heads generally try to keep all records as long as possible. When space runs out, they try to find off-site storage. At the local level, alert librarians and historical societies will offer to take records headed for destruction if they can find storage room.

The need for information and data has also created a problem of too much paper, with many government offices sinking beneath it. Government employees are sometimes unable to answer questions about information in records simply because there is too much there for one person to assimilate. To reduce frustration and more effectively plan a research strategy, public records researchers should be aware of the problems of record destruction, and of records misplaced or lost by agencies overloaded by too much information.

ROUTINE RECORDS

A014   Certain routine records are common to almost every government agency. Because they are routine and rarely change, except in format (such as microfilm or computerized), they will be described here, but not repeated in detail later. These widely available records are rich sources of information. Like other public records, the way they are organized can differ markedly from agency to agency.

A015   ***Annual Report.*** An annual summary of a department's activity. Not all annual reports are issued annually; a department's size and available money can determine frequency and format. Contents vary widely, but typically include the previous year's accomplishments, goals and objectives for the coming year, an organization chart, statistics, and details of services and programs. Note: Annual reports sometimes go by other names, including Organization and Program Overview, Fact Book, Area Plan Status Report, and Operational Plan Update.

A016   ***Audit.*** A formal examination and verification of records, usually involving finances. An auditor checks original documents, attests to their reliability, and judges the correctness of the information. Financial audit reports contain balance sheets and statements of earnings for the period covered. Internal audits are performed by government auditors. External audits, performed by outside certified public accountants, are required in some cases by state law. Special, or investigative, audits are performed if, for example, fraud is suspected. Compliance audits focus on the extent to which a program is adhering to controls and standards set by law. Other administrative audits, sometimes known as "management advisories," are done to assure that department policies and procedures to prevent fraud are being followed. If necessary, recommendations for change and warnings of future problems are presented. See also Auditor-Controller (C040).

A017   ***Budget.*** A detailed or summary financial plan of operations based on projected income and expense. Budgets are typically issued annually and include the following: estimates of funding sources (tax receipts allocated by law to individual funds, federal funds, fees received for licenses, inspections, penalties, etc.); estimates of expenditures for the coming fiscal year; outline of the year's operations based on these estimates; actual figures for the prior years and estimated figures for the immediately preceding year; a statement of function; a description of staff positions and salaries. See also Auditor-Controller (C040) and Department of Finance (S205).

A018   *Contract.* A legal agreement common to all agencies. Contracts are generally used when the agency is not qualified to perform a task or is required by law to have the job done by a non-government person or organization. Contracts can be for personal services, commodities, construction, or other services. Contents vary according to the purpose of the contract but typically include the following: date; name and address of contractor; dollar amount and term of contract; attachments including program performance standards, terms of payment, and performance bonds; insurance requirements; an audit of the contractors; special conditions (such as alternate funding, reimbursement rules, or disabled accessibility); program regulations (when and how reports must be filed, approval of changes, and records maintenance); and sanctions or penalties if regulations are not followed. A locality may also require statements of adherence to local regulations such as minority hiring, boycott of the nuclear industry, and not hiring or contracting with government employees or their family members.

A019   *Expenses, Vouchers.* Records of expenses paid for by officials and employees that have been reimbursed. Contents typically include employee's name, department no. or name, dates, destination, and reason for travel or other expense.

A020   *Grant Files.* Records of grants applied for and received by various agencies. Contents typically include application, receipts for money spent and received, and documents certifying that the funded program is being carried out appropriately. Any transfer of money for a specified purpose is sure to generate records that are public.

A021   *Licenses and Permits.* Formal certificates issued to regulate, register, and sometimes tax individuals and businesses. As used here the phrase includes certification and registration. State and local governments issue a wide variety of licenses and permits covering everything from hospitals to hog farms. Most state licenses relate to business and professional activities. Local licenses and permits may duplicate state business and professional licensing to some degree. Check the index under "Licenses and Permits" for a partial list. See also city and county Licenses and Permits (C284) and the state Department of Consumer Affairs (S100).

    Contents of application forms typically include applicant's name, residential and mailing address, phone, birthdate, related education and employment, physical description, photograph, and existence of any criminal conviction. Business applications also typically include business name, contact person, organization type, names of licensed employees or managers, corporate directors and officers, partners, residential addresses and phones, any requisite I.D. nos., related permits or licenses, and fees. Other attachments may include articles of incorporation or association, individual qualifications, disciplinary actions, and appeals. Note: Home addresses and phones of state licensees are confidential unless the home and business address are the same.

A022   **Purchase Order.** A record that a product or service has been authorized for purchase. Contents typically include the originating department, date, specifications, fund, authorization, supplier, and bid price (if any). Purchase orders must be approved by the auditor who "encumbers" the funds (verifies that the purchase is a proper one for which funds have already been budgeted and decreases that fund by the needed amount).

A023   **Reports.** Many agencies issue periodic reports outlining the goals or findings of particular projects, results of a study, recommendations for study, analysis of a problem, etc. Many reports are published and distributed free or for a small cost. For a quarterly listing of reports issued at the state level, consult the *List of Reports Prepared by State Agencies* (see Bibliography).

City and County Records

C001   Cities and counties derive their legal authority from the state, and are organized as either charter or general-law governments. Charter cities and counties are formed by a vote of the citizens and have more local control over how the government is organized. California has 58 counties, of which 10 are charter. San Francisco, a charter government, is the only combined city-county in the state.

Often the same services are provided by the city for its residents and by the county for residents of unincorporated areas. These may include, for example, parks and recreation, police, and fire protection.

Special districts are another form of local government, and are discussed in a later chapter. It should be noted that in the same geographic area a service such as parks and recreation may be carried out by a division of city or county government and also by a regional park district. An example is the East Bay Regional Park District, a special district, and the park and recreation departments of approximately 44 adjoining cities.

Commissions and boards are sometimes considered outside the regular political process. Originally they were seen as a means of getting politics out of government, reducing corruption, and increasing citizen participation. Members are typically appointed by a mayor, city council, board of supervisors, or a combination of these offices. Some boards and commissions manage or regulate their respective departments directly; others act only in an advisory capacity. When listed, boards and commissions usually appear in this guide under the area of their responsibility, such as "Police" or "Civil Service Commission."

Where local records are found depends on how local government is organized, and this can differ markedly from place to place. Airports, for example, are variously managed as separate city or county departments, as divisions of transportation departments or as independent authorities. Animal control may be organized as a separate department, or under a county sheriff's office, a city police department, a city or county health services department or a county department of agriculture. The county clerk may also be the registrar of voters, the recorder and the clerk of the superior court.

Because of the variety in local government, it is impossible to say that a function such as police or health will be found listed as such in all counties and cities. Therefore, local records are listed here by the most commonly accepted name or key word, with other names following.

Many cities and counties have established on-line computer links to a multitude of services. For example: electronic bulletin boards and Internet sites (for city public notices, listings, schedules, agendas, staff reports, license and purchasing information, and communications from various departments); electronic mail (messages to or from other system users including city council members); electronic conferences (discussion of community topics among city officials and the public); and library catalogs. Contact the city or county clerk directly to assess the status of particular government entities' on-line presence. Also see Appendix C for more information concerning on-line government access.

C002   **AGED AND AGING, AREA AGENCY ON AGING, SENIOR CITIZEN AFFAIRS**

City and County. Coordinates federal, state, local programs for seniors including day care, long-term care, legal and information services, transportation, nutrition, and ombudsman service for persons in nursing homes. Typically contracts for services with public and private non-profit organizations. May be organized separately or under Social Services, Health and Human Services, Community Services, etc. See Health Services (C232), and Department of Aging (S009) for other programs related to aging.

C003   *Area Plan Status Report.* A report mandated by the state to ensure that current operation and proposed plans conform to law. Contents: narrative, area demographics, status report for each activity (in-home services, mental health, etc.), funds awarded by recipients and purpose, objectives and target dates for each activity, and grant allocation plan.

C004   *Financial Closeout Report.* A monthly report mandated by the state to be filed for each type of service (support services, home-delivered meals or meals served) and for each contractor, showing details of costs of each type of service provided, source of funding, and reconciliation with budget. Contents (example used is for home-delivered meals): name and license number of contractor, budget period, person making report, date, expenditures, funding sources, calculation of earned funding, balance of earned funds to funds awarded and final calculation of costs over or under budget; funding, cost and earned income for each meal served.

C005   *Financial Closeout Report for Area Agency.* Results of all Financial Closeout Reports (C004) in one final report. Contents: costs, funding sources, matching and nonmatching contributions, grant income, federal share for each contractor or service provider, funding and cost per meal, and federal share of costs for each type of service (support, meals, long-term care, day care, etc.).

C006   *Management Information System Records.* Monthly data from each contractor or provider, each site and each project are used to produce a statewide computerized database. The county office receives a printout showing its performance compared to the contracted goal. Titles of required forms are: Home-Delivered Meals, Congregate Nutrition Site, Supportive Services, Monthly Pooled Resources and USDA Report—Nutrition Project Information. Contents (example used is Monthly Home-Delivered Meals Report): reporting agency and provider nos.; provider name; date, total meals prepared and delivered to seniors and non-seniors; number of days meals delivered; number of seniors on waiting list; total number of meals denied; number of nutrition counseling contacts; number of outreach contacts made in month; number of hours spent on outreach efforts; dollar amount of contributions; characteristics for each new senior served (age group, ethnicity, disability, non-English speaking, living alone, low income).

C007   *Program Monitoring Summary Report.* A summary of each contractor's performance. Contents: contractor's name, names of those present during examination, programs, monitoring date period, degree of compliance, recommendations, required action, name of program coordinator, comparison with previous review period, degree to which contractor is meeting service objectives and observations of activities (see Management Information System, C006).

C008 **AGRICULTURE**

County. Often combined with Weights and Measures. The Office of the Agricultural Commissioner is mandated by state law to enforce laws concerning insects injurious to agriculture, rodents, birds, predatory animals, weeds and plant diseases; control pesticide use; regulate produce and egg quality and the nursery industry; conduct pest-detection surveys; provide crop acreage and production statistics; give garden information and advice to homeowners; regulate "farmer's markets." All records are state mandated. See University of California Cooperative Extension.

C009 *Agricultural Pesticide Use Report.* For use of a product by pesticide control operators. Contents: location, application method, commodity or site treated, operator's name and address, date, time, equipment used, area or units treated, use permit number, customer, product used, label information, total amount used, targeted pest. Note: Growers/farmers file this report only when using restricted materials (C014). See also S520.

C010 *Agricultural Pesticide Use Report—Monthly Summary.* A monthly summary of the Pesticide Use Reports (C009).

C011 *Apiary Inspection Certificate.* For shipment of hives. Contents: control no., date, no. and size of hives, brands, if diseased, when destroyed, owner or shipper name and address, destination, inspector's name, address, phone.

C012 *Apiary Inspection Report.* A report of daily inspections. Contents: brand or I.D. no., county, date, colonies (no. of, number diseased), location, remarks, owner's name and address, inspector.

C013 *Apiary Registration.* A request by a beekeeper for prior notice of pesticide application. Contents: name, address, location, size of apiary, phone nos., date, signatures.

C014 *Application—Restricted Materials Permit.* Contents: same information as Notice of Intent (C016), plus justification for non-agricultural use, special restrictions, map (if agricultural properties involved).

C015 *Inspection Reports.* A record of inspection made at egg processors and at wholesalers of seed, nurseries, fruit, vegetable's, and honey. Contents: name, address, phone, quality of product, quarantine warning, non-compliance warnings.

C016 *Notice of Intent to Apply Restricted Materials.* For pesticide use. Contents: county, permit no., operator's name, address, name, address, location of application, size of area, method, pest, pesticide, environmental changes, date and time. Note: Not all pesticides are restricted.

C017 *Nursery and Seed Inspection.* Contents: nursery name and location; owner's name and mailing address; inspector's name; date; recheck of infested stock; areas for reception and isolation; whether producer or retailer; name of host stock; degree of infection; pest name; disposition; location, size and number of plants involved.

C018 *Pest Control Records Inspections.* A record of inspection and/or audit of types of business operations involving pesticides. Contents: permit no.; name, address, phone; location; date; time; compliance of operator, dealer, adviser, certified applicator; employer headquarters; pesticide storage site; remarks; follow-up (if required); acknowledgment of inspection; deadline for correction.

C019 *Pesticide Use Monitoring Inspections.* A record of inspections made at site of application. Contents: pesticide, registration and dosage; user's name, address, location, phone and permit no.; date and time, inspection of pre-application site, application,

(AGRICULTURE, CONT.)

field worker safety, mix/load, equipment, pesticide storage site, remarks, recommendation, signatures.

C020   **Structural Pest Control Inspection Report.** A record of inspection of applications made around or in buildings. Contents: name, address, license no., phone, date and time, type of inspection, location, area/pest, pesticide, usage details, specifics of application, safety procedures, equipment, etc.

C021   **Other Agriculture Licenses, Permits and Certificates.** Agricultural Pest Control Business; Agricultural Pest Control Operator; Farmer's Market Certificate; Maintenance Gardener Pest Control Business; Pest Control Adviser; Pest Control Aircraft Pilot; Pest Control Equipment; Pesticide Dealer Business; Pesticide Dealer's Designated Agent; Producer's Certificate.

C022   # AIRPORTS

City, County, or Regional. Airports may or may not be publicly operated. The City of Los Angeles has an independently chartered Department of Airports with authority for all airports in the metropolitan area; the San Francisco Airports Commission is appointed by the mayor; the Oakland airport is administered by the Port of Oakland, an autonomous city agency; the City of San Diego's Airport Division under General Services develops and operates two airfields; the Regional Airport Planning Committee coordinates airport planning for the San Francisco Bay Area. There are seventeen special districts that function as airports. Note: Airports are closely regulated by the U.S. Federal Aviation Administration. See state Department of Transportation, Division of Aeronautics (S656), for records required at that level.

C023   **Airport Leases.** Many different forms are used: termination of agreement, lease completion form, preferential nonexclusive use permits, disposition and development agreement, rent credit property department invoice, lease inspection sheets, etc.

C024   **Airport Maps.** Maps and plans of airport's and surrounding buildings and roads.

C025   **Noise Monitoring Reports.** Quarterly sampling statistics required by the state if the county has designated the airport as a noise problem. Reports are filed with the county, then forwarded to the state. Contents: monitoring site, date, time, data.

C026   **Weather Reports.** Contents: surface observations (U.S. MF1-10C), river and climatological observations (Weather Service Form E-15), Station Inspection Reports (Weather Service Form B-33).

C027   # ANIMAL CONTROL, ANIMAL SERVICES, ANIMAL REGULATION

City and County. Enforces state and local laws concerning animals. Main responsibilities include controlling stray animals (domestic and farm livestock), promoting spay and neuter clinics, issuance of licenses (may be handled by police or others, see Licenses and Permits, C284), collection of fees, operation of animal shelters, humane trapping of wild animals, elimination of predatory animals. May be organized under Police, Sheriff, Health, Veterinarian, Agriculture or separately.

C028   **Animal Bite Report.** Copies are kept at police and health departments. Contents: date and time of report and occurrence, location, victim's address, phone and occupation, location of wound, description of animal and license no., circumstances of attack, where animal is impounded, where victim was treated, whether a citation was issued, name of police officer and badge. Reports of rabid animals are turned over to Health Department, Vector Control.

C029   *Complaint Report.* A complaint of a nuisance or danger due to an animal (usually a dog). Contents: name, address, phone of owner and reporting party; details of complaint; date; breed and color of animal; record of attempts to contact owner; comments; dog license no.; citation or warning issued; final status.

C030   *Impound Record.* For animals brought to animal control center or shelter if there is no identifiable owner. Contents: finder's name, address and phone; breed and description of animal; where found, dates (in, adopted or destroyed), surrender statement (signer releases city or county from all liability), fees, owner notification.

C031   *Other Animal Control Records.* Rental of humane traps; placement of humane traps; wild animal capture and relocation; contracts for animal shelter services; business licenses (kennels, stables, pet shops, acts, shows and exhibitions, circuses, horse shows, rodeos, aquatic shows, etc.).

C032   ## ASSESSMENT APPEALS BOARD, BOARD OF EQUALIZATION, TAX APPEALS BOARD

County. Hears protests to the assessed value of property (application for equalization) and determines taxable value for all property in county. May be composed of and under authority of the Board of Supervisors.

C033   *Assessment Appeals Case Files.* Records of property tax appeals. Contents: application no., name, address, phone of applicant or applicant's agent, description and location of property, date of purchase and price, assessor's reference no., tax bill no., taxes due, applicant's opinion of taxable value, reason for appeal, assessor's reply, disposition.

C034   *Assessment Appeals Hearings.* A stenographic or tape recording of the hearing. Contents: a verbatim account of hearing proceedings.

C035   ## ASSESSOR

County. Locates and determines the value of all taxable property, both secured (land, houses, factories) and unsecured (boats, aircraft, mobile homes), and gas and mineral rights, except public utilities; prepares property-tax rolls and administers property-tax exemptions; reassesses upon transfer or improvement. Note: Assessors and Tax Collectors maintain many of the same records. This guide lists records usually maintained by both under Tax Collector (C521–C533).

C036   *Annual Statistical Report on Exemptions (Form R802).* A county summary of tax-exempt property forwarded to the State Board of Equalization. Contents: county name, assessor name, date, number and assessed value of secured and unsecured property belonging to: private and parochial schools, hospitals, other religious and charitable groups, disabled and blind veterans' homes, churches, private colleges. Also includes low-value property exempted by county ordinance, homeowner's exemptions, cemeteries. Arranged by year.

C037   *Assessor's Maps.* Secured property maps for assessment purposes. Contents: Assessor's no., street outlines, block outlines, lot or parcel (outlines, dimensions, reference no.), old boundaries, mergers, splits and dates of revision, name of city/town, owner's name, amount of holding, subdivision and street names, property boundaries, footage and estimated value of land.

(ASSESSOR, CONT.)

C038 **Sales Ledger-Secured Property.** A history of property ownership. Contents: Assessor's reference no. (usually block and lot no.), current owner, previous owner(s), dates of title transfers, recorder's book and page no. The date of the most recent sale and the recorder's book and page no., may be found on the Secured Assessment Rolls. Indexing is usually done by address and name. Note: Commercial services are available to research these records.

C039 **Tax-Exemption Applications.** An annual filing required of schools, churches and nonprofit organizations. Contents: application no., articles of incorporation, organization name, by-laws, statement of purpose, financial statement, locally owned property, date, officers' names, addresses, phones, result of appraisal, state Board of Equalization decision. May be arranged by name of organization or occasionally by parcel no. Indexed by Secured Property Indexes (C524, C528). The index will show the amount of exemption.

C040 **AUDITOR-CONTROLLER**

City and County. The auditor monitors accounting systems, conducts regular audits, documents fiscal transactions, computes tax rates and corrects tax rolls. The controller approves payments and issues warrants (checks) for goods and services purchased, issues the payroll, handles accounts receivable (central collection), estimates revenue for the budget of city or county offices, agencies, schools and special districts (unless the district controls its own finances). Often combined into a single Auditor-Controller office and organized under a Department of Finance. Pensions and retirement may be handled here or in a separate pensions department. See also Purchasing and Treasurer.

C041 **Accounts Payable.** Records of money owed by the government and paid. Contents: date, batch no., amount and account or document no.

C042 **Accounts Receivable.** Records of money owed to the government by private individuals (damage claims, returned checks, real estate transfer tax) or collected and forwarded by a department. Contents: source (name and address if an individual), amount, invoice no.

C043 **Audit Reports.** Records of regular examinations of financial statements of city or county departments, reviews of financial records for validity and accuracy, reviews of department procedures and recommendations for efficiency. See also Audit (A016).

C044 **Bond Register.** Records of revenue bonds issued by city or county. Contents: bond no., purpose or fund, purchaser, interest rate, dates paid and maturity, total amount. See also Treasurer.

C045 **Bonds Canceled or Redeemed.** Records that revenue bonds are paid off. Contents: same as for Bond Register (C044), plus final date.

C046 **Budget.** An annual summary of estimated receipts and expenditures for entire city or county, except those exempted by the charter. Usually prepared by the city manager or chief administrative officer assisted by the Auditor-Controller and subject to approval by the county Board of Supervisors, City Council or Mayor. Contents: financial summary by budget unit or fund title of revenue and expenditures for two prior fiscal years and estimates for next fiscal year, sources of revenue, capital expenditures, operating expenditures, statement of mission for each agency or department, goals and objectives, past accomplishments and future plans. Note: budget formats vary widely.

C047   **Capital Assets and Depreciation.** An annual listing of sewers, airports (if any), buildings and other structures. Contents: account no., property no., year acquired, description, value, depreciation rate.

C048   **Claims, Allowance Book.** For damages or injuries made against the city or county. Contents: claimant's name, address, phone, date, location and description; name of employee(s) involved; witnesses' names, addresses, phones; vehicular information (if needed); itemization of claim; supporting documents. Note: Local government decides the limit above which a claim must go to court. Claims records may also be filed with the Clerk of the Board of Supervisors, or the City Clerk. If the claim is not allowed, the claimant may petition the appropriate court.

C049   **Expense Records.** Claims for expenses by officials or employees. Contents: type of payment, department, document no., payee name, itemized expenditure, reason, warrant no. and date.

C050   **Fines and Forfeitures.** A record of amounts of fines and forfeitures collected by courts. Contents: source, amount and date. The actual money is deposited with the Treasurer.

C051   **Inventory of Property.** An annual inventory of equipment done by each department. Contents: department, name, description of item(s), I.D. no., serial no., purchase order no., date purchased, value, location of item. Note: also filed with the County Clerk.

C052   **Payroll.** A record of wages paid to government employees. Although payroll records are public according to state law, some auditors may refuse to reveal more than the salary range of an employee.

C053   **Pension Payroll.** Similar to Payroll (C052). Usually only the gross amount is public, not the net amount.

C054   **Police Property Tags.** Receipts issued to people arrested if their personal belongings are taken. Contents: name, address, other I.D. no., contents of property impounded, date, receipt no.

C055   **Revenue Forecasting, Financial Forecasting.** Data used to compile the budget estimates. Contents: typically include funds, accounts, prior year(s), current and future estimates of revenue and expenditures.

C056   **Vendor Master File.** A record of those paid or being paid for goods and services. Contents: name, address, vendor no. and code.

C057   **Other Auditor Records.** Auto allowance records, mileage allowances, capital improvements, labor (time spent on job orders), financial status of each department and of all programs.

C058   # BOARD OF SUPERVISORS

County. The legislative and executive body of county government. Counties are limited by state law to five elected supervisors, except San Francisco, which has eleven. The board has responsibility for services to residents of unincorporated county areas and certain services to city residents, such as: jails, health, social services, courts, law enforcement, voter registration, vital statistics, property tax assessment and tax collection. Board functions may also include Equalization or Tax Assessment Appeals, Flood Control Board, Water Conservation Board, Planning Appeals (Zoning Appeals), Redevelopment, Housing Authority, Libraries, Transit

(BOARD OF SUPERVISORS, CONT.)

Commission, Election Commissioners, etc. The clerk for the board may also serve as County Clerk. This is less often the case now, especially in larger counties.

The Board of Supervisors is assisted by a chief administrative officer who carries out board decisions, aids budget preparation and provides needed information for decision making. Other titles for this position are administrative officer, county administrator, county manager and county executive. State law requires keeping a minutes book (proceedings of the board), an ordinance book (ordinances as adopted by the board), an allowance book (claims against the county) and a warrant book (expenditures of funds). These records are maintained by the clerk of the board or the County Clerk.

C059   *Agenda.* A general description of each item to be discussed at a board meeting must be posted before the meeting. Contents: date, time, name of department, short description, agenda no., file no.

C060   *Board Minutes or Statement of Proceedings.* A record of discussion and action taken at any meeting. Contents: department name, agenda item no., description of item, decision/action (voting record for each supervisor), classification or file no. Indexed by C061. Note: The file no. is usually the same for all supporting documents related to a specific item.

C061   *Board Minutes Index.* Indexing methods vary. The most common are by project name, personal names, originating department, general subject.

C062   *Board Records, Board Files.* A history of legislative action taken by the board and board committees. Contents: project, board action, contract award, final completion. Some counties file board records by meeting dates, but if some records are computerized, the information can also be located by project, contract no., resolution no., subject or supervisors name.

C063   *Claims, Allowance Books.* A register of claims allowed against county. Contents: see (C048).

C064   *Contractor Index.* An index to contractors doing business with the county. Contents: classification no. and project name for every contract.

C065   *Contracts and Agreements.* Originals of contracts approved by the board, including franchises, bonds, plans and specifications, bids, reports and studies, correspondence, maps, memoranda and other printed material. Contents: project name, name of contractor, type of service performed, file no., board resolution no., beginning and ending dates, filing date, dollar amount, insurance (if any), compliance statement.

C066   *Real Property Leasing and Purchasing.* Records of land acquired, leased or sold by the county. Contents: name of department, location, name of owners, address, terms, time (if lease), date, amount, purpose or project title.

C067   *Other Board of Supervisor Records.* Correspondence, resolutions, reports and their indexes (increasingly now included in the Board Minutes Index, C061); statements of economic interest.

C068   **CITY ATTORNEY**

City. The legal representative and advisor for all city departments. Attends all council meetings and represents the city in all legal actions. Drafts laws and legal documents, reviews form and legality of city contracts, supervises legal aspects of municipal elections. Prosecution of violations of city ordinances or criminal cases varies from city to city. For instance, the San Francisco city attorney does not prosecute criminal cases; in Los Angeles, some misdemeanor cases are prosecuted through this office. May appear as legislative advocate before other government agencies. The same records may not be kept by all city attorneys.

C069   *City Attorney Legal Opinions.* For city departments on questions of law. Contents: date, requesting department, discussion. Confidential if the matter is pending litigation or related to attorney-client privilege.

C070   *Civil Case Files.* Records of persons accused of violating civil provisions of the municipal and state codes (zoning, housing, fire, health, litter control, noise abatement, building inspection, sign code, consumer fraud, environmental protection). Some civil case files include only a complaint due to a settlement out of court or the case being dropped. Case files should be viewed at the office of the clerk of the appropriate court. See Courts (C154).

C071   *Code Enforcement Files.* Records of development of ordinances and resolutions regarding code enforcement.

C072   *Criminal Case Files.* Same as Civil Case Files (C162) for misdemeanor criminal statutes.

C073   *Statistical Reports.* Monthly, quarterly and annual statistics of case loads, code enforcement, consumer fraud and other activities of the city attorney division.

C074   CITY CLERK

City. Serves as clerk of the City Council. Duties are similar to those of clerk of the Board of Supervisors (C058-C067). Keeps and indexes records of all city council activities, city-owned property transactions, city elections, financial records, franchises, ordinances. Administers oaths of office, provides administrative and personnel services to the city council, provides background research and documents for council members. Sometimes elected, usually appointed. For election and voting-related records, see Registrar of Voters.

C075   *Annexations.* Records of property annexed by the city. Contents: title of area, legal description, surveys, reports, maps, resolutions, Local Agency Formation Commission certificates, Notices of Intent, ordinances, resolutions.

C076   *Ballots.* Copies of official ballots. Contents: ballot listings, arguments, propositions, proposals, election date.

C077   *Budget.* Issued annually. For contents, see (C046) and Budgets (A017).

C078   *Business License Surety Bonds.* City. Applicants doing business with the city carry insurance guaranteeing they will conform to city laws. Contents: license no., date, name and address of applicant, DBA, surety bond no., name and address of insurer.

C079   *Campaign Disclosure Statements.* Records of money raised and spent by all city-level candidates and political committees under their control and by committees supporting local ballot measures. See also County Clerk and Secretary of State. The audits of these statements, conducted by the Franchise Tax Board, are also filed here.

C080   *City Charter.* The laws establishing and governing the city (if it has a charter form of government). See S624.

C081   *Claims.* Records of damage claims against the city. For contents see Auditor-Controller.

CO82   *Contracts and Agreements.* See Board of Supervisors for contents.

(CITY CLERK, CONT.)

C083   **Correspondence.** All correspondence referred to or received by the city council. Contents: source, subject, file no., where referred for action, council district(s) affected.

C084   **Council Agenda or Docket.** A list of matters to be considered at city council meetings. Contents: date, name of department, short description, agenda no., file no. (if any).

C085   **Council Files.** A history of legislative action taken by the City Council, city council committees, and any official body, such as the Redevelopment Agency, whose membership consists of the City Council. Contents: documents from other city agencies, committee reports, correspondence, action taken, project name or file no.

C086   **Council Files Index.** Systems vary. May be subdivided by general subject, city department, streets, parcel maps, plan cases, tracts, contracts or leases. Each entry usually refers to a unique file no.

C087   **Council Minutes, Journal or Digest of Calendar.** Shows action taken on each agenda item, voting record of each member. Sequence follows that of the agenda. Some cities offer audio or video tapes that are later erased or stored at the library or records center.

C088   **Council Standing Committee Files.** Records similar to those for the City Council Files (C085) are maintained and indexed for standing committees.

C089   **Deeds.** A legal record of transfers of city-owned property. Contents: Grantor and grantee names; document filing date; document no., mailing address of owner on transfer date. See Recorder for private property transactions.

C090   **Deeds—General Index.** An index to deeds of city-owned property (C089). Contents: names, document no., filing date.

C091   **Election Returns and Records.** Contents: date, candidate or issue, results (total, council district, precinct), summary statistics, certification by City Clerk.

C092   **Franchise Files.** Records of franchises granted to private companies for designated use in city. Contents: contracts, reports, maps, performance bonds, performance evaluations, hearings reports, franchise agreement.

C093   **Index on Candidates.** A record of candidates for city office. Contents: candidate name, dates and type of election, office title, election results. Note: Not all cities maintain these records. Lists are usually kept by year of election.

C094   **Index on Issues.** A record of referenda and initiatives in city elections. Contents: same as Index on Candidates (C093).

C095   **Land Records.** For privately owned property, maintained by a few cities as a convenience for citizens. Contents: present owner's name and mailing address; date deed was recorded; previous owner's name (going back three owners), mailing address, date of deed; location of microfilm copy of deed. The County Recorder has all property records.

C096   **Leases.** Agreements to lease city land or acquire land or buildings for city. See also Real Estate.

C097   **Oaths of Office.** Copies of oaths administered by the City Clerk. Contents: oath text, date, title of office.

C098   **Ordinances.** Laws or statutes enacted by the City Council.

C099   **Petitions.** The text of initiative, referendum and charter amendment petitions. Contents: ordinance no., subject, dates (filing, certification, election), total no. of signatures filed and approved. Signatures are not public.

C100   ***Planning Projects.*** Records of Planning Department projects in final form. See Planning for more detailed contents.

C101   ***Precinct maps.*** Detailed, large-scale maps of city precincts. Contents: precinct no., streets, area boundaries. See also Registrar of Voters.

C102   ***Records Disposition Schedule, Records Inventory, Records Retention Schedule.*** A list of every type of record kept by a department. Contents (may vary): department, name, date, record I.D. no., title, description of contents, retention requirements for department, and records center, final disposition, remarks. Some schedules indicate whether the record is public or not. Not kept by all cities. See C223.

C103   ***Resolutions.*** Measures passed by city council as opinion, not law.

C104   ***Statement of Economic Interests (Forms 721 and 730).*** A legally required statement of investments, income and gifts that may become the basis of a conflict of interest. City officers who must file 721 here and with the Fair Political Practices Commission are mayors, city council members, city managers, chief administrative officers, planning commissioners and city attorneys. Those designated by their city agency conflict-of-interest code file Form 730. See Fair Political Practices Commission (S201-S204) for contents.

C105   ***Summonses.*** Legal notices issued against the city to appear in court. Contents: date, plaintiff, name, address, phone, complaint, summons no., exhibits, correspondence.

C106   ## CITY MANAGER, CHIEF ADMINISTRATIVE OFFICER

City. Serves the mayor as manager and operations officer for the city. Advises, informs, recommends actions to the mayor and council. Most public records are also found with the City Clerk or with individual city departments.

C107   ***Appointment Calendars.*** Contents: appointments, meetings, miscellaneous notations.

C108   ***Department Agendas.*** For meetings with department heads. Contents: printed list of items to be discussed.

C109   ## CIVIL SERVICE COMMISSION, PERSONNEL BOARD, PERSONNEL MERIT BOARD

City and County. Appointed by the mayor or board of supervisors if voters approve a civil service measure. Recommendations are made for salary standards, rules, guidelines and salary levels. In some cities and counties, the Commission hears and decides appeals, disciplinary actions, suspensions and terminations. In others, the Director of Personnel does this. Records include agendas and minutes of meetings, hearings and decisions.

C110   ## CIVIL SERVICE, PERSONNEL, EMPLOYEE RELATIONS DEPARTMENT, OFFICE OF LABOR RELATIONS

City and County. Responsible for hiring, classification of positions, wage and salary determination, labor relations, bargaining, development, affirmative action. Under guidance of the Civil Service Commission (if any). Occupational health and safety program may be under Personnel or Risk Management. How personnel and employee relations are handled varies widely.

(CIVIL SERVICE, CONT.)

C111   **Affirmative Action Reports.** Statistics on work-force composition. Contents: classifications, percentage by race, ethnic group, sex.

C112   **Certifications of Eligible Applicants.** Contents: requests from departments for eligible applicants for open positions.

C113   **Class Titles, Classification Specifications, Job Descriptions.** Contents: summary of duties, job standards, evaluation criteria.

C114   **Employee Relations Records.** Files on collective bargaining, employee representation and union elections. Contents: union contracts, memoranda of understanding, election results. May be organized under the Chief Administrative Officer, Mayor, Board of Supervisors or separately.

C115   **Employee Verification.** A record of employment and class of job. Contents: name, verification of employment, department, current job title, current salary, current level of civil service, date of employment, date of termination (if any). Note: Employee verification is usually provided in response to either telephone or written inquiries. Requests for more detailed information are usually referred to the specific department. See also S113.

C116   **Examination Results.** Test results of candidates for jobs. Contents: name, job, scores on interviews, written exams or performance tests, final standing.

C117   **Examination Results Analyses.** Statistical analyses of applicants. Contents (for each set of exams): nos. applying by ethnicity, sex, race, score.

C118   ## COMMUNITY DEVELOPMENT DEPARTMENT

City and County. Many cities and counties set up departments to handle state and federal Community Development Block Grants, Community Service Block Grants, and housing and redevelopment projects. Community Development departments range widely: a community may have ten or twelve programs (low-income housing, food bank, energy-crisis intervention, rural development assistance). The Community Development Department in the City of Los Angeles manages dozens of programs (Industrial and Commercial Development, Human Services and Neighborhood Development, Rent Stabilization, Housing, Training and Job Development, and Community Analysis Planning). In this guide, the programs are discussed under Employment, Housing, Planning and Redevelopment.

C119   ## CORONER-MEDICAL EXAMINER

County. Investigates and determines cause of death in the county in cases of suicide, violent, sudden and unusual death, sudden infant death, police officer–involved shootings, police–officer fatalities, deaths where the deceased was not attended by a physician in the 20 days before death, and deaths where the attending physician cannot certify the actual cause. Also notifies next of kin and buries indigents. Note: May be organized with Sheriff, County Administrator or separately.

C120   **Coroner's Case Files.** Records of all deaths as noted above. Contents: case report, statement of investigator, mortuary death report, release to mortuary, certificate of death, fingerprints of deceased, inventory of personal effects, medical reports (toxicology, pathology), preliminary examination report, autopsy check sheet, full-length anterior and posterior body diagrams. The case report includes the deceased's name and address, occupation, physical description; cause of death, date, time and place; name of person notified of death, relationship to deceased; name of investigator; case no.

C121   **Coroner's Register.** Records of inquests performed at request of coroner. Contents: name of deceased, cause of death and date, case no., details about deceased from case file, date of inquest, names of witnesses and jurors, verdict.

C122   **Coroner's Register Index.** Contents: name of deceased, case no., volume and page no. Arranged by name of deceased.

C123   COUNTY ADMINISTRATOR, COUNTY MANAGER, COUNTY EXECUTIVE OFFICER, CHIEF ADMINISTRATIVE OFFICER

County. Serves the Board of Supervisors as operations and management officer for county government; advises, informs, recommends actions to the board. Records that are public can also be found with the County Clerk or the Board of Supervisors. See also City Manager.

C124   COUNTY CLERK

County. Chief duties are to collect and maintain the county legal records and documents. Historically, the County Clerk combined four functions, which are now usually handled separately. They were Clerk of the Board of Supervisors, Clerk of the Superior Court, Registrar of Voters and Recorder. Duties of one County Clerk are rarely identical to those of another. A typical combination is County Clerk-Recorder.

C125   **Appointments.** A record of all appointments approved by the board. Contents: name, position, date, term and expiration.

C126   **Campaign Disclosure Statements.** Records of money raised and spent by all candidates for office, their controlled committees and ballot measure committees are filed with the County Clerk where they are domiciled, except those for city office or one-city ballot measures (see C079). For details of record contents, see Secretary of State (S589–S591). Audits of these statements, performed by the Franchise Tax Board, are also filed here.

C127   **Corporation Files.** Records of corporations in the county where originally incorporated. Contents: file no., articles of incorporation, name, purpose, principal location, director's names and addresses, certificate no., affidavit of publication of notice, amendments of articles of incorporation, statement of dissolution. Note: For-profit corporations also have number of stock shares, class, par value and conditions for further issuance. Nonprofits include statement of activities. After 1976, these files are kept by the Secretary of State . The county may have destroyed pre-1977 records or sent them to the state archives (S617).

C128   **Corporation Files Index.** An index to C127. Contents: corporate name and file no. May have been destroyed after 1976.

C129   **Election Returns and Records.** For elections at the county level and above. Contents: date, candidates and issues, results (totals, supervisorial district, precinct and party) and other data, if computerized. May be on file at Registrar of Voters.

C130   **Environmental Impact Reports.** State law requires reports be filed for certain projects affecting the environment. Contents: project description, location, filing date, file no., notice of determination, notice of exemption, proposed subdivisions, negative declarations, hearings.

(COUNTY CLERK, CONT.)

C131   **Fictitious Business Name Statement (FBNS), Doing Business As Statement (DBA).**
Required of businesses operating under a name other than the owner's full name or,
if a corporation, not including the corporate name. Contents: file no., fictitious
business name statement (registrant's name, address, type of business, business name
and address), statement of abandonment of use of name, statement of withdrawal
from partnership in business. Retention: four years after expiration; nine years after
statement of withdrawal from partnership or abandonment. Business must re-
register every five years. There is no statewide, public agency listing for FBNS.

C132   **Fictitious Business Name Index.** For C131. Contents: business name or DBA, name
of registrant(s), file no.

C133   **Governor's Appointments.** Records of appointments made by the Governor to
county boards and commissions. Contents: personal name, dates of term, authority
code no., appointing power, number of members, qualifications, terms, bond (if
any), oath, compensation, function. (See S587).

C134   **Grand Juror Selection List.** Contents: name of juror, address, name of nominating
judge, dates of term. May be on file with Clerk of the Superior Court.

C135   **Limited Partnership Certificate.** Registration of California and foreign limited partnerships doing business in the state. For contents see Secretary of State (S613).

C136   **Limited Partnership Index.** Index to Limited Partnership Certificate (C135).
Contents: date, names of partners in business, business name and address. Arranged
by name of business.

C137   **Marriage License Applications.** Statement of a couple's intention to marry. Not
retained by all county clerks. For contents, see Recorder. Note: License applications
and certificates were formerly recorded separately; they are now combined and filed
with the Recorder.

C138   **Marriage License Applications Index.** An index to C137 and C147. Contents: names
and application no.

C139   **Naturalization, Declarations of Intention For.** Records of resident aliens in the
county who plan to become naturalized citizens. Contents: declaration no., name,
aliases, address, alien registration no. Note: Older declarations also contain the alien's
date and place of birth, nationality, physical description, name of spouse, and place,
date and manner of entering U.S. Since December 24, 1952, declarations are no
longer required by law, but resident aliens may still file the papers.

C140   **Naturalization Declarations of Intention Index.** An index to C139. Contents: name,
declaration no.

C141   **Naturalization Petitions.** A record of applications of county aliens to file a petition
for naturalization. Contents: petition no., petitioner name and address, age, alien
registration no., name change (if any), employer, marriage details, children's vital
statistics, details of all trips outside the U.S. for all family members, criminal record,
Communist or Nazi party membership, date of naturalization, plus other health and
political information. Note: Petitions for a child include date and place of birth,
name and address of parents. Older petitions may also include petitioner's date and
place of birth, marital status, number of children, date admitted to U.S., nationality,
alien registration no. Must be kept in county where naturalization occurred or at
nearest U.S. District Court.

C142   **Naturalization Petitions Index.** An index to C141. Contents: name(s) of petitioner
and petition no.

C143   **Notarial Records.** Notary records must be delivered to County Clerk if notary dies or otherwise ceases to function. The records must be kept 10 years and can be destroyed by a court order.

C144   **Notary Certification.** County Clerk certification that a notary's bond and oath of office are filed at the clerk's office. Contents: name, bond file no., date.

C145   **Notary Index.** A record of public notaries in the county. Contents: name, address, filing date, commission date, qualification date, notary bond file no. Note: See also Secretary of State, Notaries Public Information (S614)

C146   **Official Bonds.** Bonds insuring against default or failure, required of certain county officials, are filed here after being recorded. Contents: office, name, date, term of office, amount of bond.

C147   **Premarital Examination Certificates.** Contents: name, address, date, hospital, laboratory, physician, blood test results (syphilis and rubella). Arranged by date. Indexed by marriage license application index (C138). Note: As of July 1994, the legislature abolished the requirement for premarital examinations.

C148   **Process Servers Registration.** A record of persons in the county certified as process servers. Contents: name (individual or corporate) of registrant, copy of bond, process server's name, address, phone, age, bond file no.

C149   **Roster of Public Agencies.** Records of governmental agencies, including special districts, that are based in the county. Contents: name, mailing address, date of formation, officer's names, addresses (residential or business) of governing body and officers, description of boundaries (may be in Recorder's Office), statement of purpose, dates of election and/or expiration, any changes or amendments. Note: Copy is on file at Secretary of State.

C150   **Statement of Economic Interests (Forms 721 and 730).** Investments, income and gifts that may become the basis of conflict of interest must be reported to the County Clerk. Assistant and deputy county counsels and those designated in a county conflict of interest code must file 730 with the County Clerk. Supervisors, chief administrative officers, planning commissioners, and county counsels must file 721 with the county clerk and the Fair Political Practices Commission. For contents of both forms, see the FPPC (S204). Note: These records may be found in the department where the official works instead of at the office of the County Clerk.

C151   COUNTY COUNSEL

County. Provides legal advice, assistance and representation in civil legal matters to the Board of Supervisors, county officers, and departments, boards, commissions and special districts. Rarely involved in criminal matters. Attends all meetings of the Board of Supervisors and all commissions and boards for which the board is the legislative body. Not all counties have this office. The district attorney may perform this function in some counties.

C152   **County Counsel Case Files.** Contents: correspondence, minutes, reports, ordinances, court records. Closed unless the case has gone to court or the Board of Supervisors releases the information. Many records are duplicated in Courts or the Board of Supervisors.

C153   **County Counsel Legal Opinions.** Advice for county departments or their officers on questions of law. Contents: date, requesting department, discussion. Confidential if within attorney-client privilege or related to pending litigation.

C154 COURTS

For an outline of the court system above Superior Court, see S151. For sources of information on the California court system and on conducting legal research, see Bibliography. Each county is divided into judicial districts and is organized as follows:

C155 Municipal Courts

Trial courts for judicial districts as created by a county Board of Supervisors. Judges are elected and hear civil cases involving $25,000 or less; try criminal misdemeanors and infractions; hold preliminary hearings for felonies, except for juveniles; and may sit as small-claims court for matters under $5,000. Appeals of court decisions are made at the appellate department of the Superior Court. A separate small-claims court may maintain its own records.

C156 Justice Courts

Eliminated by the legislature as of January 1995. Formerly the same as municipal courts, but for districts of less than 40,000 population.

C157 Superior Courts

There is one Superior Court for each county; judges are elected. Superior courts sit as probate courts, juvenile courts and conciliation (divorce) courts. They hear appeals from municipal and justice courts, and grand jury indictments. They have trial jurisdiction over all felony cases and all civil matters involving more than $25,000. Appeals are made at the area court of appeal or, in death penalty cases, the state Supreme Court.

C158   *Categories of Records.* Case files, Indexes, Registers of Actions, and Minutes are essentially the same for each type of court. Registers of Actions and Minutes are produced in various forms and may be combined into a docket. Records are kept by the County Clerk (for superior court), Clerk of the Superior Court (if separate from county clerk), Clerk of the Municipal Court and Clerk of the Judicial Court. Public access to court records and court proceedings is governed by the U.S. Constitution's first and sixth amendments and the state constitution's guarantee of the right to a fair and public trial. Juvenile court records are generally sealed.

C159   *Abstract of Judgment.* A form issued by the Court Clerk recording judgments in civil and criminal cases. These are delivered to the beneficiary of the judgment (judgment creditor) or the sheriff to enforce the results of the judgment (a salary or property lien, or a jail sentence). Contents: case no., plaintiff, defendant, type of case, date, judge, amount, brief details of the judgment. The full text of the judgment is recorded in the Judgment Book. Arranged by case no. Indexed by Civil or Criminal Register of Actions. Note: Abstracts are not usually kept in the Court Clerk's files.

C160   *Calendars.* A chronological list of civil and criminal cases for each court day. Contents: case no., presiding judge, plaintiff, defendant, attorneys, pleading, remarks. Arranged by court date. Indexed by Civil Index and Criminal Index.

C161   *Charging Documents.* The "complaint" or "information" that reflects the original reason for a criminal case. Contents (typically at the discretion of the district attorney): defendant's name, code no., arrest warrant, affidavit, bail. Arranged by defendant's name or code no. Usually filed in the Criminal Case File.

C162   *Civil Case Files.* All papers related to civil actions or torts. Contents: case no., plaintiff's complaint (plaintiff and defendant names and summary of alleged injury and points of law); defendant's answer to complaint; declarations filed into evidence; motions, and briefs; court orders; judge's and attorneys' names; judgment; abstract of judgment; trial transcript (if appealed). May also include interrogatories and depositions. May indicate name of stenographer or court reporter to contact for copies of depositions. Arranged by case no. Indexed by Civil Index. Note: Case files are assembled with each new paper or "filing" added on top. Depositions may be public only if entered in evidence at a trial. Court Minutes may sometimes be filed in the Case File.

C163   *Civil Index, General Index Civil.* Alphabetical indexes for non-criminal cases, individuals in divorce cases, deceased individuals, minors, and incompetents in probate cases. Used to locate cases in Civil Register of Actions, Court Minutes, Court Docket, and Civil Case Files. Contents: plaintiff and defendant names, case no., filing date. Note: Superior Court Civil Case Indexes also often contain both divorce and probate cases. All plaintiffs and defendants named in a civil complaint should be listed separately in a Civil Index, but often are not. Because an index typically covers a span of years, it is necessary to check several volumes of indexes. See also Probate Index.

C164   *Civil Register of Actions.* Records actions, proceedings and papers filed in a civil suit. Contents: case no., plaintiff, defendant, and attorney names, nature of suit, title of each filing, proceeding, and judgment. Arranged by case no. Indexed by Civil Index. Note: The register serves as a useful summary of the Civil Case File. It is no longer required to be kept.

C165   *Court Docket.* There are several definitions. It can be a record of all actions and proceedings filed in civil or criminal cases, thus being another term for Register of Actions, serving as a quick index for documents in a case file. It can be another term for Calendar. Each case scheduled to appear before a judge has a special docket no. Contents depend on the purpose it is serving, but typically include dates of trial, arraignment, sentencing, etc. Arranged by case no., if as a Register of Actions; by date, if as a Calendar. Indexed by Civil Index or Criminal Index.

C166   *Court Minutes.* A brief chronological record of proceedings at each court session in each case. Contents: case no., court no., judge and clerk, defendant, plaintiff (if any), type of proceeding and brief description, jurors' and witnesses' names, exhibits named and numbered, court rulings, dates of trial. Arranged by date and filed with the case as the Minute Order. Indexed by the Civil or Criminal Register of Actions, which gives the date of the court session, or the Index, which gives the name or case title and case number. The Minute Book includes Minute Orders for all the day's cases.

C167   *Criminal Case Files.* Files of all papers related to a criminal case. Contents: case no., complaint or information (defendant, date of filing, charges and description of related actions), preliminary hearing transcript, motions and briefs, court orders, verdict, abstract of judgment, trial transcript if appealed, final disposition probation record, sentence report, court transcript, letters. Arranged by case no.; indexed by Criminal Index. Case files are assembled so that each new piece of paper is added to the top. Probation, medical and psychiatric reports are often kept in case files but removed before the file is made public. Probation reports are public only for 60 days from the date of sentence (Penal Code Section 1203.05). See also Probation, C355.

C168   *Criminal Index, General Index Criminal.* For criminal cases. Serve as index to Criminal Registers of Action, Court Dockets and Criminal Case Files. Contents: defendant, case no., filing date. Note: Because most criminal cases have a preliminary hearing at the municipal or justice court level, cases tried in Superior Court are also listed in the lower court records under different case nos.

C169   *Criminal Register of Actions.* A record of each action, proceeding and paper filed in a criminal court case. Contents: case no., defendant, defense attorney and prosecutor names, dates, charges, title of each filing and proceeding, verdict. Arranged by case no. Indexed by defendant's name in the Criminal Index. Note: The register serves as a useful summary to the Criminal Case File.

(COURTS, CONT.)

C170   **Dissolution of Marriage, Divorce Records.** Divorce is a civil action carried out in
Superior Court, although some counties have separate divorce courts. Divorce records
(indexes, registers, minutes and case files) are essentially the same as other civil case
files. They are often integrated into the general civil records of the Superior Court or
may be in a separate set of records. Contents: date and location of marriage, date of
separation, reasons for divorce, property held by each spouse and jointly, names and
ages of children of the marriage, estimate of earnings of both spouses, mailing addresses
of both parties, lawyers' names, addresses and phone nos., judgment. Note: For indexing
purposes, the party suing for divorce is the petitioner, and the other spouse is the
respondent. The County Recorder keeps divorce records if property is involved. Certificates of Dissolution of Marriage, Judgment of Nullity and Legal Separations are sent
to the State Registrar of Vital Statistics, Department of Health Services (S381).

C171   **Exhibits.** Written evidence, sometimes found in case files. Material exhibits are
usually kept separate from court records in an "evidence room." Indexed by Civil
Index or Criminal Index. See also Police.

C172   **Fees and Fines Records.** Money paid for court hearing fees and fines. Contents: date,
payer's name and address, I.D. no. or case no., amount, date forwarded to Treasurer.
Note: Records are maintained by the court where the fine was levied.

C173   **Probate Records.** Probate is a civil action carried out in Superior Court to prove that
a will is valid. Proceedings include establishment of wills, settlement of decedent's
estates, supervision of guardianship proceedings, supervision of habitual drunkards
and persons of unsound mind, and control of property of wards of the state. Categories of records, case files, indexes, registers and minutes serve the same purposes as
in other courts. Contents (of a case file): will, inventory of estate assets, claims
against estate, disposal of estate. Note: Probate records may be integrated into the
general civil records of the Superior Court but usually are kept separate.

C174   **Probate Indexes.** Contents: case no.; filing date; names of deceased, incompetent
individual or minor and petitioners; name of estate; administrator; executor or
guardian; heirs; brief description of proceedings. Arranged by name of estate or case
no., then chronologically.

C175   **Small Claims Court Records.** Small claims actions are civil suits for less than $5,000
carried out at the municipal or justice court level and are usually handled by a special
"small claims" division of the court. Small Claims Registers of Action and Court
Minutes are found in the Small Claims Case File. Small Claims Indexes are similar to
other civil indexes and are maintained by municipal or justice court jurisdictions.

C176   **Wills.** Wills are the legal expression of how individuals wish their property to be
disposed of after death. Copies of wills are entered as part of an estate settlement.
Contents: dates of will and recording, name(s) of testator(s), heirs, witnesses, description of bequests, signature. Arranged chronologically. Indexed by Probate Indexes.

C177   **DISTRICT ATTORNEY**

County. Handles criminal prosecution of adults and juveniles in municipal and
superior courts, advises grand juries, investigates complaints against any county
department, may defend suits against the county or the state in the county, provides
legal advice to the county, district or township, investigates paternity and custody
disputes in the process of enforcing delinquent child support, investigates consumer
fraud cases. In small counties, the D.A. may be combined with the Public Administrator and the County Counsel. Case files are confidential until a case goes to court.
See Courts (C154–C176) and grand jury. If the case is settled out of court, records
are not public unless subpoenaed.

C178 **ECONOMIC DEVELOPMENT. CITY AND COUNTY**

An umbrella title that may include employment training, redevelopment and rehabilitation, and sometimes is contained within another agency such as Community Development. For programs that are largely employment related, see Social Services. For programs related to housing rehabilitation, see Housing. See also Redevelopment.

C179 **EMERGENCY SERVICES**

City and County or combined. Coordinates with state and federal programs to provide for defense-related and disaster-related civil defense. May be organized under Risk Management, Public Works, Planning and Community Development, County Administrator, Sheriff, Police, or as an independent unit.

C180 *Administrative Plan.* An annual emergency plan submitted to state Office of Emergency Services (S167) to qualify for planning and readiness funds. Contents: name of local agency, date, general plan (legal codes, organizational charts, evaluation methods, etc.), operational plan (testing, training, public information), finances (accounting and disbursement procedures, property management, etc.). Attachments include local enabling legislation, job descriptions, personnel expenses.

C181 *Damage Assessment Summary—FEMA Form 9.* Details of damage with cost estimates. Contents: persons dead or injured; homes and businesses damaged or destroyed; impact on agriculture, hospitals, schools, utilities; roads and government facilities affected; types of government assistance programs needed; amount of assistance needed from government agencies and kinds of work required.

C182 *Emergency Management Assistance Program Expenditures.* Various forms submitted by a local agency to claim salary, benefits, travel and other reimbursements. Contents: staff names and salary/benefits due, travel dates, other expense details.

C183 *Federal Assistance—FEMA Form 90-4.* A summary sheet for all grant, insurance, and loan applicants. Contents: I.D. nos., legal applicant (a government official), address, phone, program being applied for, title and description of project, type of applicant and assistance, Congressional district, certification, date, federal action taken, starting and ending dates.

C184 *Financial Contributions Request—Form OES 26.* A request for Emergency Management Assistance Expenses during the fiscal year using figures from FEMA—Form 85-17 (C189). Contents: name of local agency, population served, budget figures for salaries, benefits, travel, federal share of total.

C185 *Private Sector Damage Assessment—FEMD Form 7.* Estimates of extent of damage in a small area. Contents: area, date, person reporting, structures (low-cost homes, mobile homes, farm homes, etc.), degree of habitability, damage to utilities, basements, details of water damage, other assessments.

C186 *Private Sector Damage Assessment—FEMD Form 8.* A summary of damage estimates for the county, based on FEMD Form 7 (C185).

C187 *Registration for Disaster Recovery Assistance.* An application by private individuals for loans from the U.S. Small Business Administration and the U.S. Farmers Home Administration, or for an Individual and Family Grant. Contents: name, address, phone, Social Security no.; employment status; type and amount of loss; insurance; housing details.

C188 *Situation Report—FEMD Form 14.* An on-site assessment of an emergency. Contents: name and jurisdiction of person reporting; date; description including number of

(EMERGENCY SERVICES, CONT.)

dead, injured, evacuated, homeless, at risk; transportation affected; proclamations; state of communications; type of assistance and equipment needed; special problems.

C189   ***Staffing Pattern—FEMA Form 85-17.*** Details of personnel expenses for local emergency services. Contents: organization name, date, job description, annual salary and range of salary, whether matching funds are needed, full- or part-time status, appointment date, when vacancy will be filled.

C190   ***Other Emergency Services Records.*** Application to state for project funds; certification of work done; claims for costs of disaster work under state Natural Disaster Assistance Act, federal inspector's recommendation of work amount and cost; legal appointment of local official as coordinator; requests for advances or reimbursements.

C191   EMPLOYMENT, JOB TRAINING

City and County. Uses state and federal funds to assess, train, and place eligible people in jobs. Local governments are allowed some flexibility in use of these funds. May be organized under Social Services, Community Development, Economic Development, etc. Some counties and cities have employment programs funded locally and do not depend on state money or requirements. Education and vocation functions are contracted out and may be listed under Job Development, Remedial Education, Job Preparation, etc. The state requires data from a local area before allocating funds for employment development programs. Funding programs include Greater Avenues for Independence, Family Economic Security Act, Summer Youth Employment Training Program, Work Incentive Demonstration and Job Training Partnership Act (see C192, as an example). Records for these programs are similar, but not identical. They also include grant reporting, contracts and audits (see A016, A018, A020).

C192   ***Job Training Partnership Act (JTPA) Program Plan.*** A two-year plan to qualify for grant. Contents: source of funds; advisory council (if any) members' names, job titles, occupations; program performance standards; employment rate (by age, sex, race, employment background, eligibility); processing of invoices (contractor's name, project, title, period covered, date); audit records; monitoring of subcontractors; statistics on enrollees and terminees by sex, age, education, ethnicity, language, disability, criminal record, veteran status, goals. Records on individuals are confidential.

C193   ***Other Employment Records.*** Private Industry Council List; Program Performance Standards; Program Performance Measure; Performance Monitor of Contractors (semi-annual). See also Routine Records (A014–A023).

C194   FIRE DEPARTMENT, FIRE PROTECTION, PUBLIC SAFETY DEPARTMENT

City and County. Responsible for fire suppression, prevention, building inspection, issuance of licenses and permits (if fire hazard involved), arson investigation, emergency medical service (paramedics) and training programs. Rural areas are organized into "fire districts" (see also Special Districts, R001–R005) that may overlap city boundaries. Small cities may contract with the county for fire protection. Some counties contract with the state Department of Forestry. Volunteer fire companies are regulated by state health and safety codes. Organization is documented at the County Recorder. Other services may include bicycle licensing, voter registration, weed abatement and fireboats (See Emergency Medical Authority , S162).

C195   ***Construction Plan Review Records.*** Inspection reports of fire code compliance. Contents: a coded report for fire inspectors with type of building and occupancy;

minutes of meetings between fire inspectors, building inspectors and owners and architects involved with the proposed construction.

C196   *Daily Register or Alarm Record.* A daily summary of fire and non-fire incidents, including false alarms, trash fires, etc. Contents: incident no., time, location, category of incident.

C197   *Fire Commission Files.* Records of commission meetings, which discuss matters such as personnel, budget, training, recruitment, rules, regulations, violations, complaints, disability injuries, and monthly reports submitted by various divisions. Contents: agenda and minutes.

C198   *Fire Incident Reports.* A record of incidents involving a fire. Contents: incident no., engine no., address, names, date, description of incident, description of property, extent of damage, cause and area of origin, injuries, deaths, response record, length of time to extinguish fire.

C199   *Fire Inspection Reports or Street Address Files.* Records of inspections made in response to a problem or complaint. Contents: complaint location, business or resident name, complainant name and address, type of complaint, owner or manager name and address, date, area of inspection, descriptions and notations, status of permit.

C200   *Fire Investigation Reports.* Investigative reports of fires involving death or injury, accidental or suspicious fires, explosions resulting in fire (arson investigations are not public). Contents: description of incident, witnesses' statements, evidence obtained, date, type of building, owner, type of occupancy.

C201   *Fire Loss Records.* A monthly estimate of lost property value. Contents: type and contents of property, date, loss estimates.

C202   *Fire Protection District Files.* Routine records include all contacts with other county fire departments and fire districts, their own formation (see Local Agency Formation Commission reports) and ongoing administration. See also Special Districts (R001–R005).

C203   *Location Index for Fire Incidents.* A daily summary of fire incidents (C198) compiled by month. Contents: location, date, time, incident no.

C204   *Non-Fire Incident Reports.* A record of incidents not involving a fire. Contents: incident no., engine no., date, name, address, description of incident, description of aid administered, by whom, deaths and/or injuries.

C205   *Permit Files.* Permit applications from businesses (garages, service stations, restaurants, places of public assembly). Contents: type of permit, permit address, business name, owner's name and address, contractor's name, address, and license no., fee amount, reasons for granting or denying. See also Licenses and Permits (C284).

C206   *Sprinkler and Fire Alarm Plans.* A record of fire prevention measures in buildings. Contents: blueprints or sketches of all sprinklers, hydrants, alarms, etc., to aid firefighting.

C207   *Volunteer Fire Company Files.* Volunteer companies' routine records include contracts with county or city for use of fire equipment, and response records of calls to other company districts.

C208   *Water Consumption Report.* A monthly report on the amount of unmetered water used from domestic water supply system. Contents: gallons of water consumed, use by battalions, amount consumed from water tanks and reservoirs.

C209   *Other Fire Department Records.* Training manuals; Fire Department Fuel Consumption Reports, Monetary Receipts Records (of fees charged for permits, inspections, etc.).

C210 **FISH AND GAME ADVISORY BOARD OR COMMISSION**

County. Advises on matters of propagation, conservation, and betterment of wildlife, enforcement of laws, development of conservation and recreation areas. Organization may be under General Services, Parks and Recreation, or separate. Hunting and fishing violation fines are split with the state and must be spent by the Board of Supervisors for propagation and conservation of fish and game. The Board of Supervisors, acting on advice from the Advisory Board, determines projects such as fish hatcheries, wildlife rehabilitation, purchase of property, youth education, fish planting and tagging, and wildlife habitat establishment.

Records include agendas, minutes, purchase orders, requisitions, personnel, maintenance, etc. Citations for violations are recorded by the local police or sheriff.

C211 **GENERAL SERVICES OR FACILITIES MANAGEMENT**

City and County. Provides support or "housekeeping services" for other departments. Organization differs from place to place. Public Works often shares or provides some of the same services. This guide has entered the following functions separately: Purchasing, Property Acquisition (see Real Estate, Risk Management, and standards and quality testing (see Public Works, C389). A recent trend is to consolidate most of the above in General Services along with communications, motor pool and heavy equipment, mail, reprographics, storage, and laundry.

A Communications Division typically handles telephone installation and maintenance; microwave; radio and avionics; alarm systems; and electrical equipment such as traffic signals, underground cables, ventilation and air-conditioning equipment. Note: Communications is sometimes under Police, Sheriff, Public Works, or independent and called Telecommunications or Electricity.

C212 *Accident Records.* See Risk Management.

C213 *Architectural Service Files.* Records of government-owned projects, sometimes excluding those for large buildings. Contents: name of facility or building, project name (if any), relevant dates, anticipated savings, total cost, funding source.

C214 *Building and Equipment Inspection Records.* Contents: location of building, type of equipment, inspector's name, date, time, details unique to the object of inspection (stairwells, floors, mileage, tires, etc.), and quality of maintenance.

C215 *Cable Franchises.* Records of cable television franchise agreements. Contents: date, agreement, franchisee name, address, officials' names, and necessary permits for excavation or construction.

C216 *Cable Television Consumer Complaints.* Contents: date, name of complainant, address, phone, reason, resolution.

C217 *Data Processing Files.* Records of use of computers to store and process information. Contents: usually include department, job no., file or control no., date in and out. If the job involves installation of a new computer system or software, a separate file or project will exist with supporting documents.

C218 *Equipment Maintenance Files.* Contents: may include name of equipment, I.D. no., controlling unit or department, work order no., date, problem, type of work done, numeric file no., manufacturer's model and serial nos., mileage and parts (if vehicle). Note: Different divisions, such as Communications, Buildings and Equipment, may maintain their own files.

C219   *FCC Citation Records.* Files of corrective measure taken by communications to answer citation. Contents: work order no., description, date, letter responding to U.S. FCC certifying that condition has been corrected.

C220   *Motor Vehicles Files.* Records for wheeled vehicles, boats, and planes, including fuel requests by employees, fuel issuance records, fuel costs, mileage reports, and vehicle parts purchased for maintenance.

C221   *Motor Vehicle Use.* A record of level of use. Contents: location or department no., serial or equipment no., make or description of vehicle, date, mileage, purpose, user. Note: Related records, sometimes maintained on computer, include license registration files, master files, and roadside care files.

C222   *Radio Logs.* Emergency messages sent by radio. Contents: text of message, date, time, name of operator, name and phone of caller, responding department (medical, sheriff or police, fire, etc.), time of response.

C223   *Records Retention Schedules, Records Storage.* Old warehoused records requiring little access. Contents: depositing department no., records center control no., date, circulation record (retrieval dates). Note: Not all records centers have complete inventories of department records or use the same indexing system. Usually, individual departments are responsible for knowing records contents and retention requirements. See C102.

C224   *Rent or Use of Government-Owned Buildings.* Records of agreements for public use of government-owned buildings (e.g., Veteran's Memorial rented out for meetings). Contents: fees charged and paid, name of user, purpose, cost to city or county, and permit agreement.

C225   *Reprographics or Duplicating Files.* Records of printing, reproduction, microfilming, binding, graphics, and forms design services. Contents: name of requesting department, work order no., date, description of work, completion date, cost.

C226   *Salvage Records.* Files on repair, recycle, sale, discard or auction of unusable or unneeded items. Contents: department no., inventory no. or equipment I.D. no., description, original cost, action needed (repair, discard, transfer, store, recycle, etc.), reason, disposition. If auction or sale takes place, the amount received is added with a copy to the Auditor.

C227   *Storage, Warehouse, and Mail Files.* Voluminous and repetitious records, not detailed here, keep track of supplies and equipment needing storage and in-house mail delivery. Computerized records now show where an item is, how much there is, and when it must be re-ordered.

C228   *Other General Service Records.* Purchase orders and inventories, and files on equipment depreciation, equipment rental, equipment replacement, fixed-asset acquisition and depreciation, equipment income and cost reports, major repairs.

C229   GRAND JURIES

County. Drawn and summoned once a year in each county, grand juries have 19 members except in Los Angeles, which has 23. Their civil function is to investigate county government operations. Their criminal function is to investigate possible crime. They are advised by the District Attorney in criminal matters. Deliberations are closed. Reports are made public after filing with the Superior Court.

(GRAND JURIES, CONT.)

C230   **Grand Jury Report.** An annual report made to the presiding Superior Court judge that may include civil or criminal investigations. In some counties, civil and criminal (or indictment) grand juries are separate. The report is available to the public, but not all details of the original investigations are included. Criminal Grand Jury transcripts are made public 10 days after delivery to defendants or their attorneys, unless ordered otherwise by the court. Some reports are made at the end of the fiscal year, others at the end of the calendar year. Contents: Committee Reports, background, findings, recommendations, copies of letters sent.

C231   **Civil Grand Jury Report Response.** A response must be made within a specified period of time by the governing body or head of the affected agency. Contents: responses to the Committee Reports, findings, recommendations.

C232   # HEALTH SERVICES, HEALTH CARE

County and City. Very few cities in California have a health department. State law mandates the county to provide medical service for indigent residents. Low-income access to health care is provided by the state through Medi-Cal. County service areas are typically divided into communicable disease (AIDS, venereal disease, tuberculosis), environmental health (sanitation, hazardous and solid waste), hospitals, mental health, public health (nursing, clinics, disease prevention), and substance abuse.

Specific programs include: biomedical laboratory services; child health; disability prevention; disabled children's service; emergency medical services; family planning; hazardous materials; immunization; inpatient and outpatient programs; medical service in correctional institutions; mental health clinics; nursing home inspections and referral; nutrition supplements; pre-natal care and well-baby care; prevention and community education; primary care clinics; sanitary regulations for food, milk, drinking water and waste disposal; TB clinic; VD clinic. Other services that may fall under Health include pest control (see Agriculture, C008), mosquito abatement (see Regional, R001–R005), Animal Control (C027). Organization varies from county to county. Many services are contracted out to private companies.

Money for most programs comes from the state, which requires periodic reports. Records of individuals enrolled in services such as Refugee Health, Family Planning, Mental Health, and AIDS are confidential. Statistical reports and other records of contracted services, inspection of facilities, and contract monitoring are public. As examples, this guide examines typical records from five areas: communicable disease, hazardous materials, licensing and inspection, statistical records, and vital records. These areas may not always appear as listed here.

C233   **Communicable Diseases**

Involves efforts to control disease transmission among humans, such as AIDS, venereal disease, measles, tuberculosis, typhoid, etc.

C234   **Block Grant Money Record.** An activity report to the state from the county. Contents: money received; description of priorities (surveillance, blood studies, testing data); past and future activities for each priority area; comments and recommendations; needs assessment; remarks.

C235   **Project Progress Report.** Reports from the county on specific projects, such as "Home Health, Attendant, and Hospice Care" or "AIDS Education and Prevention." Contents: project title, dates covered, contract no. and dollar amount, name of agency and responsible officer. Also, for each project goal: description, progress to date, statistics, problems, and crisis issues.

C236 **Hazardous Materials**

State law requires counties and permits cities to take responsibility for enforcement of hazardous-materials handling. Because there is no standardization of how this is to be managed, records may be found in various agencies, though usually in health services.

C237 *Hazardous Materials Business Plan.* Contents: business name, mailing address, phone; owner's name; Standard Industrial Classification code; nature of business, emergency contact persons and phones; building and street plan showing where hazardous materials are stored, plans for response and evacuation in case of accident, training plan for employees. Plans must be indexed by street address and company name and be available for public inspection, except maps of precise location of hazardous materials. Additional statements required are Hazardous Material Information (chemical category, maker's name, etc.) and Hazardous Waste Information (chemical category, conditions of storage, etc.).

C238 *Hazardous Materials Inspections.* Contents: Site I.D. no.; name, address, phone; date; type of inspection; details (treatment, maintenance, buffer zone for containers and tanks, etc.), comments, signatures of inspector and contact person; date and time.

C239 *Hazardous Materials Negative Response.* A signed verification form stating that the facility does not handle or store materials falling within the hazardous materials guidelines.

C240 *Other Hazardous Materials Records.* Registration of underground storage facilities; underground tank closure or modification plans; notification of or emergency response to release of hazardous materials (may be confidential if clean-up indicates future litigation); annual inventory (chemicals, types of waste, amounts, information for fire, health, safety personnel, responsible person and phone in case of emergency).

C241 **Licensing and Inspection**

Most inspections are done by an environmental health division. If violations are found, those records are not made public until corrections have been made or the case goes to court.

C242 *Apartment Inspections.* Contents: case no., date, address, owner, licensee, or manager, number of units, checklist of areas inspected (windows, water, stairs, laundry, heating, etc.), description of action needed, re-inspection date, and date of file closing.

C243 *Food Program Inspections.* Contents: date, report no., business (DBA) name and address, owner/operator's name and address, inspector's name, details on food protection, employee sanitation and health, vermin, equipment, food storage methods, water, waste, permit license, recheck, action taken.

C244 *Prosecution Files.* Reports of inspection cases that went to court. Contents: case no., address, date of filing, defendant's name or DBA, defendant's address and occupation, type of business, complainant, court, judge, complaint, law or ordinance in question, plea, verdict, disposition, any prior history.

C245 *Solid Waste Facilities Permit Application.* Contents: I.D. no.; facility name, address; description and general location; types of waste received; beginning date; property owners' and facility operators' name, address and phone; certified signatures; fees. Evaluation of certain factors (geologic, hydrologic, biotic, noise, cultural/esthetic, public service and utility, socio-economic) is required.

C246 *Solid Waste Facility Inspection Form.* Contents: facility file no.; inspection date; facility name, location, inspector's name; owner/operator's names; compliance or violation record checks, personnel, physical conditions, safety measures, equipment, maintenance, conditions of noise, litter, odor, and traffic conditions.

C247   ***Solid Waste Transfer Station Inspection.*** Contents: file no., date, facility name and location, inspector, check-up of operations, physical conditions, noise and odor, record keeping, safety factors, comments.

C248   ***Swimming Pool Inspections.*** Contents: business address, owner's name and DBA, mailing address, permit license, date, details of: recirculation equipment, construction type, safety equipment, restrooms, pool quality (chlorine, cyanurates, test kits, pH, etc.), action to be taken, inspector's signature.

C249   ***Other Health Inspections.*** Contents vary but are generally similar to other inspections listed in this section. Not all the following are done in every county:

> air pollution
> disaster
> sanitation (water, toilets, dead animals)
> ionizing radiation
> land use
> milk and dairy products
> noise
> occupational health (industrial hygiene, injury-illness data)
> rabies and animal control
> recreational health (beaches, trailer parks, mobile-home parks, campsites)
> safety (housing, trailer parks, abandoned excavations, refrigerators)
> vector control (diseases transmitted by insects or animals)
> waste (community treatment plants, septic tanks, waste-water reclamation, industrial waste sites, etc.)
> water supplies (public and private wells, ice plants, backflow of waste water into public systems)
> miscellaneous (public drinking cups, infected packing material, common towels, public toilets, wiping rags)

C250   Statistical Reports

Statistics originate at the county level and are used for determining funding and hospital needs, and alerting physicians to health conditions.

C251   ***Annual Live Birth and Fetal Death Report Tables.*** Statistical reports based on county birth records broken down by "health planning area," census tract, ethnicity, age of mother, complications of pregnancy, labor, and delivery, hospital where birth occurred, and various combinations of the above.

C252   ***Annual (Disease) Tally.*** Statistics for each disease by age group and ethnicity.

C253   ***Annual (Infant) Death Reports.*** Same tables as above (C252) for infant deaths.

C254   ***Morbidity Report.*** A weekly and monthly report of the number of deaths in the county, by specific disease and location.

C255   ***Public Health Clinic Reports.*** Half-yearly statistics for clinic visits. Contents: type of clinic, percentages for ethnicity, Southeast Asian refugee status, sex, age, clinic location, and whether visit is first-time or repeat.

C256   ***Public Health Clinic Visits Report.*** A statistical report of visits to county health clinics by type of clinic. Contents: totals by month and year for each clinic (pregnancy testing, family planning, child health, disability prevention, teen pregnancy, immunizations, sexually transmitted disease, premarital blood test, TB skin test, chest, hypertension screening, prenatal, primary care, children's primary care, podiatry, Southeast Asian, dental health, and children's dental).

C257   **Vital Registration (Births and Deaths)**

The approved full-time local health department usually functions as the local registrar of vital statistics (births and deaths), or, lacking such a department, there is a state-appointed local registrar. This function is mandated by state law.

C258   *Birth Certificates.* Registration of births. Contents (of the public portion): child's name and sex; birth date and hour; hospital name, address, city or county; mother and father's names, places of birth and ages; certification; date; attending physician's name, address, license no., date; death date (if any); local registrar's signature and date, certificate no. Note: Original certificates are indexed and filed with state Registrar of Vital Statistics (S381). After two years copies are sent to the county Recorder.

C259   *Death Certificates.* Registration of death after five days from death date. Contents: deceased's name, sex, race/ethnicity, birthplace, birth date, citizenship, social security no., marital status, surviving spouse, last occupation, employer; usual residence; death date, place, cause, related injuries; parents' names and birthplaces; physician or coroner's name, address, license no.; burial type, date, place, names of embalmer and funeral director, certificate no. Note: Original certificates are indexed and filed with the state Registrar of Vital Statistics (S381). After two years, copies are sent to Recorder. See also Coroner in cases where the cause of death is under investigation.

C260   *Fetal Death Certificate.* Contents: same as above (C259) plus funeral director's name, disposition of body, cemetery or crematory address. Note: Copies available from county recorder after two years. Original indexed and filed with state Vital Statistics Registrar (S381).

C261   *Other Miscellaneous Health Records.* Drugs and Vaccines Destroyed; Drug Inventory; Emergency Medical Services—Communications Equipment Failure (not public if filed as an "incident report"); Emergency Medical Services—Certificates (issued, suspended, or revoked).

C262   # HOUSING

City and County. Uses state, federal and local funds to acquire or construct low- and moderate-income housing, rehabilitate blighted housing, control or stabilize rents, subsidize rents and loans, give housing advice and information, enforce building codes and lending laws and help with minor repairs. Departments that usually include housing programs are Community Development, Planning, and Redevelopment Agency. See also state Department of Housing and Community Development (S388).

The U.S. Department of Housing and Urban Development (HUD) has some 66 programs that assist housing through funds, research, surveys and anti-discrimination laws. In 1988, the state Department of Housing and Community Development had 23 loan and grant programs used by local governments and nonprofit organizations. These were aimed at small cities, rural counties, and Native Americans. Because some degree of local choice is available in using the funds and carrying out projects, local organization and record keeping vary. Records for persons receiving assistance are confidential. Audits and other reports are done by HUD. See also Housing and Community Development Department (S388).

(HOUSING, CONT.)

C263   ***Community Development Block Grant Funds Application.*** An application for state money to fund various projects (purchase of property, construction of public buildings, rehabilitation of property, grant-in-aid programs, relocation assistance, industrial or commercial property expansion, historic preservation, community planning). Contents: city or county and contact person; application type; names, addresses of all district state and U.S. legislative representatives; budgets; activity and program description; maps; letters; joint powers agreement (if needed); local governing resolutions; local population and housing data; documentation of need; sources and uses of funds.

C264   ***Grantee Performance Report—HUD Form 4949.*** An annual report sent by the county or city receiving Community Development Block Grant funds to HUD. Contents: city or county, grant no., responsible official and phone, dates covered, each activity with description, date begun, economic level of those benefiting, amount spent, statistics on units completed, sites purchased, and loans processed; summary of funds received and spent; block grant funds directly used for acquisition, construction or rehabilitation of property for housing by individual project, number of units, number occupied by low and moderate income; block grant funds used for staff and administration. Also includes reports on efforts to further fair housing, on households displaced (by census tract and ethnicity); and on housing issues and problems unique to the reporting city or county.

C265   ***Pre-Rehabilitation Report (HUD Form 400-14A).*** A record required by HUD for a rental project prior to rehabilitation. Contents: date, project no., owner name, address, phone, grantee no., funds requested, total estimated cost, estimated number units after rehabilitation, type of ownership, size and rent per unit, economic level of tenants, ethnicity and size of household, whether headed by a woman, whether receiving rental assistance.

C266   ***Project Completion Report (HUD Form 400-14B).*** A record required by HUD for a rental project after completion of rehabilitation. Contents: date, project no., owner's name, project address, source, amount and terms of loans, amount spent for relocation, economic level and number of recipients, size and rent per unit, economic level of tenants, ethnicity and size of household, whether headed by a woman, whether receiving rental assistance.

C267   ***Project Files.*** Records of housing department activity such as rehabilitation of a block or area. Contents: project name, text of legislation, surveys (address, type work to be done, comments), census data, site drawings, agendas and minutes of community meetings, administrative reports, lists (of property owners, mailings), maps, relocations, construction bids and awards, assessed value of properties, deeds, notes, encumbrances, invoices, inspection records, periodic and final staff reports.

C268   ***Rehabilitation Contracts.*** Agreements with a city or county to facilitate loans and pay the difference between a borrower's ability to pay and a lender's willingness to loan. Contents: project no. or name, location and owner of property, assessed value, building permits, bank or lender financial documents, plans and specifications.

C269   HOUSING AUTHORITY

City and County or combined, and Native American tribes. Housing Authorities are independent entities set up by state law that issue tax-exempt bonds to acquire land and build, manage, maintain, and rehabilitate rental units. They also can lease housing, operate temporary, mobile-home, and farmworker housing, pay subsidies to landlords, and conduct regular inspections in return for obtaining low-income rentals. Other activities related to property owned by the authority are housing demolition, landscaping, sewers, streets, fencing, etc.

Housing authorities may operate under a variety of U.S. HUD, U.S. Farmers Home Administration, or state-law housing programs. Reports are required by the source of funds. The Board of Commissioners or Directors may be appointed by the Mayor or Board of Supervisors; or the city council or the Board of Supervisors may sit as the Housing Authority Commissioners.

C270 **Housing Authority Annual Report.** A report made to the city or county governing body and the state Housing and Community Development Department (S388) by each local authority. Contents: number of units by type of program; bedrooms per unit by type of program; number of households by ethnic origin; number of units, and number of bedrooms under construction, planned, and/or demolished.

C271 **Leased Housing Records.** Contents: landlord's name and address, location of building, number of units, payments.

C272 **Other Housing Authority Records.** Reports on maintenance, management, utilities, community services, human resources, finance, leasing, modernization, security, and administration.

C273 **INDUSTRIAL DEVELOPMENT AUTHORITY**

City and County. Sells low-interest, federal tax-exempt bonds to fund private business in constructing or purchasing industrial facilities with the object of increasing employment.

C274 **Industrial Development Bond Files.** Contents: memoranda, correspondence, resolutions, applications, reports, ordinances, cash receipts, letters of credit, and notes.

C275 **Other Industrial Development Authority Records.** Minutes, resolutions, ordinances. See also Real Estate.

C276 **LIBRARIES**

City and County or combination. Provide library services. Some counties provide services to jails, health, and community care facilities. Law libraries, separate from city or county libraries, are generally available in all counties. They typically have their own budget and report to the Board of Supervisors or Board of Library Trustees. (see also S475)

C277 **Annual Report to State Library.** Contents: name, director's name, location, phone, and telecommunication address, jurisdiction, library systems membership. Also annual statistics for: number of borrowers, bookmobiles, branches, hours of service, numbers. and staff professional levels, income sources and amount, details of expenditures, books and other materials acquired, non–English-language materials acquired, non-English holdings by specific language, circulation statistics, salary ranges for all staff, and microcomputer use.

C278 **Depository Agreements.** Agreements between library and other government departments to collect and preserve certain documents. Contents: date, donating agency, description of donation, and relevant correspondence.

C279 **Library Services and Construction Act Application.** An application submitted to the California State Library to qualify for federal grant money. Contents: fiscal year, amount, project title, applicant, telephone, school system, fiscal agent, type of program and clientele, contact person, participants, budget summary, abstract of project, civil rights certificate.

(LIBRARIES, CONT.)

C280   *Library Services and Construction Act Final Summary Report.* A report submitted to the State Library. Contents: dates covered by report, grant I.D. no., grantee, project title, date, comments, total program cost, accomplishments, plans for continuation of service, publicity results, evaluation.

C281   *Other Library Records, Reports.* Circulation Statistics, Gifts and Loans, Library Services and Construction Act Quarterly Report Narrative, Library Services and Construction Act Financial and Narrative Statement, Library Services and Construction Act Grant Award Modification.

C282   *Library Board of Trustees, Board of Library Commissioners, Public Library Commission Files.* Records of the Library Board, which advises on policies, may appoint Library Director, or may act as advisor to mayor, city council or Board of Supervisors. Contents: agendas, meetings minutes, reports.

C283   ## LICENSES AND PERMITS

City and County. Local licenses and permits vary considerably and are issued by an array of departments. Fees collected typically go to the city or county treasurer. Most state licenses and permits are related to business and professional activities, and may be duplicated by local licensing to some degree. For state listings, see entries in index with an "S" number under "Licenses and Permits."

The record may include the application along with the license or permit. Applications tend to have more information, although some parts may be confidential. Contents vary depending on use and jurisdiction, but typically include: name, address, phone; business name or DBA, address, phone; description of activity; I.D. nos. (social security, federal employer), seller's permit (if necessary), dates (beginning and expiration); record of permission received from other government depts. (fire, police); record of business license commission recommendation. Chartered cities usually require a business license or business tax certificate from all businesses.

C284   The following list is a sampling from six cities and six counties in California. Each entry is followed by the department typically requiring the license or permit.

advertising—police, zoning
aircraft repair, refueling—fire
ambulances—health
ambulance driver—police
amusement park—police
animal acts and show—animal control, police
animal feeding yard—health
antique, second-hand dealer—police
apartment house occupancy—public works
athletic, health clubs—health
auctions and auctioneers—police, city clerk
auto wrecking—police, zoning
automobile accessories—police
automobile rentals—police
automobile repairs—fire
bakery and employees—health
baths, bathing—police, health, city clerk

bicycle—fire or police
billiards—police, city clerk
bingo—city clerk, charities, police
blasting or explosives—fire
business—city clerk, tax collector, treasurer
cabaret—police, city clerk
cable television—Board of Supervisors, city council
camping—parks & recreation
card room—police
carnival—city clerk
carpet cleaning—health
cemetery—planning
charitable solicitation—city clerk or social services
chemical use—fire
chemical toilets—health
cigar factory—health
circus—animal control, police
combustible materials—fire
commercial development—planning
compressed gases—fire
conditional use—planning
condominium conversion—planning
construction—public works
construction contractors—public works,
convalescent homes—police, health
cycloramas—police
dairy farm—health
dance hall—police, city clerk
demolition—fire, planning, public works
dog license—police
drilling/extracting oil, gas—planning
drive-in theater—police, fire
dry-cleaning plants—fire
dump—health
electric wiring—public works
electronic games—city clerk, planning, police
employment office—police
encroachment on property—public works
escort service—police
fires, open and outdoors—fire
fire regulations (variance)—fire
fireworks display, retail, storage—fire, police
flammable finishes, application of—fire
flammable liquid fuel oil, storage of—fire

flood control, connections to, trespassing—public works
flying fields—planning, city clerk
food preparation and service—health
food products and marketing—health
food vending machines—health
fumigation, flammable—fire
fumigation, toxic—health
garages—fire
garbage trucks—health, police
gas cylinder—fire
golf course—police, parks & recreation
grading—public works
guns, firearms, weapons, ammunition—police
hawker, peddler—police
hazardous, toxic materials—fire, health
hillside review—planning
hog farm—health
home-located business—planning
house moving-public works, zoning
horse—zoning, animal control, health
horse shows—animal control
hospital—health
hotel occupancy—public works
house moving—police
jitney bus—police, public utilities
junk/salvage dealers and collectors—police, health, city clerk, fire
laundry—health
limousines—police
liquefied gases, storage & use of—fire
liquid waste—health
lumber yard—fire
mall, covered—fire
marching—police
marriage—county clerk
massage parlors and employees—police, city clerk
matches, storage of—fire
mattress factory—health
meat delivery—health
mobile homes, parks—planning
mosquito abatement—health
noise abatement—planning
nursery school—police
nursing home—health
occupancy of building—public works

on-site grading—planning
ovens, industrial—fire
parade—police/sheriff, city clerk
parking permits—police
parking signs—public works
parking, valet—police
pawnbroker, pawnshop—police, city clerk
pedicab and driver—police, public utilities
pesticide application, retail, storage—agriculture
pet shops, kennels—health, animal control, city clerk
petroleum oils, storage of—fire
photography processing—fire
pipeline (oil, gas, water, fuel, gasoline and other)—fire
planned industrial area—planning
places of assembly—fire
plastering—public works
plumbing—public works
police, private—police
pool rooms—police, city clerk
public-address systems—police
public assembly—fire
radioactive materials—fire, health
refrigeration equipment—fire
rail transport—public utility
residential development—planning
right-of-way—planning, public works
road excavation—planning, public works
rodeos—health, police
roofing—fire
rubbish-fires—fire
school-bus drivers—public utilities
service stations—fire
septic tanks—health
sewer—public works
sidewalk cafe—planning
sight-seeing guide—police
sight-seeing vehicle—public utilities
signs (billboard, non-conforming, inflatable displays)—zoning
skating rink—city clerk
smelter-fire
soft drinks—health
stables—health, zoning
storage tanks (under or above ground)—fire
street artist—city clerk

(LICENSES AND PERMITS, CONT.)

> street meeting—police, fire
> subdivision, residential—planning
> swill trucks—health
> swimming pools, spas—health
> tattoo parlor—health
> taxicab—police, or public utilities
> tents and air supported structures—fire
> theater—police, fire, city clerk
> timber harvesting—planning
> tire recapping—fire
> top soil—planning
> tow truck and driver—police
> traveling show—police, fire
> tree planting—planning, public works
> vehicles, overweight, overwidth—police
> video games—city clerk, planning, police
> water lines—public works
> wells, construction, repair, abandonment—health, public works
> welding and cutting—fire
> windmill—planning

C285 **Licenses and Permits Index.** An index is usually arranged alphabetically by applicant name, address, or activity. There may be several indexes, each maintained by the issuing body. The index for charities may be by group name and typically is located separately from the business files. See also Public Works, Building Permits (C369–C371).

C286 **LOCAL AGENCY FORMATION COMMISSION (LAFCO)**

County. Mandated for each county by state law to discourage urban sprawl and government overlap. Reviews, approves, or rejects proposals for the creation, annexation, disincorporation or related changes of two or more cities. Has authority for independent special districts in matters of formation, merger, dissolution, and sphere of influence. May be organized under Planning Department, County Administrator, or separately. See also Regional Government (R001–R005).

C287 **Applications.** Documents filed in support of positions argued before the Commission, correspondence, legal opinions, environmental impact reports, maps, research by Local Agency Formation Commission staff as background for a recommendation on approval.

C288 **Disclosure Statement.** A statement of ownership or financial interest of applicants. Contents: names of persons with ownership interest in property; if a corporation, names of those holding more than 10% of shares; if a nonprofit corporation, names of directors or trustees; names of persons transacting more than $250 worth of business with a commissioner; names of persons contributing more than $250 to any commissioner, name of proposal, signature.

C289 **Special District Files.** Records of districts that are new (to ensure they do not overlap) or are changing their sphere of influence (for example, a water district seeking to add territory). Contents: name of district, copies of deeds, memos of understanding, correspondence, maps, resolutions, background research and information.

C290 **PARKING**

City, County, or Special District. Functions are rarely found organized in the same way. Generally responsible for off-street parking, citation issuance, ordinance and regulation decisions, parking meters (planning, administration, maintenance, revenue collection and accounting, security), intersection control, towing, radio calls for violations, crossing guards. Traffic control may be a subdivision. A Parking Authority may finance and construct a facility and lease operation back to the city or a group. Off-street parking may be administered under Public Works or Transportation, but selected and designed by a Parking Commission. Meter collection may be contracted out, be under a Public Safety Department, or under Traffic Engineering at Public Works. There may be a "special district" specifically for parking. See also Transportation.

C291 *Off-street Parking Construction Files.* Contents: legislative decision, planning, contract bid and award (if contracted out), inspections, leaseback (if any). Financial arrangements are usually part of the legislative decision. Public Works may have contract records. The City Clerk has legislative decision records. Building permits are at Public Works.

C292 *Parking Citations.* Records are kept by police or a special parking enforcement staff. Contents: date, location, license no., make of car, violation, amount of fine, issuing officer, citation no. Note: Some cities have computer-generated lists.

C293 *Parking Meter Inventory.* A list of meter location. Contents: location, serial no.

C294 *Other Parking Records.* Abandoned vehicle records, agenda and minutes of Parking Authority Meetings, Annual Report of Parking Authority, Off-street Parking Revenue, Residential Parking District Permits (permits issued to area residents that restrict parking for non-residents), Towing Records.

C295 **PARKS AND RECREATION, PARKS AND BEACHES**

City, County, and/or Special District. Park areas range from small islands to thousands of acres. Activities include sports, education, and cultural events.

C296 *Dock, Harbor, Marina Permit Files.* Records of boat mooring permits. Contents: owner's or corporation name, address, dock site, amount charged, type of boat, registration no. See also Boating and Waterways (S069).

C297 *Incident and Accident Reports.* Records of accidents, injuries, vandalism, theft, and vehicle collisions that occur at facilities. Contents: Separate forms are submitted to cover a specific type of incident and usually include date, time, place, names and addresses of those involved, extent of injuries, aid administered, witness information, location, description of damages to property, estimated value of property damaged, persons responsible for damage, diagram of accidents, general description of incident.

C298 *Lease Files, Agreement Files, Facility Lease Files, Property Management Records.* Files of long-term lease agreements between the department and private parties using the property and facilities to set up food concessions, restaurants, operate tennis and golf shops, and handle recreational activities such as rowboating and horseback riding. Contents: lease agreements, contracts, bids, revenue statements and accounting records, name of lessee, tenant or concessioneer, related correspondence, and insurance documents.

C299 *Lifeguard Administration Files, Lifeguard Facility Files.* Information on activities at municipal or county swimming pools and beaches. Swimming pools contents:

(PARKS AND RECREATION, CONT.)

weekly attendance reports, activities, costs, revenues, fee waivers, training and certification of lifeguards, incident reports or daily log of rescues, drownings, near-drownings, accidents, first-aid cases, and vandalism. Beaches: number of drownings, rescues, diving deaths, diving accidents. See also Coroner.

C300 **Open Space Acquisition and Administration Files.** Contents: memoranda, attorneys' opinions, maps, agreements, master plans, resolutions, environmental impact reports, bond status reports, soil reports, water and gas rights, estimating or appraisal sheets, related correspondence.

C301 **Park Inventory Records, Park Facilities List.** Contents: maps, park data sheets, number of acres, equipment, building blueprints, block and lot nos., description of plants and facilities.

C302 **Park Safety Inspection Reports, Facility Inspection Reports.** Inspections of park equipment and facilities by supervisory or division staff. Contents: location, date, repair or work requests, public complaints, equipment checklist.

C303 **Permits and Reservations Files, Use Permit Files, Facility Use Permits.** Records of requests for permission to use a facility. Contents: name of organization, fees, site requested, date, time, correspondence, insurance policies, bond information, registration logs, description of activities, anticipated attendance, receipts, billing.

C304 **Pesticide Spraying Files.** Contents: name of pesticide, amount used, name and certification of sprayer.

C305 **Public Service Program Files, Special Activity Files.** Records of cultural and recreational activities. Contents: description of activity, number of participants, budget, expenditures, registration forms, brochures, fees, donations and grants, insurance, equipment rentals and purchases.

C306 **Swimming Pool Management Files.** Contents: permits, billing and revenue reports, attendance, invoices, insurance documents, registration logs and forms, pool use reports for Red Cross or physical education courses, cleaning log books. Note: Sanitary inspections are performed by the Health Department (C248).

C307 # PENSIONS/RETIREMENT

City and County. Administers retirement, disability, and death benefits for all participating employees. Fire and police may have their own funds, or may, like most employees, contract with the state Public Employees Retirement Systems (S541). Some governments carry both the state and an independent, self-funded system. Some have privately-funded pension systems.

C308 **Annual Report of Board of Fire/Police Pension Commissioners.** Summary data for fiscal year. Contents: revenue, expenditures, assets, liabilities, pension distribution in categories (types of pensions, age of pensioners, number of years of service, and rank).

C309 **Investment Portfolio.** Investment activity for the fiscal year, if pension plan is private. Contents: names of corporations in which funds are invested, bonds rate of interest and year of maturity, number of stock shares held, price per share, totals.

C310 **Other Pension Records.** Registers of active and potential retirees (including deceased), medical insurance administration and statistics (including Medicare), payroll deductions statistics, election results (proposed changes in plan).

C311 **PLANNING, RESOURCE MANAGEMENT, REGIONAL PLANNING, PLANNING AND DEVELOPMENT, ENVIRONMENTAL QUALITY, LAND USE**

City and County. Mandated by state law for all counties. All cities must develop a general plan and use environmental impact reports. Responsibilities are preparation of a master plan, development review, zoning adjustment, use permits, and land subdivision. Directed by the Planning Commission, if there is one. Involves many government functions, including fire, police, building and safety, parks and recreation, transportation, utilities, housing, and community redevelopment. See also Special Districts (R003) and Local Agency Formation Commission C286).

C312 *Annexation Plans.* City. Records of new territory additions. Also see City Clerk, Annexations.

C313 *Certificate of Compliance for Property Development.* Certification for a legal building site. Contents: deeds, maps, legal description of property or assessor's reference no., builder's name, address, and phone; date and certificate no.

C314 *Conditional Use Permit.* A permit issued with the understanding that certain conditions will be met. Contents: name, address, phone of owner or lessee, purpose or need for permit, location, assessor's reference no., restrictions on use if granted (public need, proper relation to other land, etc.), supporting facts, exhibits, maps, site plan, and filing fee. Issuance of permits is determined by the city or county charter.

C315 *Developer Agreements.* Records of various aspects of property development. Contents: developer's name, address, and phone; developer's agent (if any); date, name, and location of development; placement and use of temporary facilities; agreements for public facilities to be built by developer; maps; correspondence; restrictions; expiration date for development rights; ordinances and resolutions.

C316 *Environmental Review Reports or Case Files.* Records evaluating the environmental impact of land use proposals. Contents depend on whether there is judged to be an area impact. If so, the file may contain: owner's name and address; contact person's name, address, phone; developer's name and address; zoning case file no.; project description; environmental check list or assessment (may be hundreds of pages); maps, plot plans, and picture strips; letters from health, fire, school, and water offices; assessee list (owners within a 500-foot radius of the site); correspondence; details for hearing date and disposition.

C317 *Master or General Plan.* A county or city-wide master plan mandated by state law. Contents: research reports on land use, traffic circulation (roads, transit), housing, conservation, seismic factors, noise, scenic highway, redevelopment, cultural resources, urban design, energy conservation, recreation, industrial, commercial, and public facilities, services, safety, and open space. Policies derived from the general plan may give details on functions (noise, housing, etc.) and specific geographic areas.

C318 *Planned District, Specific Area, Community Area Project Files.* Documents related to a specific project. Contents: area, time period involved, applications (new development, building modifications, etc.), resolutions, demographic analysis, uses allowed and prohibited, property owner lists, maps, notices of public hearings, reports, rezoning requests, special use permits, business licenses issued, administrative records (travel logs, staff expenditures).

C319 *Planning Index.* Cross indexes for retrieving information on subjects related to planning such as tentative subdivision maps, parcel maps, zoning ordinances, special permits. Contents: location of property, legal description, applicant's name, name of development, map nos., zoning information. Not maintained by all cities or counties.

(PLANNING, CONT.)

C320   **Special Permits.** Applications for boundary adjustment, design review, directional tract sign, major/minor variance, and surface mining.

C321   **Subdivision Case Files.** Records of land for subdivision use. Contents: application form with owner's name and address; current and proposed land use; assessor's reference nos.; number of lots; water source; sewage disposal; plans for lot grading and street improvements; environmental review or report; planning staff report; disposition; legislative decisions.

C322   **Zoning Case Files.** Records of changes in land use through zoning variances, conditional use permits, design review, planned unit development, rezoning. Contents: application form with owner, lessee, purchaser's or agent's name, address, phone; property address; assessor's reference no.; zone; census tract; land use; proposed change and reason; plot, floor plan and elevation; environmental review or report (C316); planning staff report; disposition.

C323   **Zoning Maps.** Maps of land use showing such details as community planning areas, environmental review areas, school district boundaries, annexations, height limits, historical sites, topographical features, environmental features (flora and fauna, erosion, etc.). Contents: map no., assessor's reference no., zoning districts, street names, block and lot outlines. Some planning departments may index their maps by subject. See also Public Works, Engineering Maps (C380).

C324   **Zoning Ordinances or Regulation Books.** Regulations for local land use. Contents: zoning categories, definitions and land-use restrictions.

C325   **Zoning Violation Investigations.** Records of complaints of alleged violations. Contents: file no.; complainant's name; location of property; owner's name, address and phone; reason for complaint; photographs; inspection notices; date; results.

C326   **Other Planning Department Records.** Census data, coastal area files, designated historic-site files, energy files, undeveloped area files, regional growth files, zoning appeals board minutes and decisions.

C327   PLANNING COMMISSION

City and County. The planning commission is a part of the local planning agency. Members are appointed by the Mayor or the Board of Supervisors. The commission has responsibility for content and administration of zoning laws and compliance with the General Plan, and sets general policy for the Planning Department.

C328   **Planning Commission Records.** Hearings, reviews of environmental reports, meeting minutes, appeals, recommendations to City Council or Board of Supervisors.

C329   POLICE, LAW ENFORCEMENT, PUBLIC SAFETY

City. Responsible for enforcment of laws, investigative services, traffic enforcement, and issuing, controlling and revoking certain types of business permits. In some areas, the department handles animal control, property storage, evidence collection and analysis, statistical reporting, abandoned-vehicle abatement, crime analysis, street crossing guards, and K-9 dogs. The equivalent at the county level is the Sheriff.

C330   **Arrest Register, Arrest Log, Booking Register, Arrest Cards, Blotter, Incident Report.** Records of police arrests. Contents: arrested person's name, address, occupation, date and place of birth, sex, race, general physical characteristics and special marks; description and location of offense; name of complainant or victim, unless a juvenile; time, date and place of arrest; if previously fingerprinted and photographed, bail, disposition, warrant check; name of arresting officer and booking sergeant; list of personal property taken; charges filed; time, substance, and location of all complaints or requests for assistance; time, nature of response; name, age, address of victim; case no. Note: These records may be closed to the public if disclosure endangers safety of the person involved or threatens successful completion of the investigation. Inquiries should include the arrest no. or date. See Appendix A, Section 6254(f)(2).

C331   *Auto Theft Files, Stolen Vehicle Files. Information on vehicles reported stolen and recovered.* Contents: name of complainant, description of car, when and how taken, witness information. Note: Access to these records is sometimes limited by police departments to persons involved in the investigation.

C332   *Bail Receipts.* Records for both cash or bonds are made public when posted. Contents: date, booking charge, booking and release dates, inmate name, bonding company and bond no. (if needed).

C333   *Breath Tests.* Records of breath tests for drunk driving. Contents: name, date, time, test results. Not public until the case goes to court. Breath test usage logs are sometimes also maintained. Machine number is included in the police report for the suspect. Machine log contains time, date, place, results and name of person who conducted test.

C334   *Communication Audio Tape Recordings, Voice Tapes, Broadcast Transmission Tapes.* A record of calls made to police dispatchers. Contents: time, location, type of incident, what was said, what action was taken. Sometimes is copied onto a cassette. Access to these tapes varies: in San Diego, it is confidential, in San Francisco and Oakland, it is public, in Los Angeles City, it can be obtained under court order.

C335   *Crime Report, Police Report, Incident Report.* Information on a complaint to which police respond. Contents: reporting agency, beat, incident no., number arrested; complainant's name, address, phone, business or school address, phone, and occupation; type of crime, location, time, details of loss, weapon used; location; suspect's name, address and phone, business address and phone; physical characteristics; vehicle details (if needed); domestic violence information, if any, such as type, injuries, previous incidents, restraining order; officer's signature, serial no., watch, district, supervisor; where other copies of the report were filed. Note: Access to these records varies. Permission of the police department is typically required.

C336   *General Orders, Policy and Procedure Manuals.* Information on department rules and regulations that govern police actions. Contents: department directives outlining standard operating procedures for all situations (buying gas, making narcotics arrests, crowd and riot handling). Note: Regulations are frequently revised and updated.

C337   *Gun Registration Files, Dealer's Record of Sale Files.* Reports of handgun purchases. The original forms are sent to the state Department of Justice, which considers them confidential. However, some police departments, such as San Francisco's, retain copies and make them publicly available. Contents: name, address, date of birth, type of weapon; name, address and business license no. of firearms dealer.

C338   *Incident Logs, Crime Complaint Logs, Serious Incident Reports, Daily Complaint Logs.* A synopsis of crimes reported within the previous 24 hours. Contents: date, incident, type of crime, name and address, beat, location, case no., arrests made, suspect description, description of incident, information on parties involved. If computerized, it is possible to get data by geographic area.

C339   *Internal Affairs, Citizen Complaints, Inspection and Complaint, Complaint Investigation Reports.* Information on complaints against individual police officers is confidential. Contents (of summary statistics): number of complaints, disposition of cases, where incidents occurred, types of complaints. More detailed information can be obtained through a court order.

(POLICE, CONT.)

C340   **Monthly Crime Summary, Monthly Crime Index.** A summary of total crime activity for the month. Contents: year-to-date comparisons and percentage change for crimes by FBI Index categories, tally of reported and actual offenses and clearances; number of arrests made according to type of offense, breakdown of arrestees by sex, age, and race. Not included are certain offenses (worthless documents, missing persons, stolen, recovered, or towed vehicles, lost or found property, or matters investigated by other agencies).

C341   **Parking Ticket File, Parking Violation Notices.** Information on vehicles cited by police for parking violations. Contents: date, location, license no., type of car, type of violation, amount of fine, name of issuing officer, and citation no. Copies of tickets may be kept by the police department. The originals are sent to the municipal court or sometimes to the City Treasurer. See also Parking. Note: Los Angeles City parking matters are handled by the Department of Transportation.

C342   **Police Auction Records.** Sales records of unclaimed property are usually kept by General Services.

S343   **Police Permits and Services, License Files.** See Licenses and Permits (C284). The license or permit name will be found alphabetically listed, followed by the word "police."

C344   **Property, Chain of Custody, Continuity of Evidence Files.** Records of property or evidence taken in relation to a case. Contents: date evidence is checked into a police department property room and by whom; date it is checked out and to whom; date it is returned and its final disposition. Such files are considered confidential by some police departments. Note: Evidence or property collected is usually stated on a police report (C335), which may also be public.

C345   **Recruiting and Training Files, Recruitment and Retention Records, Police Academy Files.** Information on the recruitment and training of police officers. Contents: number of recruiting trips (where, when, who), number of applications processed, and results; annual training statistics, type of training, name of school, hours spent in courses, number of students, statistics on retention of women and minorities (if available), academy training manuals, academy curriculum files (courses on search and seizure, evidence law, deadly force, mob and riot control, etc.).

C346   **Subpoena Logs.** Records of criminal and civil subpoenas served on the police department for police records and appearances by police officers in court. Contents: court, name of litigants, case no., officer to whom subpoena is directed, court dates, type of record requested and why.

C347   **Tear Gas Registration Files, Mace and Tear Gas Gun Records.** Information on purchasers of tear gas. The state Department of Justice maintains records of licensed schools that train people in the use of tear gas and mace (S438). Local police may keep copies. Contents: student's name and address, permit no., date of course, name of school.

C348   **Towing Contract Records.** Information on companies that handle towing services for the police department. Contents: name of company; duration of contract; towing fees; rate schedules; data on police department requirements such as amount of tow trucks, lot space for storing cars, response time. Contract negotiations and setting fees and rates are usually handled by the city or police commission.

C349   **Traffic Citations, Uniform Citations.** Police citations of people for moving violations. Contents: citation no., time, location; driver's name and address, license no., date of birth, signature; vehicle license plate no., model, registered owner; type of violation; signature of issuing officer. Like parking tickets, the police department may keep copies of citations issued; originals are sent to Municipal Court.

C350   ***Uniform Accident Reports, Vehicle Collision Reports, Traffic Collision Reports.***
Contents: arrest and citation no. (if any); location, date, officer's I.D. no.; information on parties involved such as name, address, phone, business address, phone, and
driver license no.; physical characteristics; insurance; vehicle type, license no. May
also include information about injured and witnesses; hospital where people were
taken; sketches of damage to vehicles; property damage, property owner's name,
address, and phone. Other report forms include serious injury, death, driving under
the influence of alcohol or drugs. Access to these records varies.

C351   ***Voided and Dismissed Citations.*** Contents: ticket or citation no.; date; name, and
address of vehicle's registered owner; date of requested dismissal, reason for
dismissal, who approved dismissal, and additional remarks. Also for traffic citations:
type of violation; name of person cited; name of issuing police officer. The records
may also be maintained by Municipal Court.

C352   ***Warrant Files, Notify Warrant Files.*** Written orders from a court to a police officer,
bailiff, or court officer to take a specific action. Types of warrants include criminal
arrest, traffic bench, and search. Outstanding warrants (those that have not yet been
served) are confidential. Warrants already served are returned to the clerk of the
court from which they were issued and become part of the court record (and therefore public). Contents: name listed on the warrant, physical description, last known
address, criminal record, case no., related docket nos., registered warrant no., charge,
bail, and signature or stamp of judge. Search warrants include information on the
place to be searched and the person or thing to be seized. See Courts.

C353   ***Other Police Records.*** Financial reports (money collected for permits and licenses
and sent to Treasurer), administrative reports (activity during month of arrests,
investigations, miles traveled, court visits, etc.)

C354   POLICE COMMISSION, BOARD OF POLICE COMMISSIONERS

City. Supervises, regulates, and controls police activities, depending on the city
charter or action taken by the City Council. Records include meeting agendas and
minutes, hearings and decisions, and various reports.

C355   PROBATION

County. Responsible for adult and juvenile probation, coordinating juvenile crime
prevention, supervising juvenile institutions, collection of restitution for crime victims,
and unresolved child custody case reports. Adult probation function provides information to a criminal court before sentencing. See also Criminal Case Files (C167).

C356   ***Probation Pre-sentence Reports.*** Only public for 60 days after sentencing but become
public again if a defendant is sentenced for a new crime. Contents: defendant's name,
address, previous arrests, present offense, length of probation, and court case no.

C357   PUBLIC ADMINISTRATOR, GUARDIAN, CONSERVATOR

County. Protects property of deceased when there are heirs or a will; acts as guardian
of legally and medically incompetent persons. Cases are referred from county welfare
or social service agencies. Note: Sometimes combined with the Coroner.

C358   ***Public Administrator, Guardian, Conservator Records.*** Case files are confidential.
Once submitted in court, documents are public. See Courts.

C359 **PUBLIC DEFENDER**

County. Represents all indigent persons charged with a crime in the county, mentally ill persons, involuntary conservator or guardianship proceedings and developmentally disabled matters. Note: The operation may be contracted out with the county bar association and called a Private Defender program.

C360 *Public Defender Records.* Case files are confidential. Once submitted in court, documents are public. See Courts.

C361 **PUBLICLY OWNED UTILITIES**

City, County, or Special District. Provides services for gas, electricity, water, garbage, transportation, and sewers. Legislation by the Board of Supervisors or City Council determines the extent of control over budget, fees, staff, etc. Records relate to the type of utility. See Transportation for transit records and Public Utilities Commission (S543) for records of privately owned systems.

C362 *Hydrological Conditions Report.* A report required by the state Water Resources Control Board (S695) of water stored and water flow. Contents (of reservoir storage): acre feet, gain or loss each day, amount released, and surface area. Contents (of river flow within watershed): number of cubic feet per second at specific check points, calculations of available water for each reception point.

C363 *Quarterly Fuel and Energy Report.* A report required by the state Energy Commission (S174) from power generation agencies. Contents: dates covered, reporting agency, customers' names, Standard Industrial Classification, location, total usage, type of service (parks, airport, industrial, household).

C364 *Other Energy Records.* Analysis of pre-treated water for radioactivity, purgeable organics, and chemicals; climate; construction and maintenance of power transmission lines, contracts for sale or purchase of power, ground water basin test records, nuclear and alternative power generation (solar, thermal, co-generation), pipeline inspection and repair, power plant generation, powerhouse release estimates, and seepage of dams.

C365 *Water Quality Reports.* A report required by the state Department of Health (S332). Contents (for drinking water, after purification): date, measurements of turbidity, microbiological contaminants, inorganic and organic chemicals, radiological contaminants, fluorides, and trihalomethanes. Contents (for source water, before purification): date, measurements of bacteria, chlorine residues, temperature, pH, chloride, turbidity, specific conductants, and color.

C366 *Other Water Records.* Contracts for sale or purchase of water to cities, companies, and irrigation districts; files on fire hydrants, dams, pipes, reservoirs, and other waterworks.

C367 *Other Public Utility Records.* Files on customer complaints, customer connections and accounts, equipment maintenance, and real estate and right-of-way purchase. Note: A Public Utilities Commission or Board of Water and Power Commission is responsible for administration of the utilities. Records include agendas, minutes, and hearings.

C368 **PUBLIC WORKS, ENGINEERING SERVICES**

City and County. Manages planning, design, construction, operation, and maintenance of public facilities. These include public buildings, roads, tunnels, bridges, flood control, storm drainage, sewers, and waste disposal. Building permits and inspection for private construction are usually within Public Works, but may be separate. Maintenance may be under General Services (C211). The following are often separate: Airports (see C022), Transportation (C534), Parking (C290), Animal Control (C027), and Real Estate (C411).

This guide groups public works records into five areas: building permits and inspections of private construction; planning, engineering, and design of public construction; traffic management; construction of public facilities; and streets, sewers, flood control, and waste management.

Building Permits and Inspection of Private Construction

C369 *Building Permits.* Permit requirements vary. Contents: building address, tract, block page, and lot parcel; owner's name, address, and phone; contractor and architectural engineer's name, address, phone and license no.; owner exemptions; worker's compensation certificate; lender's name and address; dates; type and extent of work; energy calculation; land survey; structural calculation; soils and geologic report; permit status, construction drawings or building plans, inspection dates and status, and fees. Note: Related permits requiring the same basic information include electrical, plumbing, gas, demolition, house moving, plastering, roofing, sewer, on-site grading, and windmill.

C370 *Building Permit Appeals Board, Board of Examiners and Appeals, Housing Advisory and Appeals Records, Building Appeals Files.* Records of appeals on interpretation of the building code, housing regulations, use of alternative materials and construction methods. Contents: date, application, hearing no., description, relevant documents and permits, and disposition.

C371 *Certificate of Occupancy, Permit of Occupancy.* A permit required to show correction of code violations (health, fire, mechanical, plumbing, etc.) for buildings and new construction. Contents: inspector's report, owner's name and address, property address and description, violations, assessor's designation, signatures of all necessary inspectors, date, certificate no.

C372 *Grading Permits.* A permit for grading and excavation, usually issued by the department's engineering division. Contents: permit no.; name, address, and phone of applicant and property owners; names of contractor and geotechnical engineer; location; assessor's designation; dates; fees; equipment required; impact on water (above or below ground); noise and dust controls.

C373 *Housing Code Violation, Housing Abatement and Demolition, Housing Code Compliance Files.* Records of substandard conditions housing (including apartments and hotels). Contents: inspector's report (owner's name and address, property address and description, violations with code no. and description); assessor's designation; complaint; photographs; record of corrective actions; fire or police inspection reports. Note: In some cities and counties these files may be maintained in a Housing Department (C262) or with Building Permit Files (C369). Related information will be found in records for demolition or rehabilitation.

C374 *Housing Inspection Litigation Files.* Records of legal action taken for failure to correct violations. Contents: name, address, property description, date, copy of notices sent, case history, photographs, correspondence, notice of corrections, and disposition.

(PUBLIC WORKS, CONT.)

C375   **Road Excavation Permits.** A permit for excavation on a public highway or right of way, usually needed by utility companies. Contents: permit or control no., date, description of work, road name, applicant's name, address, phone, dates, fees, and map or sketch.

C376   **Soils and Geologic Reports, Completed Materials Reports.** Required by the state for subdivision development, and performed by a licensed civil engineer. Contents: location and size of area with major geologic features, name of person doing study, date, reason for doing study, other related investigations, topography and drainage, description of earth exposures, and subsurface information.

C377   **Other Building Permits.** Mobile home parks, noise abatement. Not required in all cities and counties.

Planning, Engineering and Design of Public Construction

C378   **Architectural Files.** Contents: all documents related to the project, including building plans and specifications, architects' names, results of inspections, correspondence, and memos. Tracings, blueprints, and specifications are stored in numbered tubes.

C379   **Assessment Records.** A record of special city or county assessments made against property owners for improvements or demolition. Contents: job description, properties affected, owners' names and addresses, amount assessed, if and when paid, dates, if and when bond was issued. The bond and accrued interest become a lien on the property to be settled when the property is sold. Information is then sent to the County Recorder (C420). Note: Related files may include assessment district maps (boundaries and individual parcels), assessment rolls (owners, properties, assessments, contractor's payments, and list of unpaid assessments).

C380   **Engineering Maps.** Maps for use by Public Works and other departments and for public sale. Examples include Aerial Photos, Annexations, As-Built or Cut Sheet, Assessor's, Base Maps, Cadastral (survey), Cemetery, Coastal Strip, Communication (for police and fire), Condemnations, Condominium Conversions, Deed (to or from government), Environmental (plastic overlays of flora, fauna, archaeological sites, and soils), Historic Site, House Nos., Contour, Parcel, Parking Zones, Permits (related to construction), Pipelines, Planning, Plat, Public Parks, Railroad Crossings, Rights of Way and Easement, Road Survey, Sanitation Districts, Scale Maps, School Sites, Seismic, Sewer Lines, Special Assessment Districts, Streetcar Tracks, Streets and Alleys (Paving, Lighting, Name Changes, Gradients), Tie Point (survey), Topographical, Tract, Traffic, Traverses and Boundaries, Utility Lines, Waterlines, and Zoning. Arrangement and indexing vary according to purpose of the map. Finding appropriate maps usually requires help.

C381   **Surveyor Records.** Maps and related documents prepared for the county by a licensed land surveyor. These include a record of survey (property lines, land boundaries, etc.); parcel map (subdivision of land into four or fewer parcels); tract or final map (subdivision of land into five or more parcels); right-of-way drawings (roads, easements, drainage, road section, and flood section); corner record (re-establishment or restoration of public land survey markers or other property markers); field notes (notes, readings, and drawings made by the surveyor while in the field).

Traffic Management

C382   **Street Excavation Permits.** A permit required for private construction or utility excavation. Contents: requester's name, location, estimate of work area needed, start and stop dates.

C383   **Traffic Control Records.** Contents: maps, permits, reports on specific problems (fuel efficiency, police collision reports), and traffic counts.

C384   **Traffic Planning Records.** A typical project may involve interdepartmental committee agendas and minutes, narrative descriptions, design specifications, consultants' reports, cost estimates, coordination of grants with local, regional, state, and federal programs.

C385   ### Construction of Public Facilities

State law mandates that construction costing more than $25,000 must be contracted out.

C386   **Contract Compliance Records.** Affirmative action information. Contents: federal I.D. no., company policy, payroll and employee records.

C387   **Contract Plans and Specifications.** Plans for construction done on government property. Contents: job no., originating department, date, title description of job, costs, specifications and blueprints.

C388   **Contractor's Work Force Roster.** Contents: A list of contractor's work force by sex, job level, and ethnicity.

C389   **Materials Testing or Field Engineering and Testing Files.** Results of construction materials tested against specifications, soils, sidewalk, trench, and street tests for subdivision developments.

C390   **Nuclear Radiation Exposure Records.** Records of radiation exposure when employees use radioactive tools in soil testing. Contents: name, date, and amount of exposure.

C391   **Project Files.** Contents: job no., project name, site acquisition, enabling legislation, plans and specifications, permits, ads, award, contract, fee negotiations, progress payments, inspection reports, acceptance of contract, warranty, testing results (of work in progress), "as built" changes, compliance certificates, completion notice. Note: Files for completed construction are kept permanently and also include photos, correspondence, permits, proposals and contracts, reports, surveys, enabling legislation, funding, environment reports, and special conditions.

C392   **Project Requests.** Contents: requesting department, project no., location, description and sketch, justification, budget and cost details.

Streets, Sewer, Flood Control, Waste Management

C393   **Bridge and Tunnel Maintenance Records.** Contents: similar to those of Street and Sidewalk Inspection Reports (C398).

C394   **Chemical and Biological Laboratory Records.** Reports of waste water treatment analysis are sent weekly, monthly, and annually to the state Department of Health and U.S. Environmental Protection Agency to measure plant efficiency and compliance. Other records include tests of overflow during wet weather and biological analysis of incoming and treated waste water. Contents (of tests of incoming and treated waste water, including industrial waste): date, source of sample, amounts of nutrients (ammonia, nitrogen phosphate), suspended solids, metals, chlorine residual, trace organics (pesticides), phenols, flow, coliform bacteria, biological oxygen demand, pH, and grease and oil. Contents (of tests of disposal area of treated waste water): date, location, amounts of coliform bacteria, turbidity, nutrient level and dissolved oxygen, number and condition of bottom-dwelling organisms, pH, conductivity, ammonia, odor, and appearance.

(PUBLIC WORKS, CONT.)

C395 **Electrical Equipment Maintenance Records.** Maintenance reports on electrical equipment at water pump stations, at government-owned buildings, street lighting, park lighting, fire and police call boxes, and parking meters. Contents: similar to those of street and sidewalk inspection reports (C398). Note: Often organized under General Services (C211) or separately.

C396 **Solid Waste Disposal Records.** Contents: trash route maps, gross weight and transaction amount for each truck, no. and weight of vehicles before and after leaving site per day, permits issued, fees collected, exempt, or protested, landfill contour drawings, inspection reports, remaining capacity, and recycled materials. Note: Services may be contracted out.

C397 **Street and Sewer Repair or Maintenance Files.** Records of work done in response to inspection reports or long-range plan. Contents: work order no., date, location, description, cost, man-hours, maps, engineering reports and inspections. Records vary from place to place.

C398 **Street and Sidewalk Inspection Reports.** Contents: reason for report (complaint, observation, damage claim) street address, diagram of area, notice no., date, block and lot no., owner's name and address, and block and lot no.

C399 **Street Cleaning Records.** Contents: permits for tree planting, litter citations, maps, statistics of work done (on streets, sidewalks, parking area, traffic dividers), location, personnel and equipment, work done for other departments.

C400 **Waste water, Storm Water, Water Pollution Project Records.** Files on handling polluted street water without overloading the sewer system. Federal law requires that sewer facilities meet certain standards. Usually, this involves large construction projects and federal funds. Contents (of a project file): job order no., project title, construction contracts (including planning and design), contract modification (if any), reason for using outside contractor, approval of proposal, financial details, target dates, signatures, copies of U.S. EPA forms, grant information, as-built drawings, certification of payrolls and statement of compliance, completion certificate, final payment recommendation, and maps.

C401 **Other Public Works Records.** Construction Contracts Monthly Status Reports; Critical Deficiency Reports (reports of engineering deficiencies); Hydrology Reports (surface and subsurface water); Material Data (soil compaction tests, concrete mix designs, quantity calculations, etc.); Purchase Order File (daily inspector's records for construction costing less than $10,000); Radiation Safety Data File (surveys of equipment, storage, personnel exposure measurements); Well Digging Permits.

C402 PURCHASING

City and County. Buys materials, supplies, equipment, and services in bulk. A related service is storage and delivery of requested supplies. May be found in Public Works, General Services, shared, or as a separate department. Purchasing procedures vary greatly, as do related record systems. Copies of all purchasing records are also kept by the Auditor-Controller (C040).

C403 **Purchase Order.** A record that a vendor has been awarded the contract to sell supplies to the department. Contents: order no. or code, description, brand, price, amount, vendor, date, cost, and fund source.

C404 **Registry.** A list of supplies and equipment out for bid. Contents: bid no., description, date due, and name of requesting department.

C405   ***Request for Quotation or Bid File.*** Prices quoted for supplies. Contents: description, date, brand, price, item amount, requesting department, control and bid nos., delivery requirements, accounting details, total cost, vendor's name, address, and phone.

C406   ***Requisition or Purchase Orders.*** Orders for supplies, materials, etc. Contents: requesting department, control or purchase order no., description, quantity, price, vendor, address, terms, and delivery information.

C407   ***Testing Records.*** Product testing records maintained by some cities and counties. Products such as labels, paint, telephone equipment and asphalt are pre-tested; the results are written into purchase specifications. Contents: product, requesting department, date, conditions of testing, prerequisites, and job no.

C408   ***Vendor Files and Warrants.*** Payments for goods and services. Contents: purchase order, invoice, warrant no. and date. Note: Where Auditor and Controller are separate, the warrant is kept in the Controller's office. The warrant system is being abandoned in favor of bank checks.

C409   ***Vendor Indexes and Logs.*** Indexes of Vendor Files and Warrants (C408). Indexing systems vary greatly. The following are the most common: vendor name, vendor no., department, name, purchase order no., warrant no., amount and date, and document reference no.

C410   ***Other Purchasing Records.*** Business Affirmative Action Compliance (firms doing business may have to submit a certificate of compliance), Copy Machine Rent/Lease Agreement, Inventory Record (usually a computer list of supplies available and requisitioned), Invoice Status (status of department stocks in storage at a central warehouse).

C411 REAL ESTATE LEASING, PURCHASING, AND SELLING

City and County. Acquires publicly owned property, disposes, sells, and leases property no longer needed, provides appraisals and relocation assistance. This function is implemented in many ways and rarely centralized in one place. Airports, Harbor, Parks and Recreation, Redevelopment, School Districts, and Water Departments may have their own Property Management Division. In some cases, General Services handles transactions pertaining to city or county-owned property while Public Works handles buying, selling, or leasing of right-of-way or easements for flood control or streets. Sometimes one department handles short-terms leases, while another takes care of long-term leases.

C412   ***Annual Report of Real Property.*** A record of property owned by the city or county. Contents: summary of acreage, land and improvement value by department; details of blocks owned with description, area, land value, improvement value, block nos. Not maintained by all cities or counties.

C413   ***Appraisals.*** Estimates of the financial worth of property being acquired or sold. Contents: file no., photographs, assessor's reference no., legal description of property, former use (if government), correspondence and memos, final transaction notification.

C414   ***Leased Property Management Plans.*** Plans of developments or facilities on land leased from the government. Contents: blueprints, plans, photographs, etc. Usually for stadium, recreation park or facility.

C415   ***Purchase, Sale, or Lease Files.*** Purchase or lease contracts for property needed by the city or county, or a sale contract for property no longer needed. Records are confidential until the transfer is completed. Contents: project or file I.D. nos. (right-of-way, engineer's document, project no.); principals' name and address; agent's name, address, and phone; board or council resolution; legal description; appraiser's report; location; purpose; amount; dates; term (if lease); map and sketch; copies of legal documents, payments, authority for expenditure from controller; correspondence; title clearance, and requesting department.

C416   ***Real Estate Indexes.*** An index to the government's real estate transactions maintained by some cities or counties. The indexing system may be cards, books, computer, etc.

C417   ***Relocation Records.*** Records of families and businesses forced to move by government action. Individual files are closed unless action is appealed and a "release of confidentiality" is signed by the appellant. Summary reports and statistics related to a project are filed here and with the project; see Redevelopment (C472).

C418   ***Revocable Encroachment Use Permits.*** A permit for temporary use of unneeded property. Contents: applicant's name, address, phone, owner's address, contractor's address, date, location, purpose, fees, cash or bond, inspection, materials used, plans, maintenance, start/finish dates, permit no., street name, or zone and line (if related to watershed land).

C419   ***Other Real Estate Records.*** Request for change in allotted office or building space; lease abstracts; annual lease revenue; property taxes (paid to city for city-owned property, then, via Treasurer, paid to county); maps; miscellaneous records related to government-owned property such as cemetery plot and burials; building plans; appraisals.

C420   RECORDER

County. Responsible for recording, indexing, maintaining, and issuing copies of all recordable documents for the county. State codes provide for the recording of more than 300 documents. The most important and heavily used are land ownership and debts secured by that property, vital statistics such as marriage, birth, and death certificates, and certain official maps. Each document is given a sequential filing no., the date, hour, and minute of reception is stamped along with a Recorder's number and the name of the person requesting the recording. The original is returned to the owner after a copy is made for the Recorder's permanent record. Documents are commonly copied and stored on microfilm. The Office of Recorder is often combined with that of the County Clerk.

Real and personal property documents and claims or liens against that property are recorded and arranged in chronological order in a master list usually called "Official Records." The all-important index to this is usually called the "General Index." Some records (deeds, leases, mortgages, notices of actions, patents, etc.) used to be kept in separate books and had separate indexes for each book. Others, called "Miscellaneous" or "Promiscuous" records (military discharges, enlistment records, bills of sale, wine certificates, tax sales, mining locations, separate property of married women, official bonds, candidates' statements, and declarations of trust), were kept in a single book with its own separate index. Many recorders now combine all records in one sequence with one index. Vital statistics are kept in a separate sequence with a separate index, but are listed alphabetically below.

C421   ***Abstract of Judgment.*** A record of monies owed and a claim against real property. Contents: court location, case no., plaintiff, defendant, date, creditor (usually the plaintiff), debtor (usually the defendant), amount, certification and signature of court deputy.

C422   **Affidavit—Death of Joint Tenant.** A record of the death of person holding title to property as a joint tenant, see Grant Deed (C425). Contents: names of survivor and the deceased, date, grant deed date and no., legal description of property, person requesting recording, signature of notary and survivor, and death certificate.

C423   **Divorce or Dissolution of Marriage Records.** Divorce records are filed with the Recorder only if property changed hands. For contents, see Superior Court (C170).

C424   **General Index or Grantor-Grantee Index.** An index of Official Records (C439). Some counties split the General Index into a General-Grantor Index and General-Grantee Index. Contents: names of grantor (seller) and grantee (buyer), title of record or instrument, reference to volume and page numbers in Official Records or microfilm/fiche locator, and recording date. Arranged by name and date. The Grantor lists seller, defendant, judgment debtor, lessor, etc. Grantee lists buyer, plaintiff, beneficiary, lessee, etc. In some counties, the General Index includes all names in one list and distinguishes between grantor and grantee by use of a coding system. Note: Uniform Commercial Code Filings (C446) and Military Discharges (C432) may be included in the General Index. Care should be taken to check all possible alphabet listings.

C425   **Grant Deed.** A record of the exchange of property. Contents: names of grantors and grantees, addresses, person requesting recording (usually the grantee) and address, legal description of property, transfer tax (if any), mailing address (for tax statements), date of execution, and signature of notary and grantors. Other types of grant deeds are Association (bank or other creditor sells property from an estate), Corporation Grant (a corporate exchange of property), Corporation Joint Tenancy (two or more corporations exchange property), Grant Conservator (sale or purchase of property by a person representing someone unable to act legally), Joint Tenancy (two or more parties buy or sell to another party), Quitclaim (a person or entity gives up claim to a property).

C426   **Homeowners Association Statement.** A statement of association for condominium owners. Contents: organization name, address, officers' names and titles.

C427   **Land Patents Records.** Records authorized by federal and state land offices granting transfer of title to real property. Contents: grantee name, property location and description, fees, recording date, proof of claim, map.

C428   **Lien.** A charge against property to secure an unpaid debt, usually property taxes. Following are some types: federal tax lien, lien agreement, lien contract, mechanic's lien, notice of lien, tax lien. Contents (of a mechanic's lien): name of claimant (person who performed work), name of person (contractor or owner) who requested work, property owner, legal description of property, amount due, description of work done, date, signature of claimant. See also Reconveyances and Lien Releases (C442).

C429   **Limited Partnership Certificate.** A statement of partnership agreement. Contents: general partners' names and addresses, limited partners' names and addresses, partnership name, terms of agreement, and amendments (names of additional limited partners). Note: Since July 1984, certificates must also be filed with the Secretary of State (S613).

C430   **Maps.** Land division and use maps as required by the state. Contents: subdivision or tract, parcel, survey, assessment boundary districts, assessor's and cemetery maps. Note: Other maps in the Recorder's office may include irrigation districts, judicial districts, railroads, state highways, right of way, and tidelands.

C431   **Marriage Certificates.** Marriage licenses, combined with the Certificate of Registry, are issued by the County Clerk. The certificate is recorded by the recorder and the

(RECORDER, CONT.)

original is sent to State Registrar of Vital Statistics (S381). Contents: bride and groom names; birth date and place; indication of previous marriage; occupations; years of education; parent's names and birthplaces; parental consent, if needed; license no. and date; witnesses' names and addresses; name, address, and denomination of person performing ceremony; marriage date and place.

C432   **Military Discharges.** Records of discharges from the armed services. Contents: name, branch of service, service no., social security no., rank, birth date, type of discharge, home address at time of entry into service, decorations, medals, education and special training, related civilian occupation, mailing address. Note: Older forms also contain a physical description.

C433   **Military Discharge Index.** An index of discharge records (C432). Contents: name, recorder's book and page no. Arranged by name and date. Note: The index may be integrated with the General Index (C424).

C434   **Mining Location Claims Notice.** A legal description of the mine location. Contents: claim or lode name; locator or miner's name, address, measurements of vein or lode; date of posting of notice; description of nearby permanent objects.

C435   **Notice of Completion.** A legal record of completion of work. The contractor has only a certain no. of days to file a lien. Contents: owner's name, and address, legal description of property and street address, date of completion, contractor's name, verification of statement, signature of notary and person requesting recording.

C436   **Notice of Default.** Notice by a trustee (usually a title company) that the borrower has failed to pay, thus initiating a foreclosure proceeding. Contents: names of trustee, borrower, and lender, date, legal description of property, type and amount of obligation defaulted on, description of default, signature of lender (beneficiary), and name of person requesting recording.

C437   **Notice of Liquor License Transfer.** A notice of intention to transfer a liquor license. Contents: current licensee (vendor) name and address, buyer (vendee) name and address, license type, addresses of licensed premises, name and address of escrow holder or guarantor, purchase price, amount and method of payment. See also Alcoholic Beverage Control (S039).

C438   **Notice of Pending Action (Lis Pendens).** Recorded notice of pending civil court action involving property. Contents: plaintiff's and defendant's names, date of notice, purpose of action, property location and description, recording date, plaintiff attorney's signature.

C439   **Official Records.** Since 1920, what had been separate volumes of records have been combined into one volume, titled Official Records. It includes attachments, brands, certificates of tax sales, contracts, decrees, deeds, easements, homesteads, indentures, leases, mechanic's liens, miscellaneous records, mortgages, notices, notices of action, orders, patents, pre-emption claims, powers of attorney, releases, satisfactions of judgment, sole trader and separate property of married women, stipulations, transcripts of judgments, and trust deeds. Contents: grantor and grantee names, type and text of instrument, recording date. Arranged by recorder's no. Indexed by the General Index (C424).

C440   **Partnership Agreement (General Partnership).** Contents: partners' names, partnership name, amendments (names of new or retiring partners).

C441   **Power of Attorney.** A legal document authorizing one person to act for another in ordinary business transactions. Contents: name of person making authorization, name of person given authorization; description of powers authorized, signature of person making authorization, and date.

C442   **Reconveyances and Lien Releases.** Legal records that remove claims of debt against property. Examples include: Full Reconveyance, Deed of Reconveyance, Release of Lien, Release of Tax Lien, Certificate of Release of Inheritance Tax Lien, Recission (cancellation) of Election to Declare Default. Contents vary. The following elements are usually found: trustor, trustee, beneficiary, legal description of property, court where case was held, and appropriate details. See also Lien (C428).

C443   **Request for Notice.** A legal record asking to be informed of any notice of default or foreclosure sale. This protects the filer's lien interest in the property. Contents: description of deed of trust (recorder's no., date, names, etc.), requester's name, address, and signature.

C444   **Satisfaction of Judgment.** A legal record that a debt or obligation as recorded in an Abstract of Judgment (C159) is paid in full. Contents: location of court, case no., plaintiff (creditor), defendant (debtor), reference to where Abstract was recorded, date, and creditor's signature or signature of attorney for creditor.

C445   **Trust Deed.** A record of property sale where a mortgage loan is involved. There are various types. Contents: borrower (trustor) name, address, lender (beneficiary) name, address, trustee (usually a title company), person requesting recording, legal description of property, amount and rate of loan, date of execution, signature of borrower, and mailing address for tax statements.

C446   **Uniform Commercial Code (UCC) Filings—Financing Statement.** Uniform Commercial Code or UCC was adopted to assure national uniformity when describing goods, timber or crops that are pledged as security for a loan. These records are filed in the county where the debtor lives if consumer goods are pledged, where the goods are located, or where the crops or timber are grown. Debts secured by business and farm equipment, accounts payable, inventory, and trust receipts are filed with the Secretary of State (S618). Contents: debtor and lender (name, mailing, residential, and business addresses, and social security or federal tax no.); trade name or style; description of assigned property or collateral; signatures; amendments to statement. Note: See also Chattel Mortgage (C458).

C447   **Uniform Commercial Code (UCC) Index.** For C446. Arranged by name of debtor. Contents: debtor's name, and file no. Note: may be integrated with the General Index (C424).

C448   **Unincorporated Association Statement.** A statement of association for benevolent, fraternal or labor organizations. Contents: organization name, officers' names and titles.

C449   **Vital Statistics Records.** See Births (C258), Deaths (C259, C260), Divorce (C423), and Marriage (C431).

C450   **Vital Statistics Indexes.** Separate indexes exist for Marriages, Births, and Deaths. Contents: name (of bride or groom, child, or deceased), Recorder's book and page no. or microfilm/fiche locator. Arranged by name and date. Note: For marriages there may be separate indexes for brides and grooms. See also state Registrar of Vital Statistics (S381).

C451   **Other Recorder Records**

There are many other types of documents, and their titles may vary from place to place. Following is a partial list with brief descriptions:

C452   **Affidavit of Death.** Recorded upon the death of one co-owner of property or beneficiary of trust to transfer interest to surviving party.

(RECORDER, CONT.)

C453   **Agreement to Convey.** An agreement regarding the conveyance (transfer) of property from one party to another.

C454   **Assignment of Leases.** Assigns either party's interest in a lease.

C455   **Assignment of Trust Deed.** Changes the person to whom the money is owed.

C456   **Attachment.** A court order to "attach" or seize property to provide security for a debt or until ownership can be determined.

C457   **Cancellation of Notice of Default.** Issued after the trustor has cured the default under a deed of trust.

C458   **Chattel Mortgage.** An old term for a lien against personal property to secure a loan. Replaced by the Uniform Commercial Code (S618).

C459   **Construction Deed of Trust.** Same as Deed of Trust (C445), but issued for construction, with the building to be constructed as part of the security for the loan.

C460   **Declaration of Trust.** Establishes a trust.

C461   **Declaration of Homestead.** Indicates intent to use property as a place of residence. Provides some protection against debts. A related record is Abandonment of Homestead.

C462   **Judgment.** A judgment awarded by a court may be recorded to establish a lien against any property the losing party may own.

C463   **Letters of Conservatorship.** Formal written evidence of the court appointment of a conservator of the person, or of the estate, or of the person and the estate of the conservatee.

C464   **Levy.** Seizure of property by judicial process.

C465   **Notice of Bulk Transfer.** Notice of the intended transfer of unsecured property associated with a business, such as equipment or inventory, in sale to another.

C466   **Notice of Substandard Building.** A notice issued by the Department of Public Works that a certain building is substandard (not in compliance with the building codes).

C467   **Notice of Trustee's Sale.** Notice of an intended sale at auction of real property by the trustee under a deed of trust when the trustor has failed to satisfy a default under a deed of trust.

C468   **Order.** Miscellaneous court orders. The subject of the court order is shown as a cross reference to the named party.

C469   **Release of Judgment.** Releases a previously recorded judgment.

C470   **Release of Mortgage.** Evidence of full repayment of the amount due under a mortgage.

C471   **Substitution of Trustee.** Used to change the trustee (the person holding property in trust as security) under a deed of trust.

C472   # REDEVELOPMENT AGENCY

City and County, or combined. Operates under state law as a legally separate entity. Uses state and federal funds to rehabilitate blighted areas. The agency can purchase land and provide low-interest loans to businesses to carry out commercial, industrial, public redevelopment, and housing rehabilitation. Money to repay the loans comes from increased tax assessments due to property improvement. The City

Council or Board of Supervisors may sit as the Redevelopment Agency. Agency staff may also work for the Housing Authority. Except for administration, the work is contracted out. Most of the records involve planning and contract monitoring.

C473   ***Project Records.*** Summary statistics for each project. Includes project dates, investment, assessed valuation, and tax revenue before and after redevelopment, acreage, population before and after, and new units.

C474   ***Redevelopment Project Area Records.*** Contents: project name, housing complex and/or buildings, facilities by name and location, developer/sponsor, architect, contractor, financing, number of bedrooms (if housing), square footage (if office space), meeting minutes, resolutions, reports on project construction, financial reports, property descriptions, exhibits, and petitions. Also may include contracts, maps, blueprints, budgets, certificates of insurance, etc.

C475   ***Statement of Revenues and Expenditures.*** Contents: revenue (tax increment, government aid, assessments, sales/use tax, interest, rentals, leases, sales, grants, other), expenditures (administration, professional, planning, survey, design, real estate purchase, operation of property, relocation costs and payments, site clearance, project improvement/construction, disposal, rehabilitation, interest expense, fixed-asset purchase, subsidies for low/moderate housing, other), payments on bond debt.

C476   ***Other Redevelopment Records.*** Agendas, meeting minutes, resolutions. Some agencies provide a list of names and addresses for all tenants in a project. See state Department of Housing and Community Development (S388).

C477 REGISTRAR OF VOTERS

County. Registers eligible voters; conducts all elections in the county except in certain cities and certain special districts; maintains precinct rosters, indexes, and voter lists; maintains and adjusts precinct boundaries; receives political nomination papers, campaign statements, and contribution reports; checks petitions. The office is traditionally part of the County Clerk. May be organized under General Services, but is usually separate.

Note: Access to some voter registration information was limited as of January 1, 1995 by SB 1518. The home address (number and street address only), phone, occupation, precinct number and prior registration of a registrant as contained on precinct lists, voter registration affidavits and voter registration rolls are no longer public. Among those specifically excluded from access to this information are "persons seeking to locate lost relatives" and "persons (such as private investigators, skip tracers, process servers and attorneys) seeking to locate individuals" unless they are working for a public agency. People seeking this information for election, scholarly, journalistic, political or governmental purposes may still be granted access upon approval of a written application by the County Registrar of Voters. The elections division of the Secretary of State's office is responsible under this law for developing guidelines defining the scope of these purposes.

C478   ***Declaration of Candidacy, Nomination Papers.*** A declaration required by law for candidates in local, state, school district, and special district elections. Contents: name, address, party affiliation, occupation or employer, years living in California, previous addresses, public offices held, office sought and election date. Note: Candidates may also file various Sponsor's Certificates with name, address, and signature of a certain number of sponsors.

C479   ***Precinct Lists, Books, Rolls.*** Records of registered voters in each precinct. Contents: street address and voter name. See note above regarding access.

(REGISTRAR OF VOTERS, CONT.)

C480   ***Voter Registration Affidavits.*** Contents: same information as registration rolls (C481) plus voter's signature, date and place of birth, social security no. (optional), and previous address (if changing registration). Note: Older affidavits may contain date of naturalization, and petitions and initiatives signed. When a voter fails to vote in certain elections, the affidavit is purged and kept in a separate file. See note above regarding access.

C481   ***Voter Registration Rolls.*** Alphabetical lists of registered voters. Contents: name, address, phone (if given), zip code, date, political affiliation, precinct no., whether person voted in primary and general elections of even years. Indexed by Assembly, Senate, or Congressional district, by precinct in street address order or alphabetical by name, political affiliation, and household. For previous elections, lists are available of voters, those registered but not voting, and absentee voters. Fees are charged. Some lists are on microfiche at lower cost. Note: Early rolls were organized by year, voting district, and then name. See note above regarding access.

C482   ## RENT STABILIZATION AND ARBITRATION BOARD

City and County. Enforces local rent-control laws; hears appeals from renters claiming excessive rent increases or unfair landlord actions.

C483   ***Landlord's Response Form.*** A formal response to a Tenant's Petition for Rent Review. Contents: case no.; landlord's name, address, and phone; tenant's name and address; reasons for rent increase; rental history of other apartments, dates, and amounts; business license; hearing fees (if paid); capital improvements to common areas and units (type of work, date completed, and cost); landlord's signature and date.

S484   ***Tenant's Petition for Rent Review.*** Contents: case no.; name, address, phone for tenant and landlord; number of units in building; rental history (dates of moving in, all increases and amounts); utilities and services; hearing fees (if paid); tenant's signature and date.

C485   ***Other Rent Stabilization Board Records.*** Meeting minutes, hearings, case files, rental histories, and legal rent ceilings.

C486   ## RISK MANAGEMENT/SAFETY

City and County and combined. Controls personnel and property losses; administers self-insurance programs; handles insurance claims; does safety training and inspections; insures conformance with U.S. Occupational Health and Safety Administration and Cal/OSHA (S403) regulations; may be involved with employee benefit programs. Sometimes responsible for emergency and disaster plans and hazardous-materials exposure. See also Emergency Services. May be organized under the City or County Administrative Officer, General Services, the City Attorney, or independently.

C487   ***Accident Report Form.*** A report filed when any employee is involved in an accident. Contents: report no. (if any), date, time, type of accident, location, description, action taken, hospital, names of all persons involved, and signature.

C488   ***Benefit Plan Reports, Self-Insured Plan Reports.*** Records of health, life, medical, and dental plans. Contents: statistics, invoices, payment requests, vendor updates, and enrollment information.

C489   ***Cal/OSHA Citations and Correspondence.*** Citations for unsafe conditions or failure to follow safety rules. Contents: date, occasion, description, details of regulations, action needed, and names (if any).

C490   **Cal/OSHA Logs.** Records of employee injuries or illnesses if there is loss of consciousness, hospitalization, or other medical care.

C491   **Citizen Complaint.** Statement of damages or lack of affirmative action by the government. Contents: form no., date, name of complainant, description of complaint, and amount of reimbursement claimed.

C492   **Departmental Safety Problem Reports.** Investigations of complaints about unsafe conditions. Contents: department description of condition, complainant, date, action taken, and other relevant information.

C493   **Injury Reports.** A record of employee injuries. Contents: date, employee's name, incident, other report forms (police, medical, fire, etc.) as required by government.

C494   **Public Liability Files.** Claims for compensation filed against the government. Contents: requests of action, claim no., invoices, correspondence, record sheets, name of claimant, description, and disposition. See also Auditor-Controller, Claims (C048).

C495   **Recovery Files.** Claims made by the government against others. Contents: correspondence, invoices, police reports (if any), incident reports, photographs (if any), and names of persons involved.

C496   **Safety Training Program Attendees.** A list of employees attending safety training classes. Contents: employee name, other employment information, and title of class.

C497   **Worker's Compensation Reports.** A record of claims, investigations and compensation for job-related illness or injury. Contents: name of employee, type of injury or illness, dates, claim form and no. (if any), correspondence, medical reports, and other forms as required by the government.

C498   **Yearly Safety Audit.** Contents: summary of findings; statistics of worker's compensation loss by type of injury; survey by department, notation of hazards, and correction required.

C499   ## SHERIFF

County. Provides law enforcement in unincorporated areas of the county, maintains jails, transports prisoners upon written warrant, serves civil papers, provides bailiffs and marshals, assists other public safety agencies in the county, and provides services to Superior Court. May issue certain licenses (bicycle) and permits (parade). Note: All counties must elect a Sheriff. Some counties combine the offices of Coroner and Sheriff. Separate units may include Major Crimes Task Force, Marijuana Eradication Unit, Constables (in outlying districts), Juvenile Hall, Probation Officers, and Animal Control.

C500   See Police (C329–C354) for the following records maintained by both police and sheriff: Arrest Register, Arrest Log, Booking Register, Arrest Cards, Blotter, Incident Report; Auction Records; Auto Theft Files; Bail Receipts; Breath Tests; Communication Audio Tape Recordings; Crime Reports; General Orders; Gun Registration Files; Incident Logs; Internal Affairs or Citizen Complaints; Licenses and Permits; Monthly Crime Summary; Property or Custody; Recruiting and Training; Subpoena Logs; Tear Gas Registration; Traffic Citations; Uniform Accident Reports; Warrants.

C501   **Certificate of Sale of Personal Property.** A record of sales due to court action. Contents: notices of publication of sale, court order, names of owner and purchaser, legal description of property, documents related to property, and amount of sale.

C502   **Commitment Orders.** Information on where a defendant will go after sentencing. Contents: defendant's name, court case no., destination, conviction date, judge's

(SHERIFF, CONT.)

signature, charges, and length of prison term. Note: Information is located in Criminal Case File (C167) after sentencing.

C503   *Inmate Jacket.* Contents: name, I.D. no., booking no., original booking, clothing inventory, personal property inventory, court orders, funds, photos, and any miscellaneous documents. Personal details are confidential. All information is confidential once the person is no longer in custody.

C504   *Jail Census Reports, Annual Jail Bookings.* Statistics on number of people in custody sent by county jails to state Board of Corrections (S135).

C505   *Monthly Summaries.* Records of administrative statistics of writs served, arrests made, number of hours of training, complaints received, persons in jail, miles traveled, and purposes of travel.

C506   *Receipt Books, Financial Reports.* Records of money received and sent to Treasurer. Contents: date, name, address, type of permit, license, and fee or fine.

C507   *Other Sheriff Records.* Boat Accident Reports; Crime Scene Photographs (not public if in litigation); Maintenance and Calibration Records for Breath Instruments (for breath tests done in jail); Mooring Owner Files; Stolen Property (photographs of property claimed by owner). Not all counties maintain the same records.

C508   ## SOCIAL SERVICES, HUMAN RESOURCES AGENCY, COMMUNITY SERVICES, PUBLIC SOCIAL SERVICES

City and County. Administers federal, state, and local aid to needy persons. Delivery is concentrated at the county level. There is little standardization of terms denoting services, or how units are organized for delivery of services. Some related services are listed elsewhere in this guide. See Aging; Employment; Housing; Redevelopment; Veterans Services.

The following is a partial list of other social service programs, not all of which are available in all counties or cities: Adoptions, Aid to Families with Dependent Children (AFDC), AFDC-Foster Care (blind and disabled), AFDC-Unemployed, Central Intake Unit (refugees), Child Abuse Prevention, Child Support Enforcement (see also District Attorney), Family Maintenance, Family Reunification, Food Stamps, General Assistance, Greater Avenues for Independence (see also Employment), Information and Referral, In-Home Supportive Services, Intensive In-Home Therapy/Self-Care Program, Medi-Cal, Out-of-Home Adult Care Services, Permanent Placement, Protective Services for Adults, Refugee Cash Assistance, SSI/SSP (needy aged, blind, and disabled), State Children's Trust Fund Program, Targeted Assistance (refugees).

Cities and counties with large urban populations may have hundreds of records. Programs differ markedly from place to place. Information about specific persons is rarely a public record. Periodic and annual reports on individual programs and reports on use of state and federal funds are public. Following are examples of records in only four program areas: Aid to Families with Dependent Children, Food Stamps, Foster Care and Adoptions, and Refugee Resettlement.

Aid to Families with Dependent Children

C509   *Quarterly Report of Recoveries of Overpayments (AFDC)—Form SSA4972.* A report required by U.S. Department of Health and Human Services for grant award eligibility. Contents: name and address of organization, inclusive dates, numbers of cases and amounts of overpayments, money lost or recovered, date, official's title and signature. Note: The equivalent state form is CA-12.

C510   *Statistical Reports—AFDC.* Monthly or quarterly reports required by the state Department of Social Services for various activities. The contents often consist of past and current statistics for caseload, applications, requests, claims, cancellations, and completions. Areas covered include: homeless assistance and temporary shelter; emergency assistance caseload and expenditures; foster care caseload and expenditures; cash grant caseload and expenditures; reasons for stopping aid to family groups and unemployed; reasons for denying or discontinuing aid; reasons for applicant refusal to supply paternity information (e.g., harm to child or parent, incest, rape, litigation); total number of AFDC, social services and Medi-Cal cases by ethnic origin and primary language.

C511   *Summary Report of Assistance Expenditures—Form 800 series:* A state-required monthly summary of costs for the following programs: Reimbursement Claims, Emergency Assistance–Unemployed Parent, Aid to Families with Dependent Children (includes federal and state data).

Food Stamp Program

C512   *Participants by Ethnic Group and Assistance Status.* Contents: county, date, signature, title, and phone.

C513   *Participation and Coupon Issuance Report.* Contents: county, date, total number of participants (households and persons by whether or not on public assistance), total issuances by method (mail, counter), explanatory remarks, signature, title, and phone. Note: A monthly caseload report is compiled from these statistics.

C514   *Status of Claims Against Households.* Contents: county, date; previous, new, reactivated, and adjusted claims made to recoup food stamps erroneously issued (numbers and amounts); claims closed, transferred, suspended, and terminated (number and amounts); remarks.

Foster Care and Adoptions

C515   *Statistical Reports—Foster Care and Adoptions.* Quarterly reports required by the state for various activities. The contents usually consist of past and current data on caseload, applications, requests, claims, cancellations, and completions. Contents: staff time expended and services provided for out-of-county adoptions and post-adoption services; independent adoptions caseload, court reports and appearances; requests to put children up for adoption and reasons why requests were withdrawn; total number of homes approved or withdrawn as possible homes for adopted children.

C516   *Summary Report of Assistance Expenditures (Form 800 series).* A state-required monthly summary of costs for the following programs: Adoption Assistance Program/Federal, Adoption Assistance Program/Nonfederal, Emergency Assistance—Foster Care, Federal Children in Foster Care, Nonfederal Children in Foster Care. Contents: expenses (current, supplemental, prior months, cancellations, abatements) number of persons (same breakdowns), and total amount owed county.

Refugee Resettlement Program

C517   *Reimbursement Claims.* Contents: county, date, expenditures made, and individuals counted for each program (such as refugee resettlement, emergency assistance, general assistance, or foster care); calculations for federal funds, signature, title, and date.

C518   *Statistical Reports—Refugees.* Required by state on a monthly basis for refugee programs. Contents (vary according to the program): caseload (prior, current, restored, transferred, and terminated) by type of cash grant (AFDC, Refugee Resettlement, etc.); number of persons, cases and dollars no longer counted in refugee

(SOCIAL SERVICES, CONT.)

programs, and number of refugees receiving aid who arrived more than 36 months previously. An annual report gives totals refugees in the county receiving cash assistance and Medi-Cal by country of origin.

Other Social Services Records

C519   *Fraud Investigation Records—Form DPA 266.* A monthly report is made to the state on new, completed, and pending investigations of fraud for AFDC, Food Stamps, and all other programs. Individual records are confidential until the case goes to court. Contents: statistical summaries for investigations of changes in status (income, resources, assets, and family composition); misuse or illegal activity; requests for investigation; investigations begun, denied, and closed; reasons; amount of money recovered; district attorney convictions, dismissals, acquittals, recovery of money, fines, etc.; number of total complaints issued; persons disqualified for fraud or administrative reasons; staff time involved.

C520   *Other Social Service Statistical Reports.* Periodic state-required reports for various activities, including Adult Programs (Out-of-Home Care, Special Circumstances Allowances); Fraud Investigations (new, completed, and pending) Monthly Report; General Relief and Interim Assistance to Applicants for SSI/SSP; Licensing of Facilities for Children; and Title XX Social Services.

C521   **TAX COLLECTOR**

County. Often combined with Treasurer. Collects city, county, school, and special district taxes on secured property (land, houses, and factories) and unsecured property (aircraft, boats, business equipment, and mobile homes) and deposits them with the Treasurer; also submits reports to the Auditor-Controller. In some cases, especially cities, business taxes, transient (hotel/motel) taxes, and license fees are also collected. Property ownership is identified through tax collector records. Commercial services are available to research these records. Note: Tax collectors and assessors maintain many of the same records. For convenience, this guide lists records usually maintained by both under Tax Collector. The key to finding tax collector and assessor records is the Assessor's designation or reference no. See also Assessor.

C522   *Delinquent List.* A public notice of the tax collector's intent to sell tax-defaulted property. Contents: affidavit of tax default, means of redemption, name of official with authority to give information, name of assessee, description of property, total amount originally declared in default, street address (if any). Indexed by: Alphabetical and Street Indexes (C524, C528). Retained for seven years. Note: Copies of the list are typically given to the Recorder, Assessor, and Auditor. Notice of default is also given to the Controller.

C523   *Secured Assessment Rolls or Duplicate Assessor's Rolls.* A listing of taxable secured property (land, houses, and factories). Contents: assessor's reference no., owner's name, DBA, tax mailing address, property address, assessed value of land, improvements, personal property, exemptions, taxes due, tax rate area, tax rate, date and notation if sold by tax-default. Indexed by Street Address Index (C528) and Alphabetical Index—Secured Property (C524). Note: The Secured Assessment Roll or Duplicate Assessor's Roll may also show current taxes paid or tax penalties owed, the date of the last sale, or the corresponding recorder's book and page. See also Secured Property—Paid-Unpaid List (C527) and Delinquent List (C522).

C524   *Secured Property—Alphabetical Index.* An index to Secured Assessment Rolls (C523) for finding the address if only the owner's name is known. Arranged by owner's name. Contents: name of owner, and assessor's reference no.

C525   *Secured Property—Delinquency Abstract, Delinquent Rolls.* A list of unpaid secured property taxes for other than current year. All information formerly added to the Secured Rolls is now added to this list. Property records remain here for five years, at which time the tax collector has the power to sell property at auction (C522). Contents: Assessor's reference no., owner's name, taxes, yearly delinquencies, penalties, delinquent taxes paid (amount and dates), redemption certificate (if any). Indexed by Secured Property—Alphabetical Index (C524), and Secured Property—Street Address Index (C528).

C526   *Secured Property—Mailing Address Register.* A list of current mailing addresses for secured property tax assessment. Contents: Assessor's reference no., previous mailing address, and current mailing address. Note: Listing changes in mailing addresses for tax assessments may be found in a separate Mailing Address Register, the Secured Assessment Rolls (C523), or some other version of the secured rolls.

C527   *Secured Property—Paid-Unpaid List.* A list of secured property tax payments for current year only. Contents: assessor's reference no., taxes assessed, amount and date of taxes paid, and penalties for late payments. Indexed by Secured Property—Street Address Index (C528) and Secured Property—Alphabetical Index (C524). Note: Payment of current-year assessments information may be included in the Secured Assessment Rolls (C523).

C528   *Secured Property—Street Address Index.* An index to Secured Assessment Rolls (C523) for finding the property owner's name if only the address is known. Arranged by street name. Contents: street address no., Assessor's reference no. Note: Some city offices and libraries may have published directories that list addresses or telephone nos. followed by the name of the resident or owner. For example, *Haines Criss-Cross Directory.*

C529   *Unsecured Property Assessment Rolls, Duplicate Assessor's Rolls.* A list of taxable unsecured property (aircraft, boats, business equipment, and mobile homes). Contents are the same as Secured Assessment Rolls except that the account no. is used instead of the Assessor's Reference no. Indexed by Unsecured Property—Alphabetical Index (C530), Unsecured Property—Street Address Index (C532). Note: The type of unsecured property may be indicated in the rolls by a code. Boats and aircraft may be identified from these rolls by the "address for location of property."

C530   *Unsecured Property—Alphabetical Index.* An index to C529 for finding the address, if only the owner's name is known.

C531   *Unsecured Property—Delinquency Abstract or Delinquent Rolls.* A list of unpaid taxes for other than the current year. Contents: assessor's reference no., owner's name, taxes, yearly delinquencies, penalties, delinquent taxes paid (amount and dates), redemption certificate if any. Indexed by Unsecured Property—Alphabetical Index (C530), and Unsecured Property—Street Address Index (C532).

C532   *Unsecured Property—Street Address Index.* An index to C529 if only the address is known. Contents: street address (or other) Assessor's reference no. Note: This index is not found in all county tax collector's offices.

C533   *Miscellaneous Tax Records.* Tax collectors and Assessors keep a variety of miscellaneous records that are usually variations on the rolls and indexes already listed. Two useful records that may exist include a Legal Description Index cross-referencing the Assessor's reference nos. with a narrative legal description that might be used by the Recorder's office; Bank, Mortgage Company, and Tax Service Lists (listings of second parties, such as banks through which property taxes are paid). This information may exist on another roll in coded form.

C534 **TRANSPORTATION**

City, County, and Special District. Provides services ranging from small-scale para-transit programs (vans and jitneys) to multi-county systems. Regulation of privately owned public transportation that crosses city or county lines is handled by the state Public Utilities Commission (S543). Local regulation of privately owned public transportation is handled in various ways. The City of Los Angeles Department of Transportation handles parking, ground transportation planning and operation, mass transit programs, and regulation of privately owned public utilities such as taxi cabs, sight-seeing buses, and private school buses. The City of San Diego handles transportation (paratransit, Dial-a-Ride, Ride Sharing, and taxis) under a Financial Management Department. In San Francisco, the Municipal Railway (buses, street-cars, cable cars, and paratransit) is organized under the city-county's Transportation Commission. A Department of Social Services may provide transportation for handicapped and senior citizens in some cities and counties.

C535 *Equipment Maintenance.* Summary statistics for vehicle maintenance. Contents: availability for service, number, frequency, and type of repairs, elapsed time until repaired, types of vehicles.

C536 *Paratransit Permits.* A permit issued to private companies to provide specialized, on-demand service for the elderly and handicapped using vans and sedans. Contents: permit no., name, address, phone of owner, DBA, number of vehicles and types, licenses, insurance certificates, and fares.

C537 *Ridership Statistics.* Data used to change routes and improve running time. Contents: route name, date, time of day, number of passengers boarding and alighting per stop, travel distance, travel time, and transfers.

C538 *Transit Accident Statistics.* Contents: time of day, dates covered, type of vehicle, and total miles. Individual route statistics are also available.

C539 *Transit Operating Statistics.* Records of scheduling and usage. Contents: route, frequency, number and type of equipment, ridership (per day, hour, vehicle, and mile).

C540 *Transit Planning Files.* Records include financial, demographic, and traffic statistics, equipment needs, surveys and reports, environmental reviews, and maps.

C541 *Other Transportation Records.* Accident rates; car-pooling; equipment operating costs (fuel vs. electricity, number of passengers per operator); facilities maintenance; fare collection; operator training; parking tokens; special transit passes; traffic control systems (loading stops, peak congestion location, traffic-signal timing); vehicle availability and reliability. For street and curb marking, installation of signals and signs, upkeep of street surfaces see Public Works. For parking, see Parking. Note: The City of Los Angeles maintains a computer-based system with data on traffic signals, vehicle flows, curb zones, pavement markings, and street conditions.

C542 **TREASURER, FINANCE DEPARTMENT**

City and County. Receives, pays out, and has custody of all funds and securities; invests idle money; administers general revenue, district and street improvement bond issues; records delinquent property sales; may administer employee retirement system. The Treasurer may also collect and record the Transient Occupancy (hotel/motel) tax. At the county level, the Treasurer also usually serves as the Tax Collector. At the city level, the City Clerk may also be the Treasurer. See also Auditor-Controller.

C543   **Bond Interest Payments.** A record of the monthly payment of interest by city or county on revenue bonds. Contents: date, bond no. or series, amount, accounting details. See also Auditor-Controller, Bond Register (C044).

C544   **Cash Pool Investments.** Records of where idle city or county money is invested. Contents: type of security, yield, dates, amounts, name of dealer or bank, and file no.

C545   **Certificate File.** Documents relating to foreclosure sale because of non-payment of special assessment taxes. Contents: bond, trust fund or sale no., request for foreclosure; owner or assessee's name and address; copies of notices sent; money due; copy of trust deed (if recorded); Certificate of Sale (if sold); other pertinent data.

C546   **Certificates of Sale.** Copies of certificates of sale. Contents: date of issuance; bond no., date of bond issuance; buyer's name; property description; amount paid; sale no.; if redeemed; name of new owner (if any) and date. Copy of deed may be included.

C547   **Claims Data.** Duplicates of documents from other departments concerning claims owed to the city or county. See Auditor-Controller and Risk Management.

C548   **Grant funds, Grant Award File.** A record of grant money awarded to the city or county. Contents: copy of contract with grantor, third-party contract, code no., federal or state department, name or type of grant, contract no., grant no., and amount.

C549   **Improvement Bond Registers.** A record of payments on special assessment bonds for street, sewer, open space or water. Contents: date and amount due; date and amount paid; date and amount paid to bondholder; penalties; assessment nos., bond nos., county map book, page, parcel, and tract no.; whether canceled; whether foreclosed, trust fund no. and date foreclosure notification was mailed to property owner. Note: Not all jurisdictions maintain information in the same arrangement. Some keep separate records of payments of assessments, cancellation of bonds, etc. Originals are kept by the City or County Clerk.

C550   **Parking Citation Fines.** Citations issued by police or special parking police. Several types of records may be kept including out-of-state citations, bad checks, requests for court appearance, and periodic statistical reports. Contents: citation no., license no., date, place, time, issuing officer, and follow-up information if fine is not paid.

C551   **Parking Meter Collections.** A record of daily intake from parking meters. Contents: route, date, and amount.

C552   **Property Tax Files.** A record of the amount the city received from the county for property taxes. Contents: amounts, date, and origin or source.

C553   **Sales Registers, Property Foreclosure Files.** A record of property being sold for non-payment of special assessments. Contents: trust fund no. or sale no. (if sale is advertised); property description; dates of reception of legal documents, mailing of notices, ads to sell, sale, and deed; purchaser (if sold); date of sale certificate; certificate no.; last possible redemption date; amounts due on payments; name, date, and amount of redemption (if any); to whom the city paid the amount and date; sale no. Note: The owner may redeem the property until a deed is recorded with the county a year after the sale.

C554   **Other Treasurer Records.** Reinstatement of improvement bonds; records of canceled bonds; routine records of bank statements, account reconciliation, paid warrants, paid checks, cash teller sheets, and deposit receipts.

C555 **UNIVERSITY OF CALIFORNIA COOPERATIVE EXTENSION, FARM AND HOME ADVISOR**

County. Provides advice and research to counties on soil, water, land use, range management, turf and landscaping, horticulture, viticulture, livestock, poultry and wildlife, food preservation, and nutrition. Extension advisors work closely with other government and community groups such as Four-H Clubs. The U.C. Extension and county Agriculture Department operate through a memo of understanding, with the University paying salaries and counties providing office space for advisors.

C556 *Annual Report to Board of Supervisors.* Contents: memo of understanding, staffing, number of meetings and consultations, and description of programs.

C557 *Civil Rights/Affirmative Action Reports.* Statistical records by race and gender of participants in U.C. Extension programs. Contents: county, year, name of program, group type (volunteer, club, group), percentage or actual number of participants by ethnic group and sex, and methods used to reach minority groups. Note: See also University of California (E053–E080).

C558 *Comprehensive Long Range Plan Record.* Contents: name of county, extension officer's name, date, years covered, program names, descriptions, population to be served, problems, resources, and anticipated results.

C559 **VETERANS SERVICES**

County. Provides assistance to veterans and their dependents in claiming benefits, counseling, handling claims for compensation, pension, education, insurance, medical or dental care, vocational training, employment, home loans, and death benefits. Often combined with Social Services, or Public Administrator. Rarely offered by cities.

C560 *Veterans' Services Records.* Personal files are closed. Routine records (see A014–A023) such as annual reports, statistics, audits, contracts, and budgets are maintained as in other departments. Money from the state or federal government is accounted for by standardized procedures to the allocating agency.

C561 **WEIGHTS AND MEASURES**

County. Tests and seals all commercial weighing and measuring devices (including taxi meters) annually; inspects containers and packages of commercial products at wholesale and retail levels for accurate labeling, including gasoline, oil, auto transmission fluid, brake fluid, and antifreeze; investigates complaints. An official seal is placed on the device showing year of inspection and certification. May be organized under Agriculture Department or independently.

C562 *Audit Inspection Report.* Notes made at the time of inspection to determine whether packages are shortweighted. Contents: name of packer, distributor, or dealer; county; inspector; date and time; location; amount of variance; commodity.

C563 *Certificate of Inspection.* A certificate issued for measuring and weighing devices, and for quantity control. Contents: district and complaint nos., date and time, type of device, details of compliance, record of violations, disposition, name and address of location, and name and address of owner or operator. Re-inspections occur at regular intervals.

C564   **Notice of Violation.** A notice of action taken if the Package Inspection Report (C566) is ignored. Contents: county; business location and phone; owner's name, address, and phone; legal details of violations; signature of owner or agent; title; date and time.

C565   **Notice to Appear.** A legal notice to appear before a judge or clerk of the municipal or justice court. Issued if the Notice of Violation (C564) is not effective. Contents: citation no.; agency name; date and time; business name, address, business license no.; offense; issuing officer.

C566   **Package Inspection Report.** A final detailed report of an Audit Inspection Report (C562). Contents: same as Audit Inspection Report plus statistics of variance, notification of sale prohibition, and value of commodity rejected.

C567   **Test Purchase Report.** A record of commodities purchased by a plainclothes inspector. Contents: county, location, date and time, commodity, prices advertised and charged, overcharge, description of seller, remarks, violation/citation issued, and name of investigator or buyer.

# Education Records

E001   Education in California is multi-level and multi-faceted. From pre-school through graduate school and beyond to adult education, the operation can be complex and confusing. This section is organized into two divisions, Elementary and Secondary Education, and Postsecondary Education. Sub-sections briefly discuss important agencies, an overview of types of records available, and details of more important or typical records.

   For purposes of this guide, records are listed where they originate. Where copies are kept on file may vary from county to county. Often the state recombines local reports into a statewide format, such as the Performance Report for California Schools (E025). For information on access to personal student information see E044.

   State agencies closely related to public schools include: the Department of Education (E002), State Board of Education, Commission on Teacher Credentialing, California Educational Facilities Authority, California Community Colleges (E088–E093), State Allocation Board, Student Aid Commission, State Teachers' Retirement Fund, Postsecondary Education Commission (E048–E052), California State University (E081–E087), and University of California (E053–E080).

   Here are suggestions for more research, some of which are also listed in the Bibliography:

Guide to California Government (League of Women Voters of California, 1992). A handbook on how the state government operates with a good overall explanation of public education.

Organization Charts. Charts are available from a school's office of administration. These are invaluable for understanding the state Department of Education, large school districts, the University of California, and California State Universities.

Administrative Manuals. Manuals, outlining school procedures and policies, are also available from a school's office of administration. The state Department of Education has manuals on specific functions (maintenance and operations) and specific programs (child development) for school districts.

Selected Publications of the California State Department of Education. (Department of Education, Sacramento, 1995). A catalog organized by subject. Good for finding more specialized records such as "California Special Education Programs: A Composite of Laws" or "Child and Parental Rights in Special Education."

ELEMENTARY AND SECONDARY EDUCATION

E002   **STATE DEPARTMENT OF EDUCATION** (916) 657-3027

The Department of Education carries out policy decisions by the State Board of Education and provides assistance to 1,086 local education agencies through general and specialized aid programs. Two important functions are ensuring a fair distribution of funds and evaluating programs paid for by those funds. The department also provides local districts with help for children who have varying disabilities (see Specialized Programs, E040–E043).

   The State Board of Education establishes policies for public education through the twelfth grade, adopts textbooks for grades one through eight, reviews school district reorganization plans, and allocates certain federal funds. Board records include meeting minutes, agendas, hearings, and notices.

Most school district records are filed with the Department of Education, but inquiries should be made at the level where the information originated. Aggregate statewide statistics and special reports are available at the state level. See also Routine Records (A014–A023). The department annually reviews the independent audit reports of all school districts and county school superintendents, and issues an annual report based on the review. For evaluation records, see E019–E027.

E003   ***Annual Report of Financial Transactions Concerning School Districts of California.*** A comprehensive collection of data for each district, published by the State Controller (S109). Contents: income and expenditures from each fund (bond interest and redemption, special reserve, cafeteria, lease/purchase, etc.); average daily attendance; school funds under the jurisdiction of the county superintendent of schools by county; regional occupation centers by county (average daily attendance, income, expenditures, and fund balances).

E004   ***California Basic Educational Data System (CBEDS) Records.*** A statewide computerized database consisting of information on staff and students, enrollment, and hiring practices collected from all public schools (including juvenile halls and other special schools), except for adult schools, preschools, and children's centers. Information is compiled from three forms (as detailed below, E005–E007) submitted by each school. CBEDS information is available via the Department of Education's electronic bulletin board (see Appendix C).

E005   ***CBEDS County/District Information Form.*** Contents: number of classified staff (persons not holding a teaching certificate) by sex and ethnicity; adult education enrollment by program type, number of graduates and staff; high school graduation requirements by subject area; teacher shortage and demand by subject area; status of contract negotiations; numbers of administrators paid from federal funds.

E006   ***CBEDS School Information Form.*** Contents: number of classified staff by sex and ethnicity; school enrollment by grade, sex, and ethnicity; high school graduates by sex and ethnicity; high school graduates completing University of California requirements by sex and ethnicity; high school dropouts by sex, ethnicity, and grade level; enrollment in high school math and science courses by sex and ethnicity; vocational education enrollment by sex and ethnicity; instructional time (in minutes) per week by subject area and grade; alternative school/programs (if available); type of attendance area of school (rural, small town, etc.).

E007   ***CBEDS Professional Assignment Information Form.*** Data for most teachers and certain administrators. Contents: county, district, school name, name of person supplying information; highest educational level; ethnic group; social security no.; sex/birth year; years of experience; assignment or courses taught, percent time spent, enrollment by sex and grade; salary and position; types of teaching credentials, subject expertise. Note: Name and social security no. are optional. On file at the state level only.

E008   ***Civil Rights Complaints.*** Completed files of all complaints regarding specialized or categorical programs. Copies are kept by the local agency or district. Contents: complaint, summary of action taken, local reports, Department of Education reports, appeal (if any), other related and follow-up documents.

E009   ***Textbook Adoptions List.*** A list of books adopted by the state Board of Education for use in elementary schools. Contents: title, publisher, copyright year, author, and price. Note: The lists are devoted to an area of instruction such as math or fine arts and are reviewed every seven years.

E010 **COUNTY OFFICES OF EDUCATION**

Each county must have a Superintendent of Schools, who serves as the link between districts within that county and the state and is secretary of the county Board of Education. The county must provide instruction, in agreement with local school districts, for juvenile court systems, vocational schools, alternative schools, continuation high schools, special education, etc. In the following rural counties, the Office of Education constitutes the only school district: Alpine, Amador, Calaveras, Del Norte, Madera, Plumas-Sierra, Shasta, Siskiyou, Tehama, Trinity, and Yuba. San Francisco is the only city that is also a county school district.

In urban areas, the county Office of Education offers help with services and programs that small cities may not offer, including personnel, business affairs, special education, assistance for disabled students, juvenile home residents, job training, professional library, and textbook depository. Local district budgets are reviewed by the Superintendent of Schools. The County board of Education makes policy decisions for all county-operated programs.

E011 *Estimated Report of the Amount of Taxes to be Collected and Distributed in Fiscal Year.* Data reported annually by the county auditor for calculation of the portion of state aid to be given to school districts. Contents: county; estimated property taxes to be collected and distributed plus state compensation for local tax exemptions; certification. Note: Copies are filed with county superintendent of schools and state Department of Education, Local Assistance Bureau.

E012 *Juvenile Court and Community Schools Files.* Statistical data and routine records of those enrolled in the juvenile-detention system or in an interim community school are generally kept by the county. Their operation is often contracted out. Individual student information is confidential. See California Basic Educational Data System (E004–E007) for other types of records.

E013 *Private School Affidavit.* An annual statement required from private elementary or secondary, full-time day and boarding schools and filed with the local school district, county superintendent of schools, and state Department of Education. Contents: name, address, phone of school; administrator; school type and accommodations; religious affiliation (if any); grades offered; public school district in which located; whether eligible for National Defense Student Loan cancellation; tax-exempt status; enrollment and faculty statistics; programs for those with disabilities (if needed); directors' and principal officers' names, addresses, and positions; location of records; local ordinance compliance; certification. Note: Some private schools educate one student, and are sometimes called home-schooling. Some counties do not recognize a home-school unless the teacher is credentialed.

E014 *Teacher's Credentials.* Contents: name, credential type and status, and expiration date.

E015 *Other County Office of Education Records.* Board of Education meeting minutes, notices, agendas, and decisions; maps of attendance district boundaries for all districts within a county.

E016 **LOCAL SCHOOL DISTRICTS**

Local school districts are organized in varying sizes and usually cover three spans of grades: elementary (K–8), high school (9–12), or unified (K–12). Districts located in more than one county are called joint union.

Local boards of education make policy decisions on curriculum, class size, budget, and other areas within state guidelines. These are elected bodies varying

(LOCAL SCHOOLS, CONT.)

from three to seven persons who may or may not be paid. They have considerable latitude in making decisions.

For purposes of this guide, Local School District records are divided into six catagories: attendance, evaluation, financial, special education, specialized programs, and students. Information from a specific school should be requested from the school district. Some local school districts provide information via the Internet (see Appendix C).

E017 **Attendance Records**

Periodic reports on attendance are filed with the state by local school districts and county school superintendents for grades K–12. These are commonly called Average Daily Attendance (ADA) and are crucial in the determination of funding.

E018 *Annual Reports of Attendance.* Reports are filed for students according to grade level, residence, and type of school. Contents: location, county, and school district; total and average attendance for regular classes, continuation schools and classes, opportunity schools, pregnant minors and home or hospital; special education (non-public, nonsectarian); extended year (non-public, nonsectarian); regional occupational centers and programs; adult classes; number expelled; and number of pupil hours for Core Academic Programs, Students not Meeting District Proficiency Standards, Summer Programs for Graduating Seniors and 11th Graders Who Would Not Graduate with Their Class, and Total Summer School Hours. Note: Two semi-annual reports are filed, July to December and July to April.

E019 **Evaluation Records**

There are three main types of school evaluation: quality, which assesses how well the program works for the people using it; compliance, whether the program fulfills regulations; audits, where the dollars were spent and for what.

E020 *Audits.* Audits of school districts are available locally. The Annual Report of Audits of California Local Educational Agencies lists those school districts failing to file audit reports on time. See also Audit (A016).

E021 *California Assessment Program (CAP).* A statistical report on standardized achievement test results for grades 3, 6, 8, and 12. Summary statistics cover all grades and subjects tested. Contents (of a sample test: 12th grade, reading and math): district, school, grade, year, number tested, score and state rank for each subject, background factors (socioeconomic status, percentage and percentile rank for AFDC and limited English proficiency). Computerized records are arranged by county, then school district, and then individual school.

E022 *Coordinated Compliance Monitoring Review.* A survey establishing that a school is following mandated guidelines for all specially-funded programs. Every three years local school districts (or local education agencies) conduct a "self-review" (E024), followed by a "state validation" of that review (E027).

E023 *Distinguished School Recognition Program Application.* Schools applying for awards for improvement during a three-year period. Contents: school and demographic information; in depth answers to questions on school curriculum, instructional practices, improvement process, culture of school, and student outcomes.

E024 *Local Education Agency Self-Review.* Contents (summarized): county and school district; special education local plan area; migrant education region (if applicable); review coordinator's name, phone; date; programs reviewed; reviewers' names, and phones; names of schools reviewed; indication of compliance for each program; description of non-compliance; summary statements; technical assistance request.

E025   *Performance Report for California Schools.* An annual report for grades 3, 6, 8, and 12 at each school with data comparing performance to a base year and to schools with similar student populations. Contents (of grade 12 as an example): Part I—enrollment in six subject areas, graduation units required, University of California requirements, achievement test scores, Scholastic Aptitude Test (SAT) scores, and dropout/attendance rates. Part II—local and state data for: achievement test scores, English fluency, mobility (if enrolled at school after 10th grade), homework load, grade-point average if a freshman at University of California or California State University, Scholastic Aptitude Test scores, American College Testing Program scores, Advanced Placement Examination scores; ethnic distribution by grade level and in selected courses; summary. Note: Data for grades 3, 6, and 8 differ from those for grade 12.

E026   *Pursuing Excellence.* An evaluation of curriculum and instruction at the high school level. Examines teaching areas (English, mathematics, science, etc.), teaching methods, and administrative support, and makes recommendations. Contents: date, school, reviewers' names, subject area and major findings, teaching methods, and schoolwide practices (counseling, special education, subject coordination, etc.). The review is conducted jointly by Western Association of Schools and Colleges and state Department of Education. It serves as both a Program Quality Review (required for School Improvement Plan funding) and accreditation.

E027   *State Validation Review.* A three-part report done by the state of a school's compliance with specialized program requirements. Contents (summarized): Review Notification and Summary of Findings—same as in Local Education Agency Self-Review form (E024). Resolution of Noncompliant Findings—Contents: County and district name; program reviewed; responsible officer; corrective action; date. Proposed Compliance Agreement—Contents: same as Resolution, plus proposed corrective actions.

E028   **Financial Records**

Following are financial records that show budget information and examples of some records that show information supplied by schools in order to obtain funding.

E029   *Annual Report of Abatement of Expenditures—Form 44.* Accounting information on expected cost reductions for the school district. Contents: reduction of expenditures by type (salaries, contracted services, sites, building, books and media and new equipment, etc.), and allocated by fund, such as General, Deferred Maintenance, etc.

E030   *Annual Report of Accounts Receivable—Form J43A.* Accounting information on funding that the school district expects to receive. Contents: name of school district and county; income by source (federal, state, county, and local) and allocation to specific fund.

E031   *Annual Report of Current Liabilities—Form J43.* Accounting information on debts owed by the school district. Contents: name of school district and county; accounts payable (employee benefits, health and welfare benefits, books and supplies), accrued salaries, sites, building, books and media and new equipment, interfund transfers, etc.

E032   *Asbestos Removal Plans.* See General Services, Office of Local Assistance (S289). Each school is responsible for estimating the need and cost of asbestos removal.

E033   *Nutrition Funding Application.* Contents: school; location; type; dates for use of program; local approval date, contact person, title, phone, and certification; race and ethnicity of enrollment area; contracts with food vendors or food management; meal production, inventory of amounts and types of food used; number of meals (breakfasts, lunches, other) or half-pints of milk served by site and by category (free, reduced price, and full price); income, expenditures, and contributions.

(LOCAL SCHOOLS, CONT.)

E034   ***Pupil Transportation Expense Annual Report.*** Contents: There are 82 possible information entries in this record, including numbers of buses used and reasons for use; mileages; fees collected; depreciation of buses; salaries, benefits, supplies, rentals, leases, and repairs; payments to other districts; other operating expenditures; equipment costs; replacement costs; adjustments to the foregoing; proration of costs; deduction of unallowable costs, etc.

E035   ***Other Pupil Transportation Expense Records.*** School districts must supply various reports detailing costs to receive state funds for pupil transportation. These include Annual Report of Pupil Transportation Expense, Distribution of Costs for a Pupil Transportation System Serving More than One School District, County Superintendent, Private School or Agency; Report of Replaced School Bus. Note: Copies must be filed at state, county, and district levels.

E036   ***School Plan.*** An annual plan done by each local educational agency (school district, county office of education) and filed with the state. The plan serves as the basis for the district budget. Contents: goals and objectives, instruction program (teaching, special education), program evaluation (testing, California Assessment Program, Stanford Achievement Test), student enrollment (history, boundary maps), projected enrollment, construction needs, staffing patterns, facility use, site and school plans (maps, floor plans, maintenance, grounds and equipment), inventory of equipment, and budget.

E037   ***Special Education Records.*** Funds for students needing help outside regular classrooms (hearing, visually, or speech impaired, emotionally disturbed, etc.) can be requested by single-school districts or Special Education Local Plan Areas (SELPA). The Department of Education maintains six schools for the deaf, blind, and emotionally disturbed, in Fremont, Riverside, Fresno, Los Angeles, and San Francisco.

E038   ***Special Education Entitlement Forms.*** Reports filed with both the county and state Departments of Education to compute funds to pay for the following: the special education of infants; children who are institutionalized, those who have physical or developmental disabilities; and extended-year school terms. Contents: certification; six legal-sized pages of instruction; eight regular-sized and seventeen legal-sized pages of computation, coded for data entry, instructional personnel, number of classes, and hours of instruction.

E039   ***Special Education Pupil Count—Form R-30SE.*** An annual report done in each Special Education Local Plan Area (SELPA) to determine reallocation of funds and growth in special education. Contents: area name, contact person, phone, and certification; number of pupils in special instruction, broken out by age and disability. Includes a summary page of special instruction categories by ethnic group and of pupil count of those transferred out by age group and instructional category.

E040   **Specialized Program Records**

About one-fourth of a school district's funds come from specialized, or categorical, programs designed by the state or federal government to help specific groups or solve specific problems. Examples are: Agricultural Vocational Education Incentive Program, Bilingual Teacher Training Program, Class Size Reduction Program, Classroom Teacher Instructional Improvement Program, Curriculum on Birth Defects, Driver Training, Gifted and Talented Education, High School Pupil Counseling, Instructional Materials, Mentor Teacher Program, Miller-Unruh Reading Program, Native American Indian Education, and School Improvement Program. See below (E041–E043) for an example of records required for the Driver Training Program.

E041   *Driver Training Cost Data Report.* A report filed by school district to claim an allowance for the cost of driver training classes. Contents: school district and county; number of regular pupils, number of disabled pupils; instructors' salaries and benefits; cost of books and supplies; private contractor's services; all other services; equipment replacement; administrative support costs.

E042   *Report of Driver Training Vehicles and Simulators.* A report filed to keep state records current on status of vehicles or simulators added or removed during the year. Contents: school district and county; type of transaction; vehicle I.D. no., manufacturer's name; whether new or used; purchase date and price.

E043   *Report of Replaced Driver Training Vehicle or Simulator.* A report filed to support a claim for "equipment replacement." Contents: vehicle I.D. no.; simulator model no.; date of purchase; whether purchased new or used; number of days in use; vehicle miles used for instruction; other miles used, including adult classes; days of use required for replacement allowance unless vehicle has met mileage requirement; sales or trade-in value; replacement expense; estimated percent of miles or hours new equipment used for driver training classes; payments made for lease-purchase equipment; certification; computation of allowance.

E044   **Student Records**

Personal information such as health problems, disciplinary records, and grades are confidential. Students and their legal guardians may view their own records under the California Education Code, Section 49060 *et. seq.*, and the California Code of Regulations, Title V, Article 3, section 430 *et. seq.* Other student records, called "Directory Information," are public subject to the decisions of each individual school board.

E045   *Directory Information.* Contents: name, address, date and place of birth, parent or guardian address, place of business, phone, emergency phone, official activities and sports participation, height and weight of those on athletic teams, dates of attendance, degrees and awards, previous public or private school most recently attended.

E046   *Expulsion Records.* Contents: name, findings of review panel, dates, school board decision. Note: Hearings are confidential. The local district may decide whether a student's name will be available as part of the expulsion record or restricted to minutes of school board meetings.

E047   **POSTSECONDARY EDUCATION**

California supports the nation's largest public postsecondary education system. The system includes formal instruction, adult extension classes, remedial classes, research, and public service.

Postsecondary education is divided into three main branches: the University of California (UC) with 9 campuses, the California State University (CSU) with 22 campuses, and the California Community Colleges (CCC) with 106 campuses. Other state-supported institutions include Hastings College of the Law and the California Maritime Academy.

In addition, there are between 2,500 and 3,000 private colleges and universities statewide, including vocational and technical schools. These must be certified with the state Department of Education (E094—E099).

UC, CSU, and the CCCs are each mandated by the state to serve distinct roles. Anyone 18 years of age or older is eligible for admission to the CCCs. Programs include associate degree, technical/vocational training, community service, citizenship, and remedial skills. Admission to the CSU system is primarily limited to the top third of high school graduates. Instruction is focused on undergraduate programs and teacher education. Postgraduate courses are offered at the master's level and some at the doctoral level in conjunction with doctoral granting institutions. UC primarily admits students from the top one-eighth of high school graduates and has strong programs at the postgraduate level in all disciplines. UC is also the main state-supported institution for research.

Each of the three systems allows their individual campuses a great deal of administrative independence. Each system also has individual reporting require-ments and organizes and maintains records in a variety of ways. Despite differences, the shared educational missions of the three systems cause each campus to generate records in the same broad groups as described below. An exception is UC's unique research function, which includes such institutions as teaching hospitals and the U.S. Department of Energy laboratories.

E048 **POSTSECONDARY EDUCATION COMMISSION, CALIFORNIA** (916) 445-7933

Coordinates and plans for higher education in the state. Advises the governor and legislature on budget and program development, admission policies, plans for campus expansion, determining student fees and faculty salaries. Statistical date of the Commission is available on-line for a fee (see Appendix C).

E049 *California Colleges and Universities—A Guide to California's Degree-Granting Colleges and Universities and to Their Degree and Certificate Programs.* Compre-hensive listing of degree-granting institutions in California. Contents: name of insti-tution, phone, address, president, degrees offered, financial organization, average undergraduate tuition. Annual.

E050 *Fiscal Profiles.* Description and analysis of financing, appropriations and expendi-tures for California's public higher education institutions. Contents: general fund appropriations, total state spending, funding per units of student enrollment, systemwide expenditures, student fees and resulting revenues, financial aid, capital outlays, per-capita spending, and national comparisons.

E051 *California Postsecondary Education Commission Student Profiles.* Contents: undergraduate enrollment and graduation rates by gender, ethnic identity, degree granted, graduate progression to and type of advanced degree achieved.

E052 *Achievement Test Files.* Materials on achievement test, such as the LSAT, PSAT, SAT, etc., administered in the state must be made available by the testing company for review. Contents: supervisory manual, interpretive manual, summary report on test scores by ethnic background, samples of administered tests, answer keys, fees received from test takers, score reports, research and development expenses, announcements of testing dates, and press releases. Materials are available for tests administered from 1985 to present.

E053 **UNIVERSITY OF CALIFORNIA (UC)** (510) 987-9179

UC is goverened by a Board of Regents with 28 members, 21 of whom are appointed by the Governor, who is also President of the Board. The regents appoint the presi-dent of the university, and on his recommendation, chancellors and deans of the various campuses. The state provides 40% of funding. The balance comes from the federal government, student fees, private contracts, and private funds. The budget is subject to analysis by the legislature. There are eight general campuses, one health science campus, three law schools, five medical schools, two dental schools, and one school of veterinary medicine. Hastings College of the Law and the San Francisco Art Institute are affiliated, but administratively separate. There are more than 150 laboratories, study centers, institutes and bureaus for research including Lick Observatory, Scripps Institute of Oceanography, and the Air Pollution Research Center. The chancellors and laboratory directors are essentially executive heads of their institutions.

Records reflect the functions of teaching, research, and public service. See A014–A023 for a discussion of routine records. The records are generally organized as follows: administrative, auxiliary and service enterprises, fiscal, medical, personnel, physical plant, student, and applicant. See also the University of California Cooperative Extension (C555–C558). Information practices coordinators at each campus and laboratory provide overall records privacy, access policy, and procedural guidance under the authority of the Office of the President.

Administrative Records

E054   *Agreements.* Various contracts, memoranda of understanding, and other agreements covering topics such as service agreements (the University as recipient and vendor), athletics, broadcasting, concessions, occupancy and lease (the University as lessor and lessee), teacher training, work/study, financial aid, and other areas.

E055   *Applications and Requests.* Records of permission granted by the University to others for use of facilities, bicycle registration applications, and various types of insurance needed for use of facilities.

E056   *Archives.* Regents' material dates back to 1915 and Presidents' material from 1915 to 1968. Both are located at the Bancroft Library on the Berkeley campus. Contents: correspondence, reports.

E057   *Certificates, Licenses, Permits, Registrations, Warrantees.* Various documents that the University receives or confers such as: aircraft registrations, insurance, copyright assignment/registration, literature distribution permits, easements, import and export licenses, nuclear-reactor licenses, radio and television station licenses, and laboratory animal permits.

E058   *Contracts, Grants, and Agreements for Research, Training, and Public Service.* Records include notice of contracts and grant awards, proposals for non-state support, and contracts with the U.S. Department of Energy for laboratory operation.

E059   *Contract and Grant Reports.* Computer-generated reports compiled quarterly and annually and sorted by source, campus, department, and amount.

E060   *Gifts, Endowments, Private Grants Files.* Records of alumni and donor profiles; deeds for gifts, grants, and quitclaims; endowment or loan fund records; estate and will files. Contents (of reports): gifts accepted and received by campus, sorted by size and source; annual summary.

E061   *Grant Award Amounts, Annual Comparison of.* An annual report of grants awarded to the University sorted by federal, state, or other type of sponsor, and by sponsor according to total annual award amount.

E062   *Leases and rental agreements.* Lease files for contracts conferred by or obtained for the University for personal property, real property, and facilities.

E063   *Other Property Records.* Bills of Sale, Conveyances of Title to Real Property, Property Tax Exemption, Business Property Tax Statements. See Assessor (C039) and Recorder (C420–C471).

E064   *Patent Case Files.* Records of patents issued and not issued. Contents: license agreement, financial records (patent income, expenses, inventor's share of payments).

Note: Most patents are medical. A weekly newsletter lists all patents issued to the Board of Regents.

E065   *Policies, Procedures, Laws.* Documents include the bylaws for academic senate and regents; records disposition schedules (see S305, for contents); policy manuals (planning and budgeting, accounting, police, etc.); university directives and regulations; business and finance bulletins.

E066   *Radiation Usage Records.* Files kept by UC Environmental Health and Safety Offices and Radiation Facilities Offices. Contents: receipt, transfer, disposal records; inventories; instrument calibration records; sealed source leak test records; internal citations; related documents.

E067   *Reports and Rosters.* Various records including controlled substances and narcotics inventories; injury reports; fire, safety, and traffic information; police daily logs; purchasing activities, credit hour tabulation, weekly student hours, etc. See Radiation Usage Records (E066) as an example.

E068   **Auxiliary and Service Enterprise Records**

Records maintained for bookstores, computer centers, garages, housing and residence halls, intercollegiate athletics, parking, storehouses, and telecommunications. Examples of records include Revenue from Instructional Use of Computers, Vehicle Inventory Report, Vehicle Disposal Reports, Applications for Housing, Housing Occupancy Records (count control), Athletic Agreements Between Campus and Opposing Team, and Intercollegiate Athletics Complimentary Ticket Reports.

Fiscal Records

E069   *Audits.* Annual audits, done systemwide and for each campus, are performed by outside auditors. Internal audits are done by the Office of the President and by campus internal audit offices.

E070   *Other Fiscal Records.* Budgets, cash statements, registration reports, equipment inventories, financial reports, general ledger reports, purchasing, and disbursements.

E071   **Medical Records**

Student health information is confidential. Teaching and research hospital records are the same as for private hospitals (controlled substances inventories, birth and death records, admissions and discharges, communicable disease reports, inspections, staff records, unusual occurrences, tumor registry files, etc).

Payroll, Personnel, and Benefits Records

E072   *Corporate Personnel System Reports.* Statistical reports based on campus data, number of personnel, pay, titles, union affiliation, age, gender, status (part- or full-time), etc.

E073   *Faculty (Academic) Applicants Records.* Information that is specific to an individual is released only on a case-by-case basis with applicant's consent.

E074   *Personnel Records.* Files for UC employees. Records are confidential except for: name, date of hire or separation, current position title, current rate of pay, office address and phone, current job description, full or part-time and career, casual, or probationary status, and other information that the Administration may release. Note: Employment contracts for public employees are not confidential.

E075   *Other Personnel Records.* Manuals, policy guidelines, and various statistical reports.

E076   **Physical Plant Records**

Construction agreements and records, bids, planning, space utilization, maintenance, operations, long-range development, and other areas.

Student Records

E077   *Applicant Records.* Files of student applications to enter the UC system. Statistical information is released, but personally identifiable information is not unless the student is
admitted, at which time student record and directory information policies apply.

E078   *Directory Information, Student Records.* Each campus adopts policies for the release
of information and informs students when enrolling. Any of the following information may be declared confidential by the student. Contents: name, address, phone(s);
date and place of birth; major field of study; attendance dates; degrees and honors
received; most recent previous educational institution attended; official activities and
sports; weight and height of participants in intercollegiate athletics, any other information authorized in writing by the student.

E079   *Enrollment Records.* Summary computerized data used in various ways to produce
reports. Individual information is confidential. Contents: dates, gender, ethnicity,
age, veteran status, residency, citizenship, credit units, level and type of instruction,
and subject field.

E080   *Student Group Contact List.* A list of registered campus organizations. Contents:
name, campus address and phone, contact person's name and phone, and type of
organization.

E081   ## CALIFORNIA STATE UNIVERSITY (CSU) (310) 985-2740

The system is governed by a 24-member Board of Trustees who appoint the Chancellor, make policy decisions, and appoint the presidents of the 22 campuses. The
primary role is teaching, including extension programs. California State University
Records are similar to those of the UC system (E054–E080). Laws governing access to
student, employee, and faculty information are the same for both systems.

E082   *Audits.* Management and operational audits are done by state and federal officials
and by the CSU Board of Trustees, Office of the University Auditor. There is no
regular outside auditor.

E083   *Organization, Responsibilities and Staffing.* A statement by the Office of the Chancellor. Contents: mission, functional responsibilities, staffing levels, and organization
charts for the five divisions.

E084   *Personnel Records.* Same as UC (E072–E075).

E085   *State University Administrative Manual.* Contents: Summaries of administrative
procedures for Academic Affairs, Business and Finance, information resources and
technology, human resources and operations, Physical Planning and Development,
and Public Affairs. Note: Each section includes appendices, which have many
examples of standard reporting forms.

E086   *Student Records.* Same as UC (E077–E080).

E087   *Other CSU Reports.* California State Publications (Bibliography) prints notices of
reports from the Chancellor's Office and from individual campuses. Some examples
are: Enrollment by Ethnic Group; Academic Grade Report; Size, Growth and Cost of
Administration at CSU; and Lottery Revenue Budget.

E088   **CALIFORNIA COMMUNITY COLLEGES** (916) 445-8752

The Board of Governors, appointed by the governor, decides on policy. The Chancellor carries out policy and administers the system, which totals 106 campuses in 71 districts. Each college has a Board of Trustees elected from within the district, which then selects the college president.

Types of records follow those of UC (E054–E080), but reflect a teaching emphasis on vocational and adult education, and preparation for transfer to a four-year institution. Community colleges also have fewer non-state sources of funds. Records are kept at individual colleges and at the state Department of Education. Annual audits are done by the community college districts. Special audits are done by the Auditor General.

E089   *Average Daily Attendance Generated in Classes for Inmates.* An annual report of courses offered to jail inmates. Contents: community college district, course title, course no., enrollment, average daily attendance, actual current expense of maintaining classes for inmates, and jail/detention center name.

E090   *Enrollment Report.* An annual report. Contents: number of students and data by district and by college (number, percent, gender/ethnicity, age, credit units, and hours spent in class); student data by district (gender/ethnicity, age, high school graduation, academic level, and enrollment/residency/citizenship status) according to full-time, part-time, and noncredit status.

E091   *Fiscal Abstract.* An annual report summarizing statistics from each college. Contents: enrollment, base revenue (calculations based on types of students enrolled), general fund transactions, sources of revenue, and expenditures. Data are given for state total, each college, and comparisons among colleges. Note: available from the Chancellor's Office and individual colleges.

E092   *Staffing and Salaries Report.* An annual report. Contents: detailed statistical tables on age, gender/ethnicity, employment classification/status, type of employment contract, annual salary and percent change in number of hours teaching, etc., for various levels of faculty, employees, and totals.

E093   *Student Records.* Contents: See E077–E080.

E094   **PRIVATE POSTSECONDARY SCHOOLS**

Private colleges and other postsecondary schools generally consist of two types— degree-granting and non-degree institutions. Each must file a current catalog, a description of placement assistance (if any), copies of advertising, copies of student enrollment agreements or contract forms, and the name and address of a designated agent with the state Department of Education, Private Post-Secondary Division.

E095   *Certificate of Authorization of Service.* A certificate is required for all instructors and administrators of institutions offering occupational courses. It must be renewed annually. Contents: certificate no., expiration date, name, address, phone, date, occupation, and teaching subjects.

E096   *Degree-Granting Institution Affidavit.* Evidence of accreditation, filed annually. Contents: institution name, address, and phone; ownership; designated agent's address, and phone; accrediting agency; whether placement assistance is offered; copy of current catalog; signature and title.

E097   *Degree-Granting Institution Application to Operate.* Contents: institution name, address, and phone; responsible representative address, phone; ownership and address; record custodian name, address, phone; pending legal action, if any; review committee's arrangements and report.

E098   ***Non-Degree Granting Institution Application.*** Contents: name, address, and phone; ownership and address; accrediting agency; designated agent's name, address, and phone; copy of current catalog; signature and title; date; description of placement assistance.

E099   ***Private School Agent's Permit.*** A permit required for a paid recruiter. Must be renewed annually. Contents: type of application, date, name of agent, expiration date, and institution's name.

Special District and Regional Records

R001   California is home to more than 5,000 types of government variously called "special districts," "regional agencies," and "multi-jurisdictional agencies." They are authorized by several hundred types of legislation, financed in diverse ways, cover various amounts of territory, and have varying degrees of authority. They are "local" in that they are not statewide. A special district may cover just one city block (such as lighting), several cities (cemeteries, parks), or a half-dozen counties (airports, air quality basins, water districts).

    Usually, districts have powers much like those of local government, including in some cases adoption of ordinances, punishment of violators, handling of licenses and permits, and issuance of bonds. They may provide one service or several. One key difference is how they are governed: by an elected board of governors (independent) or by a county board of supervisors, city council, or state agency (dependent). Another important difference is that some charge fees and pay their own way (enterprise type), while others rely on property taxes, special assessments, and state funds (non-enterprise).

R002   Enterprise agencies typically operate airports, electric utilities, harbors and ports, hospitals, mass transit, water utilities, and waste-disposal systems. Non-enterprise agencies typically handle air-pollution control, ambulance service, animal control, cemeteries, communications, fire protection, health care, libraries, lighting, parking, pest control, planning and development, police, parks and recreation, soil conservation, and streets. Water delivery, the original special district (1887), continues as the most common type, followed by lighting, fire protection, waste disposal, and financing and construction of facilities.

R003   Councils of Government (COGs) are among the largest special districts in terms of area. They were created to promote intergovernmental planning. Transportation planning is now their most important function and source of funding. They also provide research services, are an important source of statistical data, act as a clearinghouse for grant funds, and promote area-wide services such as freeway callboxes for motorists. There are 25 COGs in California, up from 19 in 1988. Examples include the Association of Bay Area Governments (ABAG), Southern California Association of Governments (SCAG), San Diego Association of Governments (SANDAG), and Kern County Council of Governments (KernCOG).

    The California Association of Councils of Government (CalCOG) serves as an umbrella association and provides direction for all COGs. Contact this group (916) 447-6396 to determine which COG covers a specific geographic area.

    Some regional agencies are set up by the state to accomplish very specific goals. Examples include the San Francisco Bay Conservation and Development Commission, Santa Monica Mountains Conservancy, and Tahoe Regional Planning Agency.

SPECIAL DISTRICT RECORDS

R004   Special district records vary according to an agency's function, jurisdiction, and authority. They typically include annual reports, audits, contracts, and various financial records. Budgets are public record and sometimes are found in the county budget. Other records include meeting agendas and minutes, and notices. See Routine Records (A014–A023).

Because of their diversity and number, special district records are not covered in depth in this guide. For specific records, refer instead to similar agencies at the city, county, and state level listed in the index. These can provide clues to what is available.

Some state agencies create regional districts due to environmental or political factors. Significant records are listed under the state entry indicated. Examples are the Air Resources Board's 14 air basins, the Water Resources Control Board's 9 regional water quality control boards, the 5 field divisions of the Water Resources Department, the California Coastal Commission's 6 coastal districts, and the Department of Fish and Game's 5 regions.

R005   Because definitions and titles vary widely, it may be difficult to trace the location of and records for special districts and regional agencies. The following sources may offer some guidance:

Local Telephone Directory. Check the government pages in front of the white pages or directly under the name in the alphabetical listing.

League of Women Voters. Some of the local leagues have published guidebooks to regional agencies. An example is *Decision Makers* by the League of Women Voters of the Bay Area.

State Controller, Special District List. District names and mailing address by county are maintained by the Office of Local Government and Fiscal Affairs, State Controller. Includes financial summary of special districts by district, type , county and activity.

State Controller, Annual Report Financial Transactions Concerning Special Districts of California. This report lists more than 5,000 special districts in the state, with summary and detailed financial data on each state, county, and individual special district.

Secretary of State, Roster of Public Agencies. This list includes the organization name and mailing address, a statement of organization, names and addresses for members, and a contact person.

Other Sources. The City Clerk (C074) and the clerk of the Board of Supervisors (C058) should maintain lists of what special districts the City Council or Board of Supervisors, respectively, sits on as the governing body. The California Special Districts Association, (916) 442-7887, represents special districts in the legislature and pools districts for employee benefits. The California Association of Local Agency Formation Commissions (CALAFCO) has no permanent staff or location. Each county LAFCO is listed under County Government in the white pages of the phone book.

# State Records

S001   Researching information at the state level is somewhat easier than at the city or county level. State offices are generally better organized and better funded. The disadvantage is that organizations are so vast it becomes difficult to locate a given record. Another disadvantage is the apparently widespread overlapping of functions. Fortunately, state officials tend to have a greater sense of service and try to provide help—even if at times misguided—for the taxpayer.

State agencies often have special libraries that are unmatched sources of information about their subject area. They are not always staffed to handle public queries, so one should call or write first. Some examples are Aquatic Habitat Institute; Bay Area Regional Earthquake Preparedness Project—Regional Resource Center; Bay Conservation and Development Commission; Energy Resources, Conservation and Development Commission; Pest Management Library, Department of Food and Agriculture; Colorado River Law Library, Colorado River Board; CalTrans Historical Library, Department of Transportation.

Many state agencies keep track of legislation that might affect them by writing legislative analyses, testifying, and contacting outside groups to generate interest on their behalf. There is no master list of these persons. The office can be identified as "legislative affairs," "legislative liaison," "legislative coordinator," etc.

There are more than 400 boards, commissions, authorities, associations, and committees at the state government level, ranging from such obscure bodies as the Board of Guide Dogs for the Blind to the large and powerful Board of Equalization. The number has grown substantially in recent years; only a few are covered in this guide. Their functions may be regulatory (Public Utilities Commission), advisory (Advisory Commission on Special Education), administrative (California Arts Council), or marketing (California Rice Promotion Board). Wide differences exist in budgets, staffing, responsibilities, and legal authority. Records vary accordingly, but generally include meeting agendas, minutes, hearing transcripts, and routine records.

A partial list of these and other state bodies not covered here is provided at the end of this chapter. For information on those agencies' records, or for a wider survey of a particular state agency's records, consult the Records Retention Schedules kept at State Archives (S617) in Sacramento. Also, many agencies issue a "List of Publications" that is useful for reports and summaries, but not primary information records.

California State Publications, a monthly and cumulative annual publication of the California State Library, is the best source for recent state documents. It does not include primary records such as those listed in this guide, but does include the following: reports, reviews, surveys, audits, periodicals, bibliographies, catalogs, statistics, directories, publications lists, and handbooks. For other sources on state government, see the Bibliography.

The California State Operator at (916) 657-9900 can provide the public with up-to-date telephone numbers for state departments, divisions, offices, and employees.

This service is administered by the Department of General Services, Office of Administrative Services. For a published listing of state government telephone numbers, consult the *State of California Telephone Directory* (see Bibliography).

Some state agencies are moving towards making public records available on electronic bulletin boards or on the Internet. Appendix C in this guide offers advice for determining what records have been placed on-line.

S002 **ADMINISTRATIVE LAW, OFFICE OF** (916) 323-6225

Reviews all proposed or existing state regulations (except those setting a rate, price or tariff, those related to public works, those directed to a specific person or group, and building standards), and issues decisions based on certain standards (necessity, authority, consistency, clarity, and reference to specific statute or court decision). The decision may be appealed to the Governor.

S003 *California Code of Regulations Decisions.* Contents: Summaries of approved regulations includes title no. from California Code of Regulations (formerly California Administrative Code), agency, file no., title of regulation, filing date, contact person's name and phone; Decision of Disapproval includes data above plus discussion of issues involved and name of staff counsel doing review.

S004 *California Regulatory Notice Register.* Advance notice of hearing. Contents: summary digest, public hearing time, place, statement of impact, and agency contact person's name and phone.

S005 *Directory of State Regulatory Agencies.* Alphabetical list updated as needed. Contents: agency name, address, phone, director, regulations coordinator (if any), name of supervising department, and relevant title no. of California Code of Regulations.

S006 *Notice of Proposed Action.* Begins the formal process for public comment. Contents: summary of existing law and proposed changes; mailing address for comments or information; contact person; public hearing (if scheduled); small business impact; cost impact on private persons or businesses, local agencies and districts, and housing; legal citations of authority and affected laws; background information.

S007 *Regulatory Determinations.* If an agency is enforcing a rule or regulation never formally adopted (an "underground regulation"), anyone may request an investigation and decision (a "regulatory determination"). All pertinent information is published in the *California Regulatory Notice Register* (S004).

S008 *Rulemaking Files.* A complete record of review process for each regulation. Contents: originating agency; file no.; published notice; proposed and final text; initial and final statement of rule-making reasons; data, studies from agency and public; cost impact.

S009 **AGING, DEPARTMENT OF** (916) 322-3887

Manages 33 local "Area Agencies on the Aging" (see Aging, C002) to deliver funds from the state and the federal Older Americans Act. Information on individuals is confidential. Regulations, contracts, and some reports are public.

S010 *Adult Day Health-Care Application for Facility License.* Contents: applicant's name, address, phone; type of business; facility name, address, and phone; person in charge and license no.; civil offenses, if any; type of facility; capacity; age range of clients; time of operation; whether previously licensed; whether construction required; ownership of property; other care facilities owned by applicant; area health planning approval (if required); signatures; titles; date.

S011 *Adult Day Health-Care Cost Report.* Contents: facility name, address, phone, license no., administrator, any changes since last report, and person certifying report contents. Note: Related records are Licensee and Center Description and Revenue Information; Related Persons and Organizations (sharing ownership and control).

S012   *Adult Day Health-Care Monthly Statistical Summary Report.* A monthly break-down of persons served. Contents: name of facility, year covered, number of non–Medi-Cal participants served, enrolled, or disenrolled; number of Medi-Cal days scheduled and attended, days in operation, and average daily attendance.

S013   *Long Term Care Facilities Elder Abuse-Dependent Adult Abuse Monthly Statistical Report.* Contents: name of ombudsman (person handling complaints made by or on behalf of residents in nursing homes), location, date; number of reports of alleged abuse by type of program, age, and disposition; types of confirmed abuse incidents by age; confirmed number of abusers by sex and status (family, employee of facility); actions taken; number of reports of alleged self-inflicted abuse by age; types of confirmed self-inflicted abuse by age and type; actions taken; contact person's phone; date.

S014   *Long-Term Care Ombudsman Monthly Report.* Contents: location, name of coordinator; new or old complaints and investigations; origin of new complaints (patients, relatives, hospital staff, etc.); categories of new complaints by program; complaints referred to other agencies; local area data (number of facilities, visits, certified ombudsmen, etc.); community education programs; witnessing procedures (powers of attorney for health-care, property transfers); number of ombudsmen training; number of citations, reports, and conferences.

S015   *Ombudsman Certification Form.* Contents: name, address, phone, date, sex, age, hours per month, education, work experience, signature, and approval.

S016   *Other Aging Department Records.* Administrator or Program Director Application; Alzheimer's Day Care Resource Centers (list); Board of Directors (background detail); Cash Flow Forecast; Civil Rights Compliance; Disclaimer of Conflict of Interest; Medi-Cal Participation Agreement; Operating Budget; Provider Background Information; Request to Establish Eligibility in Medi-Cal.

S017   **AGRICULTURAL LABOR RELATIONS BOARD** (916) 653-3699

Conducts collective bargaining elections and hears unfair labor practice cases. The ALRB General Counsel investigates and prosecutes unfair labor practice charges.

S018   *Election Case Files.* Challenges to representation or decertification elections. Contents: election petition (name, address, and phone of filing party; employer's name, address, and phone; number of workers employed; description of bargaining unit; agricultural commodity or crop), employer's response, tally of ballots, objection petition, administrative hearing record (transcripts and evidence), investigative hearing examiner and Board decisions.

S019   *Unfair Labor Practice Charge Files, Unfair Labor Practices Dockets.* Records of prosecution of unfair labor practices. Files include complaints of labor against employer, employer against labor, and labor against labor. Contents: unfair labor practice charge (name, address, phone, of filing party and charged party, number of workers employed, crop or commodity, code section violated, and basis of charge); complaint; answer to complaint; administrative hearing record (transcripts and evidence); administrative law judge and Board decision.

S020   *Other Agricultural Labor Relations Board Reports:* Regional Director's Report on Challenged Ballots; Regional Director's Report on Unit Clarification Petition; Regional Director's Report on Selected Issues.

S021 **AIR RESOURCES BOARD** (916) 322-2990

Conducts planning and enforcement of state and federal air quality standards. Shares this responsibility with 34 local agencies, called Air Quality Management Districts or Air Pollution Control Districts. State regulates vehicle emissions (see Automotive Repair Program, S100), guides research studies, and sets emission standards for all new cars sold in the state. Local districts can be county or regional and are responsible for control of stationary sources of air pollution. The forms used may vary from district to district. The Bay Area Air Quality Management District, for example, stores information on computer for: plants with permits, pollutant by type of source, abatement devices, gasoline service stations, sites not having an assigned no., emission factors, emissions inventory, permits issued, citizen complaints, inspection and surveillance, violations, and air-contaminant monitoring. Operates under the authority of the Secretary of the California Environmental Protection Agency.

S022 *Air Quality Data.* Measurement by local monitoring stations of ambient (outside) air quality data in the state's 14 air basins. Not all monitoring stations measure all elements. Contents: basin, county, station name and I.D. code; method used; gaseous pollutants tables; soiling index tables; particulate data tables; numbers of observations and samples; numbers of days and hours when pollutants exceeded limit. Quarterly and annual summaries.

S023 *Application for Authority to Construct and Permit to Operate.* Required for new equipment that may cause pollution, modification of old equipment, change of business ownership or location of equipment, establishment of a hazardous-waste facility. Contents: plant no.; application no.; business name, address, and phone; contact person's name and phone; equipment description; reasons for making application; whether an environmental impact report was prepared and by whom; whether a violation was issued and violation no.; number of emissions by kind and amount, documentation of variances allowed or claimed; documentation of air analysis; topographical map and description of all air pollution control equipment; signature. Note: The applicant may claim confidentiality for trade secret information. Permit must be renewed annually. Records are maintained by local air pollution control district.

S024 *Asbestos Demolition or Renovation Notification.* Local districts must be informed of work related to asbestos. Contents: site address; owner's address and phone; type of building; start and completion dates; description of project and material; removal methods and amounts; contractor's name, address, phone, and job no.; disposal site address; inspection dates; observations and comments from inspector; inspector name and no. Note: If the local district does not oversee asbestos removal, it must inform the U.S. Environmental Protection Agency.

S025 *Hearing Board Dockets.* Records of regulation violators appealing district decisions or requesting exemptions ("variances"); staff requests for permit revocations or abatement orders. Contents: petitioner's name, address, and phone; type of business; company officers or owners' names and addresses; attorneys' names; nature of petition (violation, exemption, appeal of permit denial or revocation, or abatement order); type of equipment involved; reply; evidence; disposition. Note: Taped transcripts of hearings are available. Records are maintained locally.

S026 *Vehicle Code 27156 Exemption Application:* Engines and pollution control equipment may not be modified or altered unless approved. Generic name for device type is "aftermarket parts" or "add-on parts." Contents: name, address, phone of applicant, device manufacturer, and authorized representative; description and operation of device; list of compatible and incompatible vehicles; details of proposed equipment; and statement of non-polluting performance. Files are located in the Mobile Source Division.

S027   **Violation Notice.** Contents: violation no.; plant I.D. no.; name, address, and phone of recipient; name, address of occurrence (if different); source, type, and time of violation; regulations involved; signature of recipient and inspector. Note: Records are maintained locally.

S028   **Warranty Complaint Form.** Contents: complainant's name, address, and phone; date; vehicle information (license no., state, I.D. no., make, model, year, cylinders, type of gas used, and purchase date); whether complaint was resolved; who was contacted (dealer, area representative, manufacturer, Automotive Repair Program); action taken; dealership name, address, and phone; details of complaint; if repaired, where, at what cost, who paid, and remarks. Files are located in the Mobile Source Division.

S029   **Other Local District Records:** Complaint forms; inspection forms; hearings notices; hearings reports; progress reports; technical reports; public meetings; status reports; source tests; emission inventories; general air pollution source data (for each piece of equipment used by a business or industry).

S030   **Other Mobile Source Division Records.** Experimental Permit for New Motor Vehicle or New Motor Vehicle Engine; Application for Certification of Gaseous Fuel Systems; Application for Fuel Additive Testing; Auxiliary Fuel Tank Certification Application; Application for Certification for New Model [vehicle]; Application for Exemption of Aftermarket Turbochargers from Vehicle Code; and others. Note: Records of vehicles with defective smog control devices are kept by the California Highway Patrol and discarded after three months.

S031   ## ALCOHOLIC BEVERAGE CONTROL, DEPT. OF (916) 263-6900

Regulates manufacture, importation into the state, and sale of alcoholic beverages. Licenses, of which there are approximately 70 types, may be denied, suspended, or revoked for violation of law. Alcoholic beverage taxes are collected by the state Board of Equalization (S184). All information about a license or licensee is maintained in Base Files (S036) kept at each field office and partially duplicated in headquarters.

S032   **Accusation.** Contents: file no., regulation no., license no., business name and address; accusation or complaint; previous record of licensee; citation of laws violated; date; signature. Note: Information related to legal matters is maintained in the Hearing and Legal Unit until decided, then merged with Base File (S036) after administrative action has been taken.

S033   **Accusation Registration.** Contents: registration no., date, district, hearing record set, whether proposed decision was received, appeal filed, file no., charge, sections and rules violated, and decision.

S034   **Application for Alcoholic Beverage License.** Contents: applicant and business name, business and mailing addresses, types of licenses, felony convictions, violations of Alcoholic Beverage Control Act, name of person transferring license (if any), location, signature, license no., and fees. Note: Records for new applications are maintained in field offices until concluded. Copies are sent to local police and sheriff offices.

S035   **Certificate of Decision.** Record of adoption of administrative law judge decision. Contents: file no., registration no., case description, suspension or revocation notice (if any), date, and official signature. Appeals are made to the Alcoholic Beverage Control Appeals Board.

S036   **Licensee Files, Base Files.** Records of alcoholic beverage manufacturers and sellers. Contents: license application, franchise agreements, accusations (official charges of violations), complaints (brought by private parties), and appeals hearings transcripts. Note: filed alphabetically by name of licensee. There is a geographical index. Financial information is confidential.

S037   ***Notice Concerning Proposed Decision.*** Rejection of a decision made by an administrative law judge. Contents: file no., regulation no., names of parties to decision, and date.

S038   ***Notice of Defense.*** Acknowledgment by licensee of receipt of accusation (S032). Contents: file no., regulation no., licensee's name, mailing address, and date.

S039   ***Notice of Intended Transfer of Retail Alcoholic Beverage License.*** Contents: licensee's name; business and mailing addresses; transferee's name and address; type, name, no. of license transferred; escrow holder or guarantor name and address; amounts paid; signatures. Note: County Recorder (C420) keeps a copy.

S040   ALCOHOL AND DRUG PROGRAMS, DEPT. OF (916) 445-0834

Licenses, certifies and regulates alcohol and drug-abuse treatment centers operating in the state. Works in partnership with county governments and public and private agencies and organization to coordinate, develop, implement and evaluate a statewide alcohol and drug abuse education, prevention, intervention, detoxification and treatment and recovery system.

S041   ***Alcohol and Other Drug Services: A Directory of Community Services in California.*** Listing by county of alcohol and drug service providers, toll-free crisis lines, county Americans with Disabilities Act (ADA) coordinators, and county drug and alcohol program administrators. Information on service providers includes: name, address, phone, and types of services provided, e.g. alcohol; drug abuse; residential, outpatient or drop-in; group, family or individual counseling; bilingual; adolescent; women; disabled access; dual diagnosed; methadone maintenance; driving-under-the-influence). Published annually.

S042   ***California Alcohol and Drug Data System Monthly Report.*** Statistical data on admissions to alcohol and drug-abuse treatment facilities. Breaks down admissions by race/ethnic composition, sex, age, housing and employment status, source of referral, legal status (e.g. on parole, incarcerated), education level, disability, drug of choice, age of first use, drug administration route, types of treatment services used, funding source, and county of admission.

S043   ***Complaint Files.*** Contents: history of any complaints filed against a treatment facility or program, complaint report, allegation of deficiencies, finding of deficiencies, investigator's name, name of person or organization complaint was filed against, corrective action plan, notice of civil penalties, and appeal of findings if any.

S044   ***Driving-Under-the-Influence (DUI) Program Directory of Service Providers.*** A listing of licensed service providers for those required to attend a driving-under-the-influence program. Contents: license number, legal program name, business program name, address, contact person, phone number, and type of DUI services provided.

S045   ***Publications Catalog.*** An annual listing of reports and information produced by state, federal and non-governmental agencies on alcohol and drug-abuse issues. Includes information on abuse-related issues such as gangs, AIDS, older citizens, persons with disabilities, workplace, and ethnic identity. Includes publications in Spanish. Indexed by category, title, and publication number.

S046   **Licensing and Certification Branch** (916) 322-2911

The Department is charged with licensing non-medical, residential alcohol and drug-abuse recovery or treatment facilities. For chemical dependency recovery hospitals see S350. Two publications of the department, *Standards for Direct Alcohol Program Services* and *Licensing Requirements for Alcoholism or Drug Abuse Recovery or Treatment Facilities*, detail the standards and licensing requirement for these facilities. All licensing information provided by an applicant for licensing must be made available for public inspection according to Chapter 3.5, Division 7 of the Government Code unless other wise exempted by law. Licensing Applications are submitted to the department and contain the following supportive documents: Annual Line-Item Budget, Partnership Agreement, Articles of Incorporation, List of Board Members (including names and addresses), alcohol and/or drug use policy, admission and readmission policy, plan of operation, sketch of building grounds, sample menu, sample admission agreement, admission policies/procedures, general program description of services offered, and Bacteriological Analysis of Private Water Supply. Note: S047–S053 are included as part of Licensing and Applications.

S047   ***Administrator/Director Information.*** Identifies administrator and director of facility and verifies qualifications to operate facility. Contents: name, title, address, phone number, social security number, and birthdate; educational background, business and work experience.

S048   ***Administrative Organization.*** Identifies entity applying for licensure. Contents: corporation name, chief executive officer, incorporation date, home office address and phone number, and governing board of directors.

S049   ***Designation of Administrative Responsibility.*** Identifies person authorized by licensee/applicant to accept responsibility for facility.

S050   ***Facility Staffing Data.*** Lists of facility personnel, including back-up persons and volunteers providing services. Contents: employee name, title and driver's license no., date employed, total time of alcohol/drug program experience, hours worked per month, date of last TB test, and CPR and first aid-training. Note: Some information is confidential.

S051   ***Licensing and Certification Branch Status Report.*** An alphabetical list by county of all non-medical alcohol and drug-abuse recovery or treatment facilities that are licensed and/or certified by the Department. Contents: facility name, director's name, address, phone, compliance review date, license expiration date, target population, service type, funding source, capacity, and department analyst name.

S052   ***Request for Licensing.*** Identifies applicant and facility for licensure. Contents: name, address and phone number of facility; type of application (alcohol, drug or combined); parent organization (as filed with Secretary of State, if applicable); profit or not-for-profit status; type of alcohol and/or drug services provided (detoxification, recovery home services, residential treatment services); total occupancy of facility; property ownership status.

S053   ***Weekly Activities Schedule.*** Facility schedule for specific activities, e.g. education, problem solving, counseling sessions, recreation, individual and family sessions, 12-step meetings, and other activities the facility may require of its residents.

S054   **Methadone Licensing Branch** (916) 322-6682

Oversees the delivery of methadone treatment services to heroin and other opiate addicts. Performs annual on-site inspections of all licensed methadone programs in the state. The federal Drug Enforcement Agency (DEA) and the Food and Drug

(ALCOHOL AND DRUG PROGRAMS, CONT.)

Administration (FDA) also regulate methadone maintenance programs. Prior written approval from these agencies is required for licensure.

S055   *Application for Methadone Licensing.* Contents: type of license applied for (outpatient or inpatient maintenance or detoxification); name of applicant; address; telephone number; executive director; type of entity; name of clinic; address; name of program and medical directors; hours of operation; patient fees; number of slots/beds, subsidized/funded slots; funding sources; date of approval, license number, and FDA number (if applicable). The department also requires applicants for licensing to submit conviction information on all partners, officers, directors, and shareholders.

S056   *Application for Medi-Cal Certification as a Clinic Provider.* Required for those applying for licensure who intend to provide detoxification treatment services funded by Medi-Cal. Contents: name of facility; address; phone; staff names, discipline history; license numbers; types of services to be provided; source of funds and income for operation; fees to be paid by patient; treatment hours; hours of operation.

S057   *Medi-Cal Providers Data Form.* Filing requirements same as above. Contents: same as S363.

S058   **ALLOCATION BOARD, STATE** (916) 445-7880

Approves all applications for school facilities and apportions funds to school districts for building construction and rehabilitation, purchase of equipment, asbestos removal in K–12 schools. Staffed by the Office of Local Assistance, General Services Department (S289) where project records are kept. Consult the school or school district involved for specific records, such as emergency classrooms, migrant agricultural worker's schools, asbestos abatement, deferred maintenance projects, etc. See also routine records (A014–A023).

S059   **AUDITS, BUREAU OF STATE** (916) 445-0255

Formerly office of the Auditor General. Examines and reports annually on the financial statements prepared by the executive branch of the state and performs other assignments including performance and compliance audits mandated by statute. Under the Reporting of Improper Governmental Activities Act, the Bureau investigates state agencies for alleged fraud, waste, and abuse. It is also required to conduct audits requested by the Joint Legislative Audit Committee of state and local government to the extent that funding is available. Audit reports are public, and evidence supporting reports is available for review.

S060   *Financial Audit Report.* Annual single audit of the state. Includes financial statements reflecting state's financial position, the results of its operations, and compliance with federal program requirements.

S061   *Investigative Audit Report.* Semi-annual investigative report of substantiated instances of fraud, waste, and abuse in state agencies.

S062   *Performance Audit Report.* Covers program efficiency, effectiveness, and compliance with law. Contents: title, date, summary, introduction (narrative background), audit results (narrative, statistics, and corrective action), conclusion, recommendations, appendices, and responses from agencies (if any).

S063 **BANKING DEPARTMENT, STATE** (415) 263-8500

Administers state laws, regulations, and licenses for state-chartered commercial banks (as opposed to federally-chartered banks), foreign and out-of-state banking corporations, trust companies, and other financial businesses. Examinations of licensees are done as needed or at least once every two years. Oversees all local government agency deposits with banks and savings & loans. Most Banking Department records are confidential.

S064 *Annual Report.* A summary of activities. Contents: summary of applications; (statement of income; name, principal office address and phone, principal officers and directors, parent company and subsidiary, branch offices, financial statement), alphabetical index of state regulated banks, summary of inquiries, and complaints.

S065 *Application Facing Page.* The facing page of application to organize a state-chartered bank and trust company or foreign bank. Contents: organizer's name and address, occupation or business, proposed bank name and address, capitalization, and authorized representative. The rest of the application is not public.

S066 *Quarterly Report.* Quarterly summary of business of state chartered banks and other licensees. See Weekly Bulletin (S067) for details.

S067 *Weekly Bulletin.* A listing of action taken by the Banking Department during the previous week. Contents: notice and type of application filed (new branch, new establishment, new place of business, etc.), dates, name, and address of bank or representative, and status of application.

S068 *Other Banking Department Licenses and Permits.* Bank or Trust License; Business and Industrial Development Corporation License; Foreign Bank Agency Office License (includes out-of-state banks); Foreign Bank Representative License; Payment Instruments License (for money orders); Transmitter of Currency Abroad License; Travelers Checks License.

S069 **BOATING AND WATERWAYS DEPARTMENT** (916) 445-2615

Responsible for development of boating facilities, support for local boating law enforcement, promoting boating safety and education, beach erosion control, water hyacinth control and licensing of yacht brokers, ship brokers, and for-hire vessel operators.

S070 *For-Hire Vessel Operator's License.* Contents: name, social security no., address and phone, birth place and date, sex, height, weight, color of hair and eyes, distinguishing marks, type of license, type of vessel, location of operation, boating experience, U.S. Coast Guard license details, physical defects, record of any license/certificate revocation and reasons, narcotics addiction, character references, and signature.

S071 *Yacht and Ship Salesman or Broker's License Application.* Contents: name, address and phone, DBA, birth place and date, height, weight, color of hair and eyes, partner's names and titles, corporation (if any) name, incorporation date and location, corporate officers names and titles. Note: Salesman's license omits partnership and corporate information. A fingerprint card must be filed. A broker must file a surety bond.

S072 **COASTAL COMMISSION, CALIFORNIA** (415) 904-5200

Controls coastal zone development and approves coastal zone plans adopted by local governments. The commission has five district offices and a main office in San Francisco. The commission processes permits until a local government has a developed local coastal zone plan and has the plan certified by the commission as consistent with the Coastal Act. Shares some responsibility with the State Coastal Conservancy.

S073 *Application for Coastal Development Permit.* An application required for any development within the coastal zone (an area delineated on maps by the legislature: typically narrower in urban areas and as wide as five miles in rural areas, and up to three miles seaward). Contents: type of permit (improvement, over $100,000, single family, or subdivision); applicant's name, address, and phone; representative's name, address, and phone; declaration of campaign contributions; project location (map, assessor's parcel no.); description (sewage, water, roads, size, purpose, and moorings); present use of property; cost; other developments; details of project (height, paved area, and landscaping); parking; utilities; grading of land; U.S. Army Corps of Engineers and other agency permit; whether a sensitive habitat, flood plain, historic or archeological site, or source of water; required local approvals; environmental documents; geology report if near a bluff or earthquake fault; biological survey; hydrologic mapping.

S074 *Coastal Development Permits.* Permit files for regulation of coastal zone land use, including offshore oil platforms and nuclear power plants. All documents for a project are kept in one file, which may extend for many shelves. Contents: description of proposed development, environmental impact status, plans and maps, permit exemption application (if filed), special permits (as for mariculture, nuclear plants, oil/gas drilling), special reports (effect on marine life of oil drilling), federal consistency certification, deed restrictions/easements, mailing lists for agendas, findings, appeals, and other local agency approvals (planning, health).

S075 *Commission Meeting Tapes.* Commission meetings are recorded on tape; written transcripts can be made from tapes on request. Commission meetings generally address administrative matters, Coastal Development Permits (S074), Local Coastal Programs (S078), and Federal Consistency Certifications (S076).

S076 *Federal Consistency Certification.* Commission determines whether federal permits and licenses (such as offshore oil exploration and development activities) are consistent with the state Coastal Management Program. Files are organized by project no. and location. Contents: proposing company's application for consistency certification; staff report, recommendations; amendments; Commission action.

S077 *Federal Consistency Determination.* See Federal Consistency Certification (S076); the same information applies to activities or projects conducted by a federal agency.

S078 *Local Coastal Programs (LCPs) Files.* A summary status report and chart of all LCPs. Contents: plans and amendments filed by local governments; staff reports including grants, findings, and approvals of jurisdiction maps; Commission certification with findings and resolutions; notices of permits issued by local governments. Note: Copies of plans, correspondence, and comments of interested parties are usually filed in appropriate regional commission offices.

S079   **CONSERVATION, DEPARTMENT OF** (916) 323-1886

Guides development and conservation of the state's earth resources—oil, gas, geothermal, mineral, and soil. There are six oil and gas district offices, and two geothermal district offices.

Office of Land Conservation (916) 324-0850

S080   *Farmland Conversion Report.* A biennial report to the Legislature on types of farmland, total acreage, and changes in status. Contents: county; year; amount of acreage for farming, grazing, urban use, water, etc.; percent of each county mapped. Note: Not all counties have been mapped. See Important Farmland Series Maps (S081).

S081   *Important Farmland Series Maps.* A series of maps revised and updated biennially by the Farmland Mapping and Monitoring Program. Eight farmland categories (prime, statewide importance, unique, local importance, grazing, urban/built-up, water, and other) reflect current status and changes. Data on these maps is computerized and serves as the basis for Farmland Conversion Report (S080).

S082   *Mineral Land Classification-Designation Program Records.* Data on location of important mineral deposits where land development may prevent mining. Contents: geological classification; designation for protection.

Division of Mines and Geology (916) 445-5716

S083   *Mineral Land Classification Petition.* Records of requests that land with mineral deposits be classified as not-for-development. Contents: petitioner's name, mailing address; reason for interest in land; name and legal description; description of mineral deposits (geologic and economic data); description of proposed development as a threat; recorded land owner or lessee name and mailing address within area and adjoining; action requested; signatures of reviewer and petitioner; date.

S084   *Mineral Land Reclamation Plan.* A plan for land reclamation given to city and county planning departments to cope with the closing of mines. Contents: name, address of operator and agents; type and quantity of material to be mined; beginning and ending dates for mine operation; maximum depth; size and legal description of lands; boundary, topographic, and road maps; geology; type of mining; proposed use after reclamation; how reclamation will be done (contaminants, mining waste, relocated streams); impact of reclamation on future mining; statement of responsibility. Note: Reclamation plans must be filed with the city or county when the mine permit is issued. See also Planning (C320).

S085   *Mineral Property Reports.* Statements of location (township, range, section, meridian), commodity, owner of property, geological description, date, geologist's name and I.D. no. Documents locating mining claims are kept by the county Recorder (C434). Permits to engage in mining are issued by the county Planning Commission (C327).

S086   *Open File Reports.* Data sent to city or county planning departments. Types of data include fault evaluation, landslide hazard areas, timber harvest, and mineral land classification maps.

S087   *Strong-Motion Data.* Records obtained from seismographs or accelerographs installed on open land and inside structures. Contents: station name and no.; location; geology; type of structure; distance from epicenter; trigger time; peak acceleration values.

(CONSERVATION, CONT.)

S088   **Timber Harvesting Plans.** Plans to allow timber cutting and prevent erosion. Contents: name and location of timber harvesting unit; inspection date; county; map quadrangle; watershed; size of area; silvicultural method; logging system; erosion hazard rating; steepness of slope; geologic conditions; geotechnical concerns; methods to minimize damage; references, maps, photographs, geologist's signature, and no. Plans are maintained in the Santa Rosa office of the Division of Mines and Geology.

S089   **Well Sample Repository.** A collection of well core, rock samples and related data. Kept at California State College, Bakersfield. Advance appointments are needed. Fees are charged.

Division of Oil, Gas and Geothermal Resources (916) 445-9686

S090   **Basic Well Data.** A permanent file of all documents related to a specific well. Included are: Notice of Intention to Drill, Rework, or Abandon Wells (S091); regulatory reports; drilling, completion and/or plugging histories; plats; land surveys; sample and core records. Copies of records exist in district offices and in Sacramento. Access is by lease name and well no., operator's name, and location (section, township, and range). Oil and gas well prospect records are confidential for two years on request of the operator, and geothermal well records for five years. Extensions can be obtained.

S091   **Notice of Intention to Drill, Rework or Abandon Well.** Contents: well name, and type; American Petroleum Institute no., operator's name, address, and phone, type of organization, location and drilling details, map, environmental impact statement (if needed), date, signature.

S092   **Oil, Gas and Geothermal Logs, Tests, and Surveys.** Records of electrical, physical, and chemical logs, tests, and surveys of well-drilling equipment and conditions.

S093   **Production Data—Monthly Production, Injection, and Oil/Gas Disposition Reports.** Production data are available on microfiche, floppy disk, or paper printout. Make advance appointments to view records. Fees are charged. Contents: location, lease name, well no., American Petroleum Institute no., operator's name and address, pool name, date, amount, and type of production or injection. Records from 1977 to present are maintained electronically.

Division of Recycling (916) 323-3836

S094   **Recycler Certification Application:** Contents: operator's name, address, and phone; organization name, address, and organization type; previous recycling data; location and property ownership; permits and licenses; contact person's address and phone; type of program; certification no.

S095   **Other Conservation Permits, Records, Reports, Maps.** Special studies (coastal and marine, earthquake, geochemical, geothermal, landslide, minerals program, radioactive and toxic-waste site, and nuclear reactor plant site); photo archives; maps (volcanology, oil, gas, geothermal, energy-base, contour, and fault); subsurface injection permit (for oil, gas, or geothermal wells); ore buyer's license.

S096 **CONSUMER AFFAIRS, DEPT. OF** (916) 445-4465, (800) 952-5210

Charged by law with advocating consumer interests, licensing businesses and professions, recommending and proposing legislation, promoting consumer education, and investigating and mediating consumer complaints. Each regulatory entity is responsible for regulating an occupational or professional group through licensing and enforcement. Contact the individual board for information about licensees. Each licensing agency should provide information about complaints and disciplinary action against licensees and about their status, but access may vary.

S097 *Complaints.* Contents: number of complaints found to indicate probable violation; date, disposition, and average number of complaints against licensees in a given region or locality; statements of caution, if needed.

S098 *Disciplinary Action.* Contents: name, address, whether disciplined, when and reason; whether named in a disciplinary action.

S099 *License Status.* Information on all past and current license holders. Contents: name and/or DBA; license no.; address and phone; date of original license; bond or cash deposit information; date(s) of license expiration, lapse, termination, and reason. Note: Many lists are computerized and can be purchased in total.

S100 Following is a list of regulatory agencies that operate within the Department of Consumer Affairs, and the businesses and professions they license and regulate. As examples, three agencies are described in detail at the end: the Automotive Repair Program, the Contractors State License Board and the Medical Board of California.

Accountancy, Board of (916) 263-3680
Certified public accountants (CPA), public accountants (PA), CPA or PA corporations and partnerships
Acupuncture Committee (916) 263-2680
Animal Health Technician Examining Committee (916)263-2610
Architectural Examiners, Board of (916) 445-3393
Athletic Commission (916) 263-2195
Announcers, assistant matchmakers, box-office employees, boxers (professional and amateur), door persons, full-contact karate (kickboxers), gyms, judges, managers, promoters, matchmakers, referees, sparring permits, ticket sellers, timekeepers, and trainers/seconds
Automotive Repair Program (916) 445-7964, (800) 952-5210
Automotive repair facilities; lamp, brake, and smog-inspection certification stations; smog check stations and technicians
Barbering and Cosmetology, Board of (916) 445-7061
Barbers, cosmetologists, electrologists, estheticians, and manicurists
Behavioral Science Examiners, Board of (916) 445-4933
Educational psychologists; licensed clinical social workers; marriage, family, and child counselors
Cemetery Board (916) 263-2660
Cemeteries, cemetery sales agents and brokers, crematories, and cremated remains disposers
Contractors State License Board (916) 255-3985
General engineering contractors and 39 different categories of specialty contractors such as: cabinet and mill work, drywall, electrical (general), fire protection, low-voltage systems, masonry, painting and decorating, plumbing, roofing, solar,

structural steel, swimming pool, tile (ceramic and mosaic), heating and air conditioning, and welding

Court Reporters Board of California (916) 263-3660

Dental Auxiliaries, Committee on (916) 263-2595

Dental Examiners, Board of (916) 263-2300

Dispensing Opticians, Registered (916) 263-2634
Registered dispensing opticians, contact lens and spectacle dispensers

Electronic and Appliance Repair Program (916) 445-4752
Automotive radio, stereo, security system, and cellular phone installation and repair; electronic equipment and appliance repair; residential antenna installation and repair (includes satellite antennas); service contract sales and administration

Engineers and Land Surveyors, Board of Registration for Professional (916) 263-2222
Land surveyors and engineers of the following types: agriculture, chemical, civil, control system, corrosion, electrical, fire protection, geotechnical, industrial, manufacturing, mechanical, metallurgical, nuclear, petroleum, photogrammetric, quality, safety, structural, and traffic

Funeral Directors and Embalmers, Board of (916) 263-3180
Embalmers, funeral directors, and preneed funeral arrangement trusts

Geologists and Geophysicists, Board of Registration for (916) 445-1920
Geologists, geophysicists, and hydrogeologists

Guide Dogs for the Blind, Board of (916) 445-9041
Instructors, training schools, and fund-raising to establish training schools

Hearing Aid Dispensers Examining Committee (916) 263-2288

Home Furnishings and Thermal Insulation Program (916) 574-2041
Bedding and furniture manufacturers, renovators, retailers, wholesalers, custom upholsterers, insulation manufacturers, supply dealers, and sanitizers

Landscape Architects, Board of (916) 445-4954

Medical Board of California (916) 263-2388
Physicians, surgeons, and research psychoanalysts

Midwifery Licensing Program (916) 263-2496

Nursing, Board of Registered (916) 322-3350
Nurses of the following types: anesthetists, midwives, practitioners, mental health, public health, and registered

Nursing Home Administrators, Board of Examiners of (916) 263-2685

Optometry, Board of (916) 323-8720

Pharmacy, Board of (916) 445-5014
Continuing education providers; free, nonprofit , surgical clinics; hypodermic needle and syringe distributors; interns; nonresident pharmacies; out-of-state distributors; pharmaceutical wholesalers and exemptees; pharmacies; pharmacists; pharmacy technicians

Physical Therapy Examining Committee (916) 263-2550
Electroneuromyographers, physical therapists, and assistants.

Physician Assistant Examining Committee (916) 263-2670
Educational training programs, physician assistants, and supervising physicians

Podiatric Medicine, Board of (916) 263-2647

Psychiatric Technician Examiners, Board of (916) 263-7830

Psychology, Board of (916) 263-2699

Respiratory Care Examining Committee (916) 263-2626

Security and Investigative Services Program (916) 322-7530
> Burglar alarm agents, company operators and managers, firearms/baton permits, training facilities and instructors, locksmiths, private investigators, private patrol operators, repossessor employees, company managers, and security and armored car guards

Speech-Language Pathology and Audiology Examining Committee (916) 263-2666

Structural Pest Control Board (916) 263-2540
> Pesticide applicators and fumigators for wood roof cleaning or treatment, general pest and termite control, and pesticide company branch office and field representative registrations

Tax Preparer Program (916) 255-3145
> Tax interviewers and preparers

Veterinary Medicine, Board of Examiners in (916) 263-2610
> Veterinary hospitals, and veterinarians

Vocational Nurse Examiners, Board of (916) 263-7800

S101 **Automotive Repair Program** (916) 445-7964, (800) 952-5210

Registers and regulates automotive repair dealers; accepts and mediates auto repair complaints from public; investigates violations of Automotive Repair Act; refers cases to law-enforcement authorities; administers state-wide program of official smog check stations, auto repair dealers and mechanic licensing and lamp, brake, and smog inspection and repair.

S102 *Automotive Repair Facility License.* Contents: shop name, address, owner's name, date of licensure, phone, and history of complaints filed. Requests must be in writing.

S103 **Contractors State License Board** (916) 255-3985, (800) 321-2752

Regulates 105 types of contractors.

S104 *Contractor Listing.* Contents: name of contractor, name of business, business address, type of license, license no., effective dates, code section of violation(s). Note: Lists are maintained on computer locally for active licensees. Inquiries should be made by phone to nearest local office. Commercial services are available to research these records. Information on contractors certified to remove asbestos is available here and with Department of Industrial Relations, Division of Occupational Safety and Health (S401).

S105 *Disciplinary Action Files.* Contents: name on license, license no., address, date of action, specific violation, and disposition.

S106 *Licensing Files.* Contents: applicant name, address, and phone; name and address of business; type of license, type of organization; key personnel and residential addresses and dates of birth; social security no.; work history; license no.

S107 **Medical Board of California** (916) 263-2388, (800) 633-2322

Consumer service analysts supply license information and handle complaints (excluding disputes about fees and ethics) against physicians, audiologists, physician's assistants, podiatrists, psychologists, speech pathologists, and registered dispensing opticians. Accusations are public, investigative material is confidential until a finding of a violation is returned, at which time the results become public.

S108　**CONTROLLER, STATE** (916) 445-3028

Serves as chief fiscal officer and primary fiscal manager for the state. Supervises accounts payable and receivable, centralizes information on all state employees and retirees, state bonds, investments, unclaimed and abandoned property, claims against state, and taxes.

S109　*Annual Report of Financial Transactions.* Contents: detailed information on funding sources, expenditures, indebtedness for: cities, counties, special districts, community redevelopment agencies, public retirement systems, and school districts. Note: Each report is a separate volume.

S110　*Audits.* Pre-payment claims audits (for government expenditures) and post-payment field audits (of agency control and accounting systems) are made. Local governments may ask the Controller to audit special projects involving state funded programs and expenditure of state funds. Contents: see Audits (A016).

S111　*Claim Schedule Files.* Records of goods and services sold to the state. Contents: claim schedule no., invoices (payee name, address, itemized purchases, and purchase order no.). Note: Purchase orders may be examined at General Services (S296).

S112　*Departmental Revolving Funds.* A record of payments for goods and services sold to the state. Located in the fiscal or accounting sections of individual departments. Contents: "remittance advice" (copy of check issued), claim schedule, and invoice or receipts. Note: Routine and small payments and employee expense claims are usually made from individual revolving funds.

S113　*Employee Verification Information.* A centralized database on past and present employees. Contents: employee name, salary (current gross and range), current job title and classification, department, county, work location, telephone, length of service, tenure, and work history with state. Note: Fees are charged. The personnel division of employee's department may provide the same information except work history—and faster. See also C115.

S114　*Estimated Apportionment of Revenues.* Reports from sources such as federal grazing fees, forest reserve receipts, highway use taxes, motor vehicle license fees, and timber yield tax.

S115　*Payee Index.* An index to warrants register (S117) that lists individuals and companies receiving payments through the Controller's Office. Contents: payee name, amount and source of fund, warrant no. and date. Note: Claims not yet paid will not be in this index. Check the Payee Log in the Audits Division, arranged by state agency name.

S116　*Unclaimed and Abandoned Property.* Records of property (escheat) unclaimed after the death of the owner or left dormant or inactive. After being turned into cash, the proceeds are held in perpetuity by the Controller. Contents: name, last-known address, social security no., dollar amount or description, claims (if any), and Controller's account no. Note: Inquiries can be made by phone. Listings are on microfiche and are for sale.

S117　*Warrants Register.* A list of warrants (payments) for goods and services that serves as an index to the Claim Schedule Files (S111). Contents: payee name, purchasing agency, and claim schedule no.

S118　*Other Controller Records.* Insurance companies tax; corporation revivor; pooled money investment (monthly report of investments made with money from state, cities, and counties); senior citizen tax deferment; public pension reporting.

S119   ***Other Controller Reports.*** Accountability over K–12 Educational Funding; Allocations to Counties for Snow Removal, Rainfall, and Storm Damage; State of California Annual Report—Cash Basis (appropriations, expenditures, and budget); Financial Transactions Concerning Streets and Roads of Cities and Counties of California; Annual Report of Assessed Valuation of Counties of California. Note: This is not a complete list. See *California State Publications* (Bibliography) for a complete list.

S120   ## CORPORATIONS, DEPT. OF (213) 736-3481, (916) 324-9011

Charged with protecting the public against unfair business practices and fraudulent sale of financial products and services. Qualifies securities for sale to the public. Registers non-exempt franchises, licenses broker-dealers and investment advisors; regulates certain companies that lend or hold money; licenses health-care service plans including health maintenance organizations (HMOs); qualifies real estate syndicates with more than 100 investors, real estate investment trusts, and syndicates involved in oil, gas, or public mine title leasing; suspends/revokes licenses under their jurisdiction. For articles of incorporation and current listing of officers and directors of California corporations, see Secretary of State. A main regional office in Los Angeles houses divisions for securities regulation, financial services, health-care services, and enforcement. Other regional offices are in San Francisco, Sacramento, and San Diego. Paper files are retained four years; legally required documents (permits, Commissioner orders, etc.) are kept on microfilm permanently in the Los Angeles office. Information supplied by an applicant is public unless confidentiality is requested and granted by the Department.

S121   ***Broker-Dealer Certificate Application.*** For registration of securities brokers-dealers. Contents: applicant name, address; arrest record; financial statements; articles of incorporation; copy of certificate.

S122   ***California Commodity Law Notices.*** Listing of persons who file as a commodity merchant or a telephonic seller of a commodity or a commodity contract. Contents: filer's name, telephone numbers, type of commodity, and business or activity.

S123   ***Central Index.*** A computerized index of all applications for permit, license, and certificates, notices and requests for interpretive opinion. Information is available by phone from any regional office. Contents: applicant name, file no., office location, and file status (active or destroyed).

S124   ***Closely-Held Securities Notice.*** For recording issuance of securities to fewer than 36 persons and when not publicly advertised. Non-exempt issues must obtain Securities Qualification Permits (S133). Contents: notice of issuance, issuer's name and address, class and value of securities, and in some cases, names of purchasers.

S125   ***Desist and Refrain Orders.*** Administrative actions for violation of laws. Orders are maintained in investigative files (see S128) and on microfilm. (Note: Microfilmed copies are retained long after investigative files have been destroyed.) Contents: name of violator, date of order, and directive related to specific type of violation.

S126   ***Franchise Registration.*** For monitoring franchise sales. Contents: names and addresses of franchisor and agents; states where proposed registration is effective or was refused, revoked, or suspended; franchisor's projected financial requirements including proposed loans; salesmen disclosure forms, including employment and criminal history; copy of advertising (including franchisor's business; names and occupations of directors, trustees, principal officers, and litigation; fees, investments, and other obligations required of franchisee; franchisor obligations; exclusive area or territory; trademarks, logos, etc.; projected sales, profits, or earnings; franchisor

(CORPORATIONS, CONT.)

financial statements; copies of all contracts to be used in franchise). This information is entirely public.

S127   ***Health-Care Service Plan License Application.*** For licensing health-care service plans also known as health maintenance organizations (HMOs). Contents: applicant's name and address; type of plan; type of organization (corporation, partnership, etc.); articles of incorporation; contracts with affiliates and principal creditors; map of geographic service area; information on physicians, hospitals, and other health-care service providers (laboratory, ambulance company, etc.); contracts with health-care service providers; plan for evaluating quality of care, service costs, etc.; organization chart; contracts with service providers and enrollees; grievance procedure; contracts with salespeople receiving compensation; audited financial statements; usage rates for services, and usage costs; insurance policies; payment and claims system; license (if application approved); officers, directors, shareholders, and managers (employment history, stock ownership in plan, criminal record, social security no., birthdate, physical description, and affiliation with other health plans). Note: Information on payments to service providers is confidential.

S128   ***Health Maintenance Organization (HMO) Review and Investigation Files.*** The department conducts separate three-year medical surveys and financial examinations of health-care service plans. Also, an annual report of any complaint data against a plan is made. Enforcement Action files are also kept and contain: name of plan, type of complaint, how resolved.

S129   ***Investment Advisor Certificate Application.*** For licensing of investment advisers. Contents: applicant name, address, arrest record; proof of compliance with securities examination requirements; financial statements including ratio of net capital to aggregate indebtedness; copy of standard investment advisory contract; copy of certificate.

S130   ***Lender-Fiduciary Files.*** For licensing check sellers and cashers, consumer and commercial finance lenders, credit unions, escrow companies, industrial loan companies, personal property lenders and brokers, small loan companies and trading stamp companies. Contents: applicant name and address; business plan; names and "Statements of Identity" for officers and directors: title, physical description, birthdate and birthplace, social security no., driver's license no., employment history, residential address history, criminal record, bankruptcy history, any fictitious business names previously used; balance sheet; articles of incorporation; copy of license.

S131   ***Licensee Lists.*** Lists of licensed broker-dealers, check sellers, bill payers and proraters, consumer finance lenders, commercial finance lenders, credit unions, escrow agents, health-care service plans, industrial loan companies, investment advisors, personal property brokers, and trading stamp companies. Fees charged. Contents: names, addresses, and file nos.

S132   ***Security Owners' Protection Certificate Application.*** An application for certifying persons who solicit funds for holders of securities. Contents: applicant name and address; "statement of business reputation"; description of services; proposed use for proceeds of solicitations; articles of incorporation; financial statements; names, addresses, and background information (including education and employment history, criminal record, and personal financial statement) for applicant's officers, directors, agents, and managers; copy of certificate.

S133   ***Securities Qualification Permit Application.*** An application for authorization of intrastate offerings and sales of securities by corporations, partnerships, or others. See Closely-Held Securities (S124) for exempt offerings. Must be renewed annually. Contents: applicant name and address; type of security; number of shares; proposed maximum price; business description and history; intended purpose of net proceeds; distribution plan including names of underwriters and agents; disclosure of significant financial transactions with affiliates, directors, principal employees, or share-holders; type and amount of outstanding securities and options to purchase securities; information on principal shareholders; remuneration of directors, officers, and principal shareholders; copy of charter documents; sample security certificate; financial statements; copy of security prospectus; copy of permit. Note: Information varies depending on type of issue and transaction. Government bodies, private offerings, and securities already listed on the New York, American, and NASD/NMS stock exchanges are exempt from filing.

S134   *Uniform Application to Register Securities.* Contents: file no.; issuer's name, address, and phone; contact person's name, address, and phone; description of securities; commission, filing, and exam fees; U.S. SEC registration statement (if filed), amount of fees paid, and receipt no.; prospectus.

S135   CORRECTIONS, BOARD OF (916) 445-5073

Inspects local correctional facilities for compliance with state law; gives technical and financial assistance to counties for jail construction; establishes recruiting and training standards for local correction and probation officers.

S136   *Biennial Legislative Report.* Contents: county, local jail non-compliance with standards; summary, by county, of litigation against jails; compliance cost estimates; summary statistics on facilities and inmate populations. Available from Legislative Liaison Office. Note: inspection reports are filed with city or county Chief Administrative Officer (C123) and presiding judge of county Superior Court (C157). Local health officers' inspection reports and fire and safety inspection reports are filed with local officials and Board of Corrections.

S137   *County Correctional Facilities Capital Expenditure Fund.* An annual report on funding of jail construction to state legislature. Contents includes: name of jail, location, designed bed capacity, facility type, supervisor, size, construction cost, amount of state funds appropriated, completion date, architectural drawings, housing and support services, construction and finishing materials.

S138   *Jail Inspections and Costs of Compliance Report.* A biennial report to the Legislature on jail conditions and overcrowding. Contents: county and city jails, inventory of local jail cells, previous developments, future plans, issues and litigation, and non-compliance with regulations by individual facility (procedures, physical plant, and health officer's and fire marshal's reports). Note: Copies are kept at local level.

S139   *Medical Audit.* Peer review of medical procedures in all detention facilities by the Department of Health Services. Includes an audit trail for management of all legally obtained drugs.

S140   CORRECTIONS, DEPARTMENT OF (CDC) (916) 445-7683

Operates 29 institutions, including four licensed hospitals, a narcotics addiction treatment center, and 38 minimum-security conservation camps; supervises parole programs and community correctional program for parolees. Individual inmate records are generally confidential except for inmate prison no., county of commitment, age, and charge. Some information is available through the individual's court files (C167). Litigation records are exempt where the CDC is a party, as are inmate lawsuits, complaints, and investigations, and certain CDC procedures such as armory inventories.

S141   *AIDS Reports.* Contents: monthly statistics on AIDS-infected inmates; reports by CDC and other departments on AIDS among inmates. Available from Communications Office.

(CORRECTIONS, CONT.)

S142   **Construction Projects.** Individual contract files. Contents: bidding packages and
construction drawings (available once winning bidder is selected), correspondence,
monthly progress reports, change orders, specifications and as-built drawings (once
project is completed), and CDC-conducted audits. Available from Construction
Operations Office.

S143   **Five-year Facilities Master Plan.** Contents: forecasts of inmate population characteristics, summaries of construction standards, descriptions of facilities in planning
and construction stages, financing and budget information.

S144   **Health-Care Licensing Files.** CDC health-care facilities are licensed by the Department of Health Services. The inspection team prepares a licensing survey describing
needed improvements; CDC responds by preparing a Plan of Correction. Licensing
surveys and Plans of Correction are available from Department of Health Services
(S350). Also the state Department of Mental Health licenses part of the California
Medical Facility.

S145   **Offender Information Services Branch Reports.** Contents: statistics on prison population size, racial, or ethnic characteristics, custodial classification, geographic distribution, parolee recidivism, behavior, and time served. List of reports is available
from the branch. Specialized statistical reports can be prepared upon request.

S146   **Parole and Inmate Information.** Computerized records of current inmates and
parolees. Contents: name, inmate no., date of birth, offense, current prison location,
address and phone of institution or parole unit, year of discharge (if any), dates of
prison term. Requesters must state their reasons for making inquiries. To locate an
inmate in the federal prison system contact the Federal Bureau of Prisons, Inmate
Locator Service, (202) 307-3126.

S147   **Prison Industry Authority Annual Report.** Manufacturing and service enterprises
exist at more than 10 CDC institutions; products are sold to government agencies.
Contents: financial and operating statement; operating results; inmate employment
by industry and institution. Information on specific manufacturing and service
operations is available from individual institutions.

S148   **Tuberculosis Reports.** Contents: monthly report on the TB status of every CDC inmate.

S149   **Weekly Report of Population.** Contents: institution name, number of inmates,
parolees, escapees, institution inmate and staff capacity, and percent change since
previous year.

S150   **Other Corrections Records.** Inmate Classification System (a computer rating of prisoners based on criminal history, length of sentence, and tendency for violence);
Statistical Reports for Current Periodic Offenders (population, movement, parolees
returned, characteristics, behavior, time served, institution capacity, and other),
population projections, and annual escape report.

S151   # COURTS

The state is divided into six appellate districts each with a Court of Appeal that hears
appeals of municipal, justice, and superior court decisions. Cases may be appealed
from the appellate courts to the State Supreme Court. If the death penalty is
involved, a case goes directly from the superior court to the state Supreme Court.
The state court system is also composed of several ancillary organizations: the
Judicial Council of California serves as the chief administrative agency of the courts,
(415) 396-9100; the Commission on Judicial Performance considers all complaints
regarding California judges, (415) 904-3650; and the State Bar of California regulates

attorneys (see S626–S672). For a more detailed discussion of the state court system see *Guide to California Government* or *The Courts and the News Media*; for information on access to court records see the *Reporter's Handbook on Media Law* (Bibliography). For records contents, see C154–C176. Records are organized similarly throughout the court system.

California Supreme Court and appellate court opinions, calendars, and minutes are available via the Judicial Council's electronic bulletin board (see Appendix C).

S152   ***Annual Data Reference: Caseload Data by Individual Courts.*** Produced by the Judicial Council. Contains detailed statistical data on changes in judicial positions, court consolidations, and all actions heard before California courts. For example: summaries of filings and dispositions, appeals filed, heard and pending, level of conviction of criminal defendants, dispositions by jury trials, total cases awaiting trial, and civil and criminal case processing time.

S153   ***Judicial Council Annual Report.*** A two-part report on conditions in state courts, with recommendations for improvement. Part I contents: recommendations for improved court administration. Part II contents: 130 statistical tables and graphs with data by court and type of proceedings, assignment of judges, transactions for each level of court; disposition of cases; status of cases (case or appeal pending, awaiting trial, etc.); transactions per judge. Statistics for type of case (family law, motor vehicle, personal injury, juvenile delinquency, etc.) and disposition are given for each county.

S154   CRIMINAL JUSTICE PLANNING, OFFICE OF (OCJP)
(916) 324-9100

Administers federal and state grants for the following types of state criminal justice, crime prevention and control programs: career criminal apprehension and prosecution; victim/witness assistance; domestic violence shelters; rape crisis centers; child sexual abuse centers; gang violence suppression and community crime prevention.

S155   ***OCJP Program Plan and Application Kit.*** Annual document containing information regarding funding opportunities available through OCJP. Contains instructions and forms necessary to apply for more 37 different public safety and victim services programs.

S156   ***Grantee Handbook.*** For agencies that receive grant funds from OCJP, outlines the terms, conditions and procedures required of grant projects.

S157   ***Request for Proposals Response.*** Grant application packet submitted to the Office of Criminal Justice Planning (OCJP) specifying the priorities, strategies, and objectives of the applicant. The proposal, with possible modifications, becomes the grant award document if selected for funding by OCJP.

S158   ***Request for Proposal Evaluation.*** For selecting applicants for funding. Contents: rating criteria, proposal content requirement, funding information and protest procedures.

S159   ***Grant Award.*** The grant award is an agreement between the Office of Criminal Justice Planning (OCJP) and the grant recipient. The approved grant application when signed by both the Executive Director and the Fiscal Officer of OCJP becomes the grant award, which contains the terms and conditions of the grant agreement. Grant award components include: grant award condition, certification of assurance of compliance, project summary, budget information, project narrative, and project contact information.

S160   **DEVELOPMENTAL SERVICES, DEPT. OF (DDS)** (916) 654-1897.

Coordinates services under the Lanterman Developmental Disabilities Services Act for people with developmental disabilities such as mental retardation, cerebral palsy, epilepsy and autism. Establishes, monitors, and enforces policies, procedures, and standards for the delivery of developmental services. Works directly through seven developmental centers and indirectly through a state network of private, nonprofit regional centers.

Coordinates over 1,800 records for 183 program areas annually. Much of the information collected by the Department is confidential. Subjects included in these records include, but are not limited to: quality assurance; rehabilitation; psychologist and consumer surveys; project correspondence (including active treatment and staffing standards); studies (includes neuroleptic project and objective achievement); regional center evaluations; Medicaid waiver billings; educational services in developmental centers; community projects.

S161   *Numerical Listing of Developmental Services: Forms and Publications.* An index of public records generated by DDS. Includes title, form number, revision date, originating department, users, and storage location.

S162   **EMERGENCY MEDICAL SERVICES AUTHORITY** (916) 322-4336

Develops standardized guidelines and regulations for emergency medical services statewide. Promotes disaster medical preparedness and manages the state's medical response to major disasters. Operates the state paramedic testing, certification, and registry program. Sets training standards for emergency medical personnel including: emergency medical technician-I (EMT-I), EMT-II, EMT-paramedic, mobile intensive care nurses, firefighters, peace officers, and lifeguards.

S163   *Approved Prehospital Care Training Programs (for emergency medical technicians and mobile intensive care nurses).* Contents: training institution, county, contact person, phone, frequency of program, cost, and date of approval expiration.

S164   *California Air Ambulance Providers.* Listing of government-operated medical airlift providers in California. Contents: base county, agency providing service, address, telephone, equipment type used, I.D. nos., hours and days of operation, and number and type of medical staff and pilots.

S165   *Instructor Syllabus.* Approved training programs for emergency service providers including: emergency medical technicians, paramedics, and emergency dispatchers (911 and others).

S166   *Periodic Reports.* Titles include: *Disaster Needs for Disabled Persons, The Coalinga Earthquake, U.S./Mexico Earthquake Preparations,* and *The Emergency Medical Response to the 1992 Los Angeles Civil Disturbance.*

S167   **EMERGENCY SERVICES, OFFICE OF** (916) 262-1843

Develops and maintains state plans for assisting local governments during disasters; provides training and research; coordinates disaster efforts. The state is required by federal law to provide a record-keeping system for adoption by local government. Records of disasters are collected from cities, counties, special districts, and Native American tribes, and assessed by the state. Federal funds are then requested by the state and delivered to the local governments. For contents of these records, see Emergency Services (C179–C190).

S168   *California Hazardous Materials Incident Reporting System (CHMIRS).* Statistical data based on reported incidents. Contents: agency name, phone, I.D. no.; incident date; time notified; time and date completed; incident address and location; weather; property use (residential, industrial, etc.); property operator; cause of accident; equipment involved; action taken; chemicals involved (name, I.D. nos., quantity, and physical condition); extent of accident; container description; how material was identified (fire department personnel, toxic center, shipping papers, etc.); type and no. of casualties; vehicle information (if any); name of reporting officer and I.D. no.; date; comments.

S169   *Other Emergency Services Records.* Bay Area Regional Earthquake Preparedness Project; Hazardous Buildings (San Francisco); Oakland Community Preparedness; San Jose Staff Training.

S170   **EMPLOYMENT DEVELOPMENT, DEPT. OF** (916) 654-8210

Operates Employment Service (links applicants to employers); collects taxes (including withholding of personal income); pays benefits under Unemployment Insurance and Disability Insurance programs; administers job training and counseling programs, such as Joint Training Partnership Act and Greater Avenues for Independence (GAIN); prepares customized statistical reports. Appeals from insurance decisions are heard by the California Unemployment Insurance Appeals Board. Information on individuals (wages, taxes paid, medical disabilities, and ongoing investigations) is confidential. Employer or employee annual tax rate is public, not the actual amount paid.

S171   *California Labor Market Bulletin plus Statistical Supplement.* A monthly report done in cooperation with the Bureau of Labor Statistics, U.S. Department of Labor. Contents: total civilian labor force, civilian employment, and unemployment. Shows statistics for current and previous two months, by sex, race, and age. Tables give breakdowns by type of industry, agriculture, government, and by county. Supplement gives breakdowns by metropolitan statistical area. Available via the Department's BBS. (See Appendix C)

S172   *Fraud and Investigation Files.* Records of overpayment or under-reporting of Unemployment and Disability Insurance are confidential until court action is taken. Requests to the Program Review Branch for information about convictions are generally referred to the appropriate county clerk. Liens are filed with the appropriate county Recorder (C420) in cases of overpayment.

S173   *Labor Market Conditions in California.* A monthly statistical report. Contents: labor force; unemployment rates and reasons; industry employment, earnings, and hours; unemployment and disability insurance (fund, claims, rate, etc.); new applications for jobs, openings, and placements.

S174   **ENERGY RESOURCES, CONSERVATION AND DEVELOPMENT COMMISSION** (916) 654-4989

Certifies the construction and operation of major thermal electric power plants of 50 megawatts or more, forecasts energy supplies and demands, conducts research, promotes research (efficiency, new sources), and develops policies for conservation including building and energy efficiency standards. See also Public Utilities Commission.

S175   *Notice of Intention to Build and Application for Certification for Thermal Power Plants (of more than 50 megawatts).* For plants using thermal energy (not wind turbines, hydroelectric, or solar photovoltaic types). Contents: applicant's name, address, and phone; business name, address, and phone; project description; need for

(ENERGY RESOURCES, CONT.)

facilities; proposed facilities; proposed site or sites; transmission lines; facility system safety and reliability; facility system reliability; financial impacts; environmental information; compliance with other laws; air quality; water supply and quality.

S176   *Quarterly Fuel and Energy Reports.* Required of utilities and major industrial users. Contents: company name and no.; dates covered; electricity generation by type; total megawatts received or delivered; amounts and kinds of fuel received and used; dollar amounts of gas and electricity sold to residential users and to nonresidential users by type of industry; same by county; natural gas sold or otherwise used by type of sale or use; same for source of supply; dollar and actual amounts of natural gas sold by customer category; same report by county.

S177   *Small Power Plant Exemption.* Granted for plants of less than 100 megawatts. Contents: applicant's name, address, phone; business name, address, phone; project description and location; transmission lines; fuel use; power plant construction; power plant operation; environmental and energy resource impacts; project alternatives; mitigation measures; need for facility; contact persons; on-site electricity use.

S178   ENVIRONMENTAL HEALTH HAZARD ASSESSMENT, OFFICE OF (916) 324-7572

Performs risk assessment and epidemiological evaluations of chemicals and other health hazards in the environment. Responsible for implementation and administration of the state's Safe Drinking Water and Toxic Enforcement Act of 1986 (Proposition 65). Serves as scientific and technical consultant to and operates under the authority of the Secretary of the California Environmental Protection Agency.

S179   *Toxic Chemicals List.* Alphabetical listing of chemicals known to the state to cause cancer or reproductive toxicity. Contents: chemical name, Chemical Abstract Service (CAS) registry number, and date chemical first appeared on list.

S180   *Toxic Chemical Inventory Release Reporting.* Reports of release of chemical into the environment by air, water, land, or-off site transfer. Contents: company name, contact person, chemical name, and amount of release. Available on computer disk for search by zip code, street, and longitude and latitude.

S181   ENVIRONMENTAL PROTECTION AGENCY, CALIFORNIA (CAL-EPA) (916) 445-3846

Replaced the Environmental Affairs Agency in 1991. Unifies and coordinates the state's environmental protection efforts under one, cabinet-level agency. Six departments and boards are accountable to the Secretary of Cal-EPA: Department of Pesticide Regulation (S513), Department of Toxic Substances Control (S638), Office of Environmental Health Hazard Assessment (S178), Air Resources Board (S021), Integrated Waste Management Board (S430), and the Water Resources Control Board (S695). Three organizational components operate within Cal-EPA at the agency level: Hazardous Substance Cleanup Arbitration Panel (arbitrates disputes over cleanup liability for sites on the California Superfund List); Registration of Environmental Assessors (accepts the voluntary registration of environmental assessors); and Hazardous Materials Data Management (provides products and services used for the assembly and use of toxic related information). Produces reports such as: *Strategic Plan for Promoting California's Environmental Technology Industry.*

S182   *Cal/EPA Report.* Monthly newsletter with updates on legislation, funding, and activities and programs concerning the agency and its departments.

S183   *Environmental Report of the Governor.* Annual review of environmental priorities.

S184 **EQUALIZATION, BOARD OF** (916) 445-6464

Values state-assessed property, oversees local property tax assessment; collects a wide variety of state business taxes; hears appeals from the Franchise Tax Board.

S185 *Annual Report.* A statistical appendix containing information on the assessed value of property by county and by incorporated city; the value of property exemptions (veterans, religious, educational, or welfare) by type and county; assessed value of property assessed by state and subject to local taxes by company name; timber production by county; assessed value of private railroad cars by company; sales and use taxes by type of business and by county; revenues distributed to counties and cities from sales, use, and cigarette taxes; gas and jet fuel production and revenue by year; gallons of gasoline produced and taxes paid by company; taxable insurance premiums and total taxes by company. Other tables show administrative costs per $100 collected, transit district tax distributions, taxes imposed by cities, alcoholic beverage taxes, cigarette taxes, and total federal, state, and local tax collections.

S186 *Business Taxes Registration Search Service.* Listings of companies with business tax licenses and permits. Contents: business name or DBA, owner's name, business addresses, account no., active or inactive status, registration date. Note: Account Reference Section in Sacramento has a statewide register. District offices have listings for their district only. Owner's name and DBA are needed. Some districts also list by address. Some districts require sales tax permit no. in order to get specific information. Requests to Sacramento of five or more names should be submitted in writing, attention Account Reference Section.

S187 *Equalization Board Licenses, Permits, Registration.* Selling products or services includes an obligation to collect a tax or to report to the Equalization Department. Types of taxes include the Alcoholic Beverage Tax, Cigarette Tax, Emergency (911) Telephone Users Surcharge, Energy Resources Surcharge, Hazardous Waste and Substance Taxes, Insurers Registration Tax, Motor Vehicle Fuel Tax, Private Railroad Car Tax, Sales and Use Tax, Solid Waste Disposal Fee, Timber Yield Tax, and Use Fuel Tax. Most common is the Sellers Permit to sell tangible personal property. Contents: See Licenses and Permits (A021). Note: Each type of tax has different requirements.

S188 *Tax Appeals Files.* Appeals from actions of the Franchise Tax Board to the Board of Equalization, Board Proceeding Division, by individual income taxpayers, business income and franchise taxpayers, and claimants under Senior Citizens Property Tax Assistance Law. Contents: letter of appeal detailing protest; exhibits (may include copies of tax returns and other financial information); briefs by appellant and respondent; hearing transcript; opinion. Note: Income tax returns become public when under appeal. Insurance companies may file a "petition for re-determination" instead of an appeal. Only evidence and transcripts from a formal hearing are public for these petitions.

S189 **FAIR EMPLOYMENT AND HOUSING COMMISSION**
(415) 557-2325

Conducts hearings and issues decisions in cases brought before it by the Department of Fair Employment and Housing (S192). Serves as a forum and advocate for civil rights issues. Responsible for enforcing several California civil rights laws, including the Fair Employment and Housing Act, the Unruh Civil Rights Act and the Ralph Civil Rights Act (Hate Crimes Act). The Department of Fair Employment and Housing brings cases before the Commission and prosecutes them when it determines there is a basis to a claim of an unlawful practice.

(FAIR EMPLOYMENT COMMISSION, CONT.)

S190   ***Employment and Housing Discrimination Case Files.*** Contents: name of complainant, name of respondent, names of commissioners who voted and how they voted, accusations and pleadings, accusation amendments and related legal pleadings, correspondence relating to the case, exhibits, briefs, proposed decision of the hearing officer, and the Commission's final decision.

S191   ***Rule Making and Regulatory File.*** The Commission interprets laws under its jurisdiction and develops regulations for their implementation (e.g. family and medical leave laws; sex discrimination regulations; pregnancy leave regulations). This process is documented in Rule Making Files. Contents: notice of regulatory action, statement of reason for regulatory action, full text of regulations, public comments, sometimes transcripts of public hearings, when available; final regulations and staff memos.

S192   FAIR EMPLOYMENT AND HOUSING, DEPT. OF
(916) 445-5523

Administrative agency responsible for California civil rights laws including the California Fair Employment and Housing Act. Receives and investigates complaints of discrimination on the basis of race, color, religion, national origin, sex, marital status, age, physical disability, ancestry, and medical condition. Enforces discrimination laws covering employment, housing, public accommodation, and public services. Issues rules and regulations, and subpoenas witnesses and documents. Monitors the non-discrimination and affirmative action programs of state contractors. Following an investigation, complaints deemed valid where conciliatory efforts fail are referred on the Fair Employment and Housing Commission for hearing (S189).

Complaints of discrimination made under the American with Disabilities Act are investigated and forwarded to the U.S. Equal Employment Opportunity Commission (EEOC). Some of the information listed here may be considered confidential by the Department.

S193   ***Case Analysis Manual.*** A written description of the Department's framework for use in investigating discrimination complaints. Contents: case analysis procedures; summary of legal standards; evidence patterns in complaints.

S194   ***Pre-complaint Questionnaire.*** Contents: complainant's name, address, telephone number; respondent's name, address, and telephone number; basis of complaint (race, color, national origin, etc.); resulting unfair treatment; date of discrimination; why treatment was discriminatory; list of potential witnesses; employment data; whether filed before Department or U.S. Equal Employment Opportunity Commission; attorney consulted; personal data (sex, age, and ethnic group).

S195   ***Case-Related Files.*** Contents: same as above plus: response to complaint of discrimination; consultant notes, negotiation/settlement notes; telephone messages; witnesses names and statements; progress memo; pleadings.

S196   ***Disclosure Requests and Register Logs.*** Contains date of disclosure, information disclosed, purpose of disclosure, person receiving information, who authorized the disclosure, and who actually completed the disclosure.

S197   ***Annual Statistics.*** Statistical information is recorded by fiscal year and calendar year. Employment statistics include: cases filed, closed, where filed, basis, type of respondent, alleged discriminatory act, type of occupation, and disposition of cases. Housing statistics include numbers and types of accommodations made and disposition of cases. Public service/accommodations statistics include cases filed, closed, alleged basis of discrimination, type of respondent, and disposition of cases.

S198 **Appointment and Interview Logs.** Contents: appointment date; supervisor's name; consultant's name; time of appointment; name, address, and phone of complainant.

S199 **Complainant Registers.** Contents: filing date, case number, federal number, respondent, complainant, consultant, and closure code and date.

S200 **Workforce Analysis and Monitoring Reports.** Identifies a state contractor's workforce by ethnicity and gender.

S201 **FAIR POLITICAL PRACTICES COMMISSION (FPPC)**
(916) 322-5660

Regulates and enforces campaign financing and lobbying as mandated by the Political Reform Act of 1974. Oversees disclosure of campaign receipts and expenditures and disclosure of assets and income of public officials, and regulates lobbyists and disclosure of their finances. Advises public officials regarding potential conflicts of interest.

S202 **Campaign Disclosure Statement Audits.** The Franchise Tax Board audits statewide candidates, legislative and superior court judge candidates, local candidates, and controlled committees. The audits are filed with the FPPC, the Secretary of State, the Attorney General, local filing officer, or county District Attorney. Contents: name, address, type of audit, whether record-keeping and reporting is adequate, and judgment or statement. See also Secretary of State.

S203 **Enforcement Investigative Files.** Records of investigations into alleged violations of Political Reform Act by candidates and committees filing Campaign Disclosure Statements (S588–S590) or Statements of Economic Interest (S204) and by lobbyists filing reports (S594). Contents: letter or legal brief, evidence, and response. Investigative information can be made public if public interest in disclosure is deemed paramount.

S204 **Statement of Economic Interest, Financial Disclosure Statement (Forms 721, 730).** Statements on reportable investments, income and gifts are filed with the FPPC by all elected state officials; by most appointed top state officials; by members of Board of Equalization, Legislature, Public Utilities Commission, State Coastal Commission, State Energy Resources, Conservation, and Development Commission; by all state and local judges; by county supervisors, chief administrative officers, district attorneys, planning commissioners, and county counsels; and by city mayors, council members, city managers, chief administrative officers, planning commissioners, and city attorneys. Members of the FPPC itself file with the Attorney General. All of those listed above file Form 721. State and local officials not listed above file Form 730 at a location specified in their agency's conflict-of-interest code.

Both forms contain the following: official's name, address, and phone; position; investments valued at $1,000 or more (company name, type of investment, ownership percent, and dates); real property interests valued at $1,000 or more (location, type, date acquired, value, and ownership percent); income valued at $250 or more (source and location); loans (source and location, security for, amount if more than $250 except for loans through a commercial lending institutions of less than $10,000); gifts (donor, date, description, and value if aggregating $50 or more from any source during reporting period); broker or sales commission (business name and sources); income and loans to businesses if the official or spouse owns at least a 10% interest and the official's pro rata share of the income or loan is $10,000 or more; names of renters and income received if $10,000 or more during reporting period. Some reportable interests include spousal and children's interests. Note: Form 730 requires that business positions also be listed. Lobbyists and lobbyist employers file public-disclosure statements with the Secretary of State.

S205   **FINANCE, DEPARTMENT OF** (916) 445-3878

Advises the Governor on fiscal matters, helps prepare the budget and legislative programs, does financial audit and program compliance, provides economic, financial, and demographic information. The Finance Department produces valuable reports, such as Financial and Performance Audits, which are announced in *California State Publications* (see Bibliography). Customized statistical data are available for a fee.

S206   *Finance Department Reports (selected titles). California Statistical Abstract* (annual); *Final Budget Summary* (annual); *Final Change Book of Governor's Budget* (annual); *Impact of Federal Expenditures on California* (annual); *Population Estimates of California Cities and Counties* (annual); *Review of the Board of Registration for Professional Engineers and Land Surveyors; State of California Statement of Federal Land Payments* (annual). *Vacancy Rates for Housing* (based on census figures, utility company active meter data, and local government housing unit construction data) for incorporated cities and counties.

S207   **FISH AND GAME, DEPARTMENT OF** (916) 653-7664

Protects, manages state fish, wildlife, and native plants; helps local agencies develop recreation and conservation programs; reviews environmental impact reports; enforces hunting and fishing regulations. Issues over 150 different types of licenses and related documents, some of which are listed below. Maintains five regional offices.

S208   **Environmental Services Division** (916) 653-4875

Coordinates with and performs lab analyses for other regulatory agencies on fish and wildlife matters, and gives technical assistance to the department's anti-pollution activities.

S209   *AQUATOX Database.* A literature survey of toxicity information maintained on computer.

S210   *Fish and Wildlife Loss Report.* An annual report compiled by the department's Water Pollution Control Laboratory. Contents: report no., date of loss, type of animal killed, cause (suspected), site (river, lake, estuary, ocean, etc.), town/county (nearest), location (specific), species, number lost, percent game species of total lost, severity of kill, laboratory I.D. no., and action taken.

S211   *Fish and Wildlife Losses Due to Pesticides and Other Causes.* An annual report. Contents: date, species, number killed, name of chemical, county, and remarks.

S212   *Toxic Substances Monitoring Program Data Report.* An annual report on collection and analysis of aquatic organisms, forwarded to Water Resources Control Board for further interpretation. Contents: collection station location, I.D. no., date of collection; type of fish, size, amounts of metals and synthetic organic compounds found; description of sampling procedures.

S213   *Other Environmental Services Reports, Studies.* A variety of reports are done as needed on such matters as marine pollution; fish and wildlife water pollution control; hydroelectric project erosion; selenium verification study (3-year investigation); bioassays of hazardous waste samples (for Health Services); biological control organisms (for Department of Food and Agriculture).

S214   **Inland Fisheries Division** (916) 653-6194

Protects and improves conditions for inland fish; regulates and provides for recreational and commercial fishing, protects endangered fish, amphibians, and reptiles, promotes aquaculture.

S215   *Aquaculture Registration Application.* Contents: business name; owner's name, mailing address, phone; facility address; species to be maintained; location; name, description of water source, type of diversion; lot nos.; description of work (research, private consumption, or commercial); maps; sketches; signature and title; date.

S216   *TRNDATA.* Database of information from fishing tournament permits and report forms. Contents: regional office, sponsor's name, applicant's name and address, species fish caught, location, county, value of size, date and days of tournament, date of permit, type of tournament (derby, team, or draw), total number and weight of fish weighed-in, number reported as dead, species' names and number, number of hours tournament lasted, and species and weight of largest fish caught.

S217   **License and Revenue Branch** (916) 227-2244

Issues and collects more than 150 commercial license and permit fees after approval by other divisions. Note: Sport fishing and hunting licenses are sold locally. Records are kept by the government.

S218   *Fish and Game Licenses and Permits.* For contents, see Licenses and Permits (A021). Types of licenses include:

Abalone (for crew member or diver)
Bighorn Sheep
Exotic and Prohibited Species
Falconry
Fish Canning, Processing, Wholesaling
Fish Importer, Domesticated
Fur Agent or Buyer
Game Breeder
Guide, Nonresident or Resident
Hunting Club, Commercial
Kelp and Aquatic Plant
Live Fresh Water Bait
Lobster
Migratory Game Bird Shooting Area
Pheasant Club
Salmon Stamp, Commercial
Scientific Collector
Shark- and Swordfish-Drift Gill Net
Stream or Lake Alteration Agreement
Standard or Special Suction Dredging Permit (for gold mining, sand, or gravel)
Student Scientific Collector
Swordfish
Trapping (to sell furs)

(FISH AND GAME, CONT.)

S219   **Marine Resources Division** (916) 653-6281

Protects and improves conditions of marine life. Records include fish landing receipts, commercial passenger fishing vessel records, gill net fishing impact reports, and files on construction of new marine habitats (artificial reefs, kelp forest restoration, and artificial propagation of certain fish and shellfish).

S220   *Commercial Boat License.* Contents: year; boat no.; type of commercial passenger boat; owner's name and mailing address; type of fishing gear; home address; boat name and home port; California registration no.; U.S. document no.; out of state no.; length, beam, net ton, horsepower, and year built; where built; year purchased; name of captain/operator; address; type of license; signature.

S221   *Commercial Fish Dealer License Application.* Contents: dealer I.D. no.; type of application; commercial fishing license no.; business name and mailing address; location of main plant and contact person; number of plants, outlets, or fish-receiving stations in operation; fees paid; signature; date; license stamp nos.

S222   *Commercial Fish Landings.* Monthly figures for weight of commercial shipments and fish landings at the six major ports by type of fish. Monthly figures for weight landed from inland waters by type of fish.

S223   *Commercial Fishing License Application.* Contents: I.D. no.; name, address, signature, date of birth, weight, height, color of hair and eyes, complexion, citizenship, any previous fishing license, and date.

S224   **Natural Heritage Division** (916) 322-2493

Includes the Endangered Plant Project, Lands and Natural Areas Project, Endangered Species Act Coordination, and California Wildlands Program (game refuge areas supported by user fees).

S225   *Natural Diversity Data Base.* An inventory of rare and endangered animals and plants. Reports can be produced in various formats, including map overlays. Contents: (depending on how data are requested) natural community or county; element name and code; legal status (endangered, threatened, etc.); location; dates observed; road or trail directions; habitat description; ownership of site; other scientific data. Note: Fees are charged; request forms are required. Information about the location of rare and endangered species is confidential.

S226   **Wildlife Management Division** (916) 653-7203

Assesses and improves wildlife habitat, surveys and inventories wildlife and their environment, works to develop public-use programs, promotes public education. Records include wildlife inventories, censuses and observations, and for big game (antelope, bighorn sheep, deer, elk, wild pigs, mountain lions, etc.) hunting permits.

S227   *Private Lands Wildlife Management License.* Contents: name, date, legal description of land, estimate of number and type of affected wildlife and animals (cattle), description of habitat, details of planned improvements, and county land-use designation for area.

S228   *Wildlife Habitat Relationships Databank.* Based on a cooperative effort by 20 state and federal agencies, universities, and major power companies. Predictions are made on wildlife likely to occur in a given habitat and area. Fees are charged. Data are available on computer disk. Continuously updated.

S229   **Wildlife Protection Division** (916) 653-4094

Protects and monitors game and nongame fish, wildlife, and their habitat. Activities include regulation through granting of permits, enforcement through inspection and arrests (records are confidential), education programs, contingency plans for oil or hazardous spills (see also Office of Emergency Services), and supervision of use of oil cleanup agents (see also Water Resources Control Board). Length of season, bag limit, and methods of take for game animals and sport fish are decided by the Fish and Game Commission.

S230   *Wildlife Protection Records.* An annual report of division activity includes arrests for illegal sale, importation, hunting, or killing of wildlife, warden training, Klamath Indian Commercial Fishery, and plans for dealing with hazardous materials and oil spills. Applications to drive or herd birds or animals causing damage to property must be investigated and approved. Copies of these permits are also maintained by Wildlife Management Division (S226). Specific information can be obtained from the regional offices.

S231   **FOOD AND AGRICULTURE, DEPT. OF** (916) 654-0466

Shares responsibilities with county Agricultural Commissioners (C008–C021) for protecting worker health and safety; preventing introduction of new pests by inspection and quarantine; inspecting products sold by weight, measure, or count; inspecting and certifying all liquid and weight-measuring devices; providing research and marketing information to state agricultural industry; protecting and promoting plant and animal industries. Records are arranged by the six departmental divisions: animal industry; inspection services; marketing services; measurement standards; pest management, environmental protection and worker safety; plant industry.

S232   **Animal Industry Division** (916) 654-0881

Inspects livestock; inspects meat and poultry products if produced in federally exempt facilities; enforces state law on inspection and sanitation of milk products; prevents below-standard meat and poultry from reaching the market; inspects cattle brands.

S233   *Brand Registry Certificate.* A voluntary system of recording livestock brands with the state for protection against loss. Contents: owner's name, address, and phone, design and name of brand ("Lazy A"), location on animal's body, drawing of brand. Note: A weekly report is sent to law enforcement agencies in the western states of lost, strayed, or stolen livestock.

S234   *Dairy Container Brand Registry.* A voluntary system of listing brand names. Contents: name of dairy, owner certificate no., brand name, and owner's name and address.

S235   *Milk and Dairy Food Complaint Reports.* Contents: complaint no. and date; inspector's name; complainant's name, address, and phone; whether referred by county health department; illness; product name, size, and flavor; package code; whether eaten; purchase date and location; distributor or manufacturer's name, and address; narrative of investigation; result of lab work; name of lab; investigator's name; date completed and closed.

S236 ***Other Animal Industry Licenses, Permits, Registrations, and Certifications.*** For contents, see Licenses and Permits (A021).

> Animal Parts or Products Transporters
> Biologic Registration
> Brand Registration for Dairy Containers
> Butter Distributors
> Butter Graders
> Cattle Movement
> Collection Centers
> Condemned Meat and Poultry Products (permit to remove)
> Dairy Exemption (exempts dairies from inspection of animals sold for slaughter)
> Dairy Inspectors
> Dairy Substitutes
> Diabetic and Dietetic Frozen Milk Products
> Federally Exempt Locker Plants (registration)
> Feed Yards
> Feeding Garbage to Swine
> Frozen Milk Products Plant
> Garbage Collector for Vessels and Aircraft
> Horse Meat and Pet Foods
> Imitation Ice Cream or Ice Milk
> Inedible Kitchen Grease Transporters
> Livestock Meat Inspector
> Livestock Movement into California
> Meat Processing
> Milk and Cream Testers
> Milk Distributors
> Milk Handlers
> Milk Inspection
> Milk Producers, Sellers, Distributors (not retail)
> Milk Products Plant
> Modified Milk, Cream (for special nutritional requirements)
> Nonfat Milk Solids Tester
> Oleomargarine
> Pasteurizer
> Poultry Meat Inspector
> Poultry Slaughtering and/or Processing
> Renderers
> Salesyards
> Samplers and Weighers
> Semi-Frozen or Soft-Serve Milk Products
> Shipping Permits (horse meat and pet food) Slaughter Houses
> Veterinary Biologics (for any veterinary biological substance such as serum, blood, and vaccines)
> Vitamin and Mineral Additives

S237   **Inspection Services Division** (916) 654-0792

Inspects commodities not covered by marketing orders (S248) for compliance with standards for maturity, grade, size, weight, pack, and labeling to protect against substandard products reaching consumers. Chemical laboratories analyze pesticides, their residue, heavy metals, fertilizers, feed ingredients, drugs, etc., for the Department and other state agencies.

S238   *Fresh Fruit and Vegetable Inspection Reports.* Inspections may be done and records kept by county Agriculture Commissioners (C008) or state inspectors. Records of detection and exclusion of contaminated produce are kept by the Department.

S239   *Notice of Non-Compliance.* A record that a grower or producer is marketing products below standards. Confidential except for name of producer.

S240   *Request for Analysis and Report of Analysis on Materials Submitted by Collaborating Public Agencies.* Contents: laboratory no.; date; agency name, address; sample description, identification, location/source, description of problem; requester's signature and date; analysis of sample; time and to whom report is sent.

S241   *Other Inspection Services Licenses, Permits, Registrations, and Certifications.* Commercial Feed License; Commercial Fertilizing Materials License Application (required to sell commercial fertilizers in the state); Commercial Fertilizing Materials Registration Application (required to field test a new genetically engineered biotic that is a soil or seed inoculant containing live microbes); Egg Container Exchange; Egg Dealers; Fertilizing Materials Manufacturers and Distributors; Fertilizing Materials Registration (minerals, soil/plant substances, packaged soil); Livestock Drug Manufacturer; Restricted Livestock Drug Sales. Contents: see Licenses and Permits (A021).

S242   **Marketing Services Division** (916) 654-1240

Distributes regulatory information, current market reports, crop and livestock reports and forecasts; supports on-the-farm sales and certifies farmers' markets; monitors for quality and mediates processing and marketing of California-grown farm produce and dairy products.

S243   *California Dairy Industry Statistics.* An annual compilation of manufactured dairy products, milk production, use and price statistics.

S244   *Complaint Files.* Records of verified complaints against any licensee for non-payment or not harvesting, investigation and mediation, administrative hearing (if not settled), and enforcement of any decision. The license may be revoked or suspended. Contents: licensee name, address, and phone; complainant's name, and address, phone; date; documents concerning the transaction. Confidential until case goes to a public hearing.

S245   *Container Size-Supplementary Dairy Information.* Contents: sales of whole and lowfat milk by type of trade (wholesale, retail, military, etc.), by container characteristics (size), and by type of container (plastic, glass, etc.).

S246   *Farm Products Processors and Dealers License.* Required for handlers of California-grown farm products for sale, except milk and timber. Contents: name, address, type of license, fee, and financial statement (confidential).

S247   *Grade A Dairy Farmers List.* A statewide alphabetical list. Contents: name, address. Note: Grade A, or Market Milk, must conform to certain sanitary standards.

S248   *Marketing Orders.* Agreements between handlers and growers on quality standards and inspections. Produce under agreements has included cantaloupes, dried figs, Cling peaches, pears, strawberries, and tomatoes.

S249   *Milk Handler List.* An alphabetical list of all dairy processing plants in the state. Contents: name, address, phone, and type of handler (receive/not receive milk directly, cooperative association with/without a plant, etc.).

S250   *Milk Marketing Order.* A notice of minimum prices established monthly and bimonthly. Contents (partial): commercial milk production; milk production by counties; use (whole, skim, fat); sales by class of milk, by county, and of selected classes by area; manufacture of selected type of dairy products (cottage cheese, sour cream, yogurt, etc.) by month; prices per pound for classes by area.

S251   *Milk Pooling Branch Comparative Statement.* Contents: statistics by year for milk production by class; prices; number of producers and handlers; quotas and averages; volume; detail costs of audits; by county production of milk fat.

S252   *Milk Production Cost Index.* A list of costs to rancher of milk production by area. Contents (partial): processing, labor, and feed costs; market prices; transportation costs, consumer buying power.

S253   **Measurement Standards Division** (916) 229-3000

Enforces regulations at the county level of products sold by weight, measurement, or count. See also Weights and Measures (C561–C567).

S254   *Metrology Laboratory Records.* Files on maintenance of basic standards of weight and measure. Includes results of equipment calibration tests.

S255   *Measurement Standards Licenses, Permits, Certificates, and Registrations.* Includes Weighing, Measuring, Counting Device Certificate; Device Repairman Registration; Weighmaster License (required for any business where bulk product is sold by weight), Container Tares and Cab Cards (for trucks whose cargo net weight must be calculated). Contents: see Licenses and Permits (A021).

S256   **Plant Industry Division** (916) 654-0317

Protects plants from pests through inspection, quarantine, and treatment.

S257   *Agricultural Inspection Station Files.* Records of inspections made at state borders, postal and independent parcel services, airports, maritime ports, military organizations, and railroads. County inspections are made of plant material coming by post or parcel. Contents: traffic or package volume, number and types of interceptions, and number of inspections. For regulatory records of nurseries, see Agriculture (C008).

S258   *Nursery Stock License.* To sell, grow, or distribute nursery stock. Contents: business name, mailing address, and phone; sales location; type of business and ownership; kinds of stock and growing locations; whether license was ever refused or revoked; name of insurance; fees; signature and title; date.

S259   *Plant Registration and/or Certification.* Records of plant stock inspection to identify diseased and develop healthy stock. Contents (of annual report): type of plant stock, number of trees, acres of plants, grower.

S260   *Other Plant Industry Licenses, Permits, Registrations, and Certifications.* Move and Use Live Plant Pests or Insects or Noxious Weeds (required for introduction or importation into state of plant disease or organism, insect pest, or weed, including genetically engineered types); Wild Burros Capture; Wax Salvage (of bees).

S261   *Other Plant Industry Databases.* For entomology (insect identification), plant pathology (plant diseases, and physiological disorders), nematology (plant parasites), botany (weeds, poisonous plants, cultivated and native plants), seeds.

S262 **FORESTRY AND FIRE PROTECTION, DEPT. OF**
(916) 653-5121

Provides fire protection for state, private range, brushland, and timber; operates conservation camps, fire centers; regulates timber harvesting on private land; assists in forest and range management; regulates and conducts controlled burning; manages state forests; operates tree nurseries.

S263 *Timber Harvesting Plan.* Required for cutting and removing timber from non-federal land, except for Christmas trees, and fuel wood where minimal effect results. Contents: vary according to local conditions, but include a description of the harvesting operation and environmental impact. Copies are sent to the County Clerk, Fish and Game Department, Parks and Recreation Department, and Regional Water Quality Control Board.

S264 *Timberland Conversion Permit.* For timberland converted to another use, such as skiing, recreation, housing, and grazing. Contents: owner's name and address; acres to be converted; location of forest district; location of conversion; deed and recorder's no.; property owner's name; affidavit of intention to convert; estimated dates.

S265 *Other Forestry Licenses and Permits.* New Varieties, New Tree Species, Professional Forester Registration, Timber Harvesting Operator.

S266 **FRANCHISE TAX BOARD** (916) 369-4800, (800) 852-5711

Collects personal income, bank, and corporation taxes; exempts qualified non-profit corporations; provides property tax assistance and rent assistance for low-income state residents 62 years of age or older or totally disabled; audits campaign statements for the Fair Political Practices Commission. Most records are confidential. Any individual, or anyone appointed by an individual, may see his or her tax records. Requests must be in writing to the Information Security Officer. Appeals from the Franchise Tax Board made to the Board of Equalization are public. Records of Tax Board liens against individuals or corporations for non-payment or underpayment of taxes are filed with the county Recorder (C420).

S267 *Annual Report.* Personal income tax data (50-year comparisons, levels of income, adjustments to income, sorted by county, high income-non-taxable returns, etc.); bank and corporation tax data (50-year comparisons, levels of income, industry comparisons); homeowner and renter tax assistance.

S268 *Audits.* Done of lobbyists, campaign committees, and statewide and local candidates according to a mandated schedule. Results are filed with the Fair Political Practices Commission, Attorney General, and appropriate local filing officers (City Clerk, C079, and County Clerk, C126).

S269 *Corporate Tax Filing Information.* Non-confidential information contained in tax returns. Contents: exact corporate title, address, phone, date opened for business in state, officers and directors with private addresses, corporation no., tax year, filing date of return, name and title of person signing return, tax due date, and amount of delinquent taxes.

S270 *Exempt Organization Application Files.* On corporations claiming exemption as non-profits (corporations, trusts, and unincorporated associations). Contents: application for exemption; articles of incorporation and by-laws, budget. Application for Exemption contents: organization name, address, and phone; federal employer I.D. no.; representative's name, address; type of exemption claimed; activity, type of organization; incorporation date and no.; previous exemptions; date of tax returns;

description of types of membership; whether property will be transferred or shared with incorporators; whether organizers will be employed and paid by organization, organizational activities, church-related activities. Note: This information is public only if the application is granted. See also Registry of Charitable Trusts Files (S447).

S271   *Training Manuals.* Staff training manuals for field audits, collection procedures, and general procedures are available for a fee. Confidential information is deleted.

S272   **GENERAL SERVICES, DEPARTMENT OF** (916) 445-3441

Known as the state housekeeping department or business manager. It performs architectural consulting and construction, building rental, building standards, buildings and grounds maintenance, energy assessments (to reduce energy costs), site and environmental impact of new state offices, local assistance, real estate and design services, fleet administration, insurance and risk management, legal services, management technology and planning (policy, systems, procedures, and data processing services), procurement (purchasing, records management, information, protection for small and minority business, state police protection, printing, telecommunications, and support services such as office machine repair, copying, mail, and warehousing. Records are listed under 10 General Services divisions.

S273   **Administrative Hearings Office** (916) 445-4926

Conducts public hearings for some 50 state agencies related to issuance, renewal, suspension, or revocation of licenses, and disciplinary hearings for all elected and certain top non-elected officials. Evaluation, discipline, and appointment of most non-elected employees are confidential. Specialized hearing agencies exist for Workers Compensation Appeals Board, Unemployment Insurance Appeals Board, Public Utilities Commission, Public Employment Relations Board, Agricultural Labor Relations Board, Occupational Safety and Health Appeals Board, and Personnel Board. A final decision is made by the agency involved. Appeals may be made to Superior Court.

S274   *Administrative Hearings Case Files.* Records of hearings on issuance, renewal, suspension, or revocation of licenses and personnel disciplinary hearings. Cases are heard before an Administrative Law Judge. Contents: file no., pleading no. (statement of issue or accusation), notice of hearing, date, agency involved, names on license, agency case no., hearing officer, and proposed decision. Note: Copies are kept at the agency involved.

S275   **Architect, Division of the State** (916) 445-2163

Provides engineering and architectural services and inspection for state construction projects, earthquake safety inspection for schools, hospitals, and essential services buildings (those used in cases of disaster); removes or corrects hazards in state facilities (asbestos, PCBs, and underground tanks).

S276   *Application for Approval of Plans and Specifications.* Contents: project name; school district or owner, address, and person acting for owner; name of building, type of work to be done, and location; whether funded by state; description of work, names, phones, and registration nos. of architects and engineers; estimated cost; filing fee; applicant signature, address, date; application and file nos.

S277   *Application for (Hospital) Building Permit.* Contents: facility name, address, phone; administrator; description of work; legal owner, address; type of facility and number of beds before and after construction; names of architects and engineers preparing plans; plans and specifications; geological data; structural calculations; local permits and reports; fees; name, address, phone of filer; date. Note: These are also filed at the Statewide Health Planning and Development Office.

S278   **Contract Information.** For state-owned buildings and public schools. Contents: application and file nos.; project name, district, or owner; amount of contract; start date; contractor/subcontractors and addresses; testing lab and address; inspector and address; scope of contract; signature of architect or chief engineer.

S279   **Historic Architectural Files.** Working drawings of many state buildings dating back to 1900s. Contents: institution or department, location, name of building, and drawings. Note: Prior notice is needed because files are stored in a vault. Specifications are stored at Archives. Some departments (Corrections, State Colleges) have taken responsibility for their own drawings.

S280   **Hospital Contract Information.** Contents: application no.; name of facility, address, applicant's name, and city/county; contractor name, address, and phone; contract amount and changes; scope of contract; copies of required documents; signature of architect or engineer.

S281   **Hospital Project Summary.** A historical record of work done, materials used, and inspections made. Contents: county; application nos.; hospital, address, and buildings; estimated cost, fees, and actual cost; names of architect and engineers; required documents and dates; names of contractors and inspectors; verified reports (by type of work); final recommendation and certification; deferred approval items; type of construction; addenda and changes.

S282   **School Project Summary.** A historical record of work done, materials used, inspections made. Contents: county; application and file nos.; project name, address; school district or owner name, address; names of buildings; estimated cost, fees, actual cost; names of architect and engineers; required documents and dates; contractor and address; inspectors; verified reports (by type of work); affidavits of testing and inspection; completion notice; approval and deferred approval for specific items; type of construction; addenda and changes.

S283   **Structural Tests and Inspections.** A list of items needed to be checked by a testing laboratory for construction approval. Contents: testing laboratory, date, name, school district or owner, application and file nos., architect, and structural engineer. Also includes tests and inspection reports for brick and block, compacted fill, concrete, glued laminated structural lumber, grout, gunite, mix designs, mortar, reinforcing steel, structural steel, suitability tests, etc.

S284   **Other Architect Office Records.** Backcheck Worksheet; Plan Check Worksheet; Verified Report; School Recommendation for Approval of Application and Certificate of Compliance; Field Engineer's Final Recommendation for Schools; Closing Check List; Plan Check Work Sheet, Hospital; Hospital Recommendation for Approval of Application and Certificate of Compliance; Field Engineer's Final Compliance Recommendation for Hospitals; Notice to Responsible Inspector on Hospital Projects; Change Order Approval; Verified Report. Note: The last two records are also filed at the Statewide Health Planning and Development Office.

S285   **Energy Assessments, Office of** (916) 323-8777

Develops policies for reduction of energy use in state government projects, represents the state before the Public Utilities Commission, negotiates rates with utilities, and files energy related studies done by General Services.

(GENERAL SERVICES, CONT.)

S286   **Special Rate Concession Records.** Files on rate negotiations with the Public Utilities Commission and other business conducted by private attorneys under contract to the office. Access may vary.

S287   **Insurance and Risk Management Office** (916) 445-2184

Provides appropriate insurance and self-insurance for state agencies; conducts studies of accident-reducing programs for state employees.

S288   **California State Workers' Compensation and Safety Program Annual Report.** Contents: data by department for workers compensation benefits, hours worked, disabling injuries, days lost, frequency/severity rates; summary report of state driver accidents (miles driven, accident rate and type); vehicle accident rates by department.

S289   **Local Assistance, Office of.** Administers all public works programs as authorized by State Allocation Board. Most activity now concerns school construction (see also Architect, S275), site acquisition, deferred maintenance, asbestos abatement, child care (relocatable facilities), and emergency (portable) classrooms. Note: Local records for these programs are kept at local school districts (E016).

S290   **Asbestos Abatement Program Files.** Records of funds available to school districts or county offices of education. Contents: certified resolution of district's governing board authorizing action and repayment; district and school location, nature and extent of asbestos; report of project completion and cost; summary of estimated cost; authorized agent, contact person, phone, and date.

S291   **Asbestos Hazard Emergency Response Act Management Plan.** Required by the U.S. EPA from all public and private nonprofit elementary and secondary schools. A set of seven forms must be filed with the Office of Local Assistance. Contents: general data including name, address, phone, code no., signatures, and training/accreditation, address and phone of the local responsible official and management planner; for each building—name, location, existence of friable asbestos, blueprints and diagrams; assessment of physical and hazardous properties, and recommendations; operations and maintenance for entire school where friable asbestos is found; periodic surveillance plan; reinspection plan (every three years); parent and employee notification program (annual); evaluation of resources needed (money, equipment, facilities, and personnel).

S292   **Lease-Purchase Asbestos Abatement Program Files.** Records of funds available to school districts or county offices for schools closed because of asbestos problems. Contents: certified board resolution; application, location of district and school, reason for closure, description and scope of project, estimated cost, and amount requested; available rents (district money that must be contributed to project); certification of site's legal owner, legal description, if free from liens or encumbrances; district representative, date. Note: Local school districts must maintain many other project-related records.

S293   **Procurement Division** (916) 445-2500

Oversees all state purchases of equipment, materials and supplies worth more than $10,000. Individual agencies must handle their own service contracts.

S294   **California State Contracts Register.** A twice-monthly announcement of state construction and service contracts. Contents: contract category no., contract no., project or contract title, description, bid opening date, length of time estimated to finish contract, location, state agency, and contact person and phone.

S295   ***Directory of State of California Contracting Officials.*** A list of officials responsible for contracting for purchasing, construction, or services. Contents: agency name, official's name, address, and phone.

S296   ***Purchase Order and Bidding Files.*** Records of private bids, awarded or not, to provide the state with goods and data processing services. Purchase order contents: company name, address, and phone; list of items ordered; cost; ordering agency; shipping address. Bids contents: bid no., goods requested, cost, company name, and address. Note: See also Controller, Claim Schedule Files (S111). Bids are public after they have been awarded.

S297   ***Purchase Order and Bidding Files Index.*** For access to S296. Contents: agency name, requisition no., and bid no.

S298   ***Small Business Directories.*** A list of certified contractors, published in three parts: Small Business Summary of Commodity Purchases; Small Business Construction Firms; Small Service Firms. Contents: contractor no.; name of firm; owner's name, address, and phone; representative's name; district (state is divided into twelve districts), ethnic code (if provided before 1987); type of business. Note: Since January 1, 1987, a directory of small minority and women-owned businesses is maintained at Department of Transportation, Office of Civil Rights (S670–S671). Businesses may register in both places.

S299   ***Other Procurement Division Records.*** Transfer Order Surplus Personal Property; Request to Freeze Excess Surplus Property; Property Survey Report-Request to Dispose of Property; Transfer of Location of Equipment; Report of Overage or Shortage of Surplus Property; Distribution Document (for donation of surplus property).

S300   **Real Estate and Design Services, Office of** (916) 445-9693

Manages space planning and allocation, leasing, property selection, appraisal, and management for most state departments. A computerized statewide property inventory is used to keep track of all state-owned land and land leased by the Department.

S301   ***By-State Lease Files.*** Records of state-owned land leased to non-state parties and administered by agencies other than General Services or the State Lands Commission. Indexed by project name and managing agency name. Contents: lease. Note: Most land is improved. See also Property Management Files (S302); Non-Extractive Lease and Permit Files, Lands Commission (S461).

S302   ***Property Management Files.*** Records of state-owned land administered by General Services. Indexed by street address and assessor's reference or parcel no. Contents: acquisition documents, environmental impact report, improvements, repair, maintenance, and demolition, lease documents. See also Lands Commission (S454–S465).

S303   ***Proprietary Land Index.*** An index to state land purchases by assessor's reference or parcel no. and agency of jurisdiction. Contents: agency with jurisdiction, property location and legal description, grantor name, type of deed or instrument, date, recording information, cost of acquisition, and title company. Note: Not indexed here are highway property (see Transportation, S672–S675); sovereign lands and school lands (see Lands Commission, S454). The Proprietary Land Index will be phased out in favor of a statewide property inventory.

S304   **Records Management Division** (916) 445-2294

Responsible for policy on records creation, inventory, storage, and destruction. Issues standardized record forms.

S305   *Records Retention (Disposition) Schedules.* Information on inventory, appraisal, storage and destruction of executive branch records. The Legislative and judicial branches, the University of California, and the California State University are exempt. Contents: department and unit names, location, item no., volume in cubic feet, title and description, number of years to be stored and where, destruction date, confidentiality/privacy, archival value, and remarks. Note: A publicly accessible copy is kept at the State Archives (S616).

S306   *Records Transfer List.* An inventory of records transferred to the State Records Center. Contents: duplicates most information in the Records Retention Schedule (S305), except to show storage box nos. and volume being transferred. Note: Copies are kept by the issuing agency and at Records Centers.

S307   *Other Records Management Records.* Request to Withdraw or See Stored Records; Authorization to Destroy Records.

S308   **State Police, Office of**

Provided police and security for state property and officials, and air/land patrol of the California Aqueduct. As of July 1, 1995 the Office of State Police ceased to exist and its functions were merged into the California Highway Patrol (S360).

S309   **Telecommunications Division** (916) 657-9903

Reviews plans, installs, does technical analysis for all state-leased, private-line (MCI, Sprint) phone systems and interexchange carriers, manages the state 911 system, licenses all state public safety radio systems. Inquiries must be made to the specific department where system was installed.

S310   **GOVERNOR'S OFFICE** (916) 445-1455

As head of the executive branch, the Governor is responsible for appointments to the judiciary, heads of state agencies, boards, and commissions; he advises the legislature through his State-of-the-State message, submits the State budget, has line-item veto of the budget and veto power of legislative bills passed, and grants pardons and commutations of sentences. The Governor's Office of Planning and Research issues studies, reports, handbooks, and guides containing useful summarized information such as *California Planner's 1994 Book of Lists* and *California Permit Handbook, 1992.* See *California State Publications* (Bibliography) for publication notices.

    Certain records are not public, including investigations of nominees for judicial office and correspondence to or from the Governor or his employees. *Records of the Governor's Office,* State Archives, lists types of records kept in the Governor's office. Confidential records are considered public after retirement except for specific restrictions.

S311   *State Appointments List.* Contains appointments to boards and commissions made by the Governor and other appointive authorities. For a description of this record see (S586).

S312   *Statutory Index of Positions.* A comprehensive list of positions the Governor may fill by appointment. Contains name of office or position only. See the State Appointments List (S586) for details on appointments to boards and commissions. For agency and department appointments, contact these offices directly or the Governor's office and request the press release announcing the appointment.

S313   *Vacancy and Term Expirations.* A list of vacancies for appointive offices and dates that current appointments will expire.

S314   *Pardon Book.* Name and date of pardon. Note: Working papers in extreme penalty and executive clemency cases are closed until 25 years after last activity, at which time they are made public at the state archives.

S315   *Proclamations.* Date, subject, and text of Governor's proclamations. These are on file at Secretary of State, where inquiries should be made.

S316   ## HEALTH AND WELFARE DATA CENTER (HWDC)
(916) 739-7700

Provides data processing computer and communications equipment, software and expertise to the 13 departments operating under the Secretary of the Health and Welfare Agency. Records maintained by HWDC are the same as those listed in this guide for the Stephen P. Teale Data Center (S632).

S317   ## HEALTH PLANNING AND DEVELOPMENT, OFFICE OF STATEWIDE (916) 654-1606

Develops state health policy; checks that hospital and health facility construction complies with state building code for seismic and fire safety (see Architect, S275); collects cost and utilization data from hospitals; administers various health training programs. The state requires annual reports, quarterly financial and utilization reports, and disclosure reports by different types of health facilities (long-term care, home health, etc.). Fees are charged for individual and summary reports.

S318   *Annual Report of Clinics.* Data on patients, major expenditures, sources of revenue. Contents: name, address; year of operation; type of clinic; administrator's name and signature; amounts and sources of revenue; number of patients and visits; use of volunteers; number of abortions; number of surgical operation rooms; number of surgeries performed; number of operating room minutes (time used for performing an operation); equipment purchased (value, description, date, and how acquired (lease, donation, purchase, etc.); new major projects (over $1 million); ethnicity of patients; types of services provided; percent usage of different services.

S319   *Annual Report of Hospitals.* Required by law. Contents: name of hospital; reporting year; number of patient days; discharges and number of beds; surgery utilization; visits to the emergency room; type of ownership; cardiac catheterization; surgery utilization; age and reimbursement source for psychiatric and long-term care patients; licensed level of emergency service, radiation therapy equipment and usage; service; birth and abortion data; major capital expenditures.

S320   *Financial Disclosure Report.* Required for each state acute care hospital. Contents: name (legal and DBA), address, and phone; state facility and Medi-Cal provider nos.; type of ownership, number of beds; inventory of services; utilization of services; balance sheet; changes in equity; income statement; revenues and costs by cost center; expenses; revenue amounts by payor; allocation of non-revenue producing center costs to revenue-producing centers; employee wage rates and productive hours by employee classification and cost center.

S321   *Hospital Discharge Data.* Report on acute care, psychiatric and alcohol/drug rehabilitation, skilled nursing, intermediate care, and rehabilitation. Contents: number of

(HEALTH PLANNING, CONT.)

discharges, days, lengths of stay by age and sex, major diagnostic categories, use and charges by payor, admission sources and types, and disposition statistics.

S322   **Notice of Intent.** A notice to construct, increase, or convert the license of a skilled nursing or intermediate care facility. Contents: facility name, address; person or organization giving notice; authorized person, business name, address, and phone; type of project; estimated cost; beds (presently licensed, to be added or changed); zoning approval; source of funding; signature; title; organization; date.

S323   **Quarterly Financial and Utilization Report-Hospital.** Contents: discharges, patient days, and outpatient visits (shown separately for Medicare, Medi-Cal, and other payors); number of beds, total operating expenses, gross inpatient and outpatient revenue; deductions from revenue; net patient revenue by Medicare, Medi-Cal and other payors; capital expenditures and fixed assets; physician costs (optional). Some parts available on computer disk.

S324   **Summary Individual Disclosure Reports.** Computerized calculations on original Disclosure Reports (S320-S323). Contents (in addition to original data): expense per patient day, discharge, and outpatient visit; occupancy rates; employee average hourly rates and hours shown by employee classification and by cost center; average length of stay; profitability; other financial ratios.

S325   **Other Health Planning and Development Records.** Long-Term Care Facility Integrated Disclosure and Medi-Cal Report; Home Health Agency Annual Report; Annual Report of Skilled Nursing or Intermediate Care Facilities.

S326   # HEALTH SERVICES, DEPARTMENT OF (916) 445-0174

Provides financial aid for medical services to needy residents through Medi-Cal, handles licensing and certification of facilities that provide medical services and health-care, provides counties with money and technical assistance, regulates medical and low-level radioactive waste handling and disposal. The Department also regulates and provides services for: foods; drugs; medical devices; cosmetics; shellfish; biotechnology products; radiation machines and workers; public water supplies; epidemiological research; vector-borne diseases; physically and developmentally disabled children; family planning; genetic or congenital disorders; maternal and child health; food vouchers for low-income mothers and children; air and industrial hygiene including pollutants; clinical chemical, microbial, viral, and rickettsial diseases; sanitation and radiation; infectious disease outbreaks; heart disease; cancer; epidemiological research; rural farm workers and laborers; public health nursing; hospitals in rural areas; care of medical indigents. See also Health Services (C232–C261). Note: Individual medical records are confidential.

AIDS Division (916) 445-0553

S327   **California AIDS Update.** A quarterly summary of statistics from a computerized reporting system of statewide data on the spread of AIDS. Includes number of new cases by disease type, age, race/ethnicity, patient group, and adolescent/pediatric group.

S328   **Other AIDS Records.** Individual records are confidential. See also Health Services (C233). Summary statistics are kept for grants contract management, project development, epidemiology, and information services. Reports of new cases and incidence per 100,000 population by county are issued monthly. The office can design specialized reports using the computerized reporting system on request.

Communicable Disease Control, Division of (510) 540-2566

S329   *California Morbidity.* A weekly report giving a count of specific reportable diseases by state, county, and year-to-year comparisons, with narrative discussion of specific infectious-disease problems.

Chronic Disease and Injury Control, Division of (916) 445-1102

S330   *California Cancer Registry.* Incidence data from doctors, hospitals, and clinics.

S331   *Preventive Health-care for the Aging Files.* Statistics of persons 60 years of age or older served by the program. Contents: sex, race, age, health assessment, health habits, nutrition, and living arrangement.

Drinking Water and Environmental Management, Division of (916) 322-2308

S332   *Public Water Supply Monitoring Reports.* Each water company has a file and is self-monitoring. Reports of water analyses are filed with the Department. Contents: company no., permit; well nos.; results of annual inspections (biological, chemical, and physical factors are tested by the utility and by state-approved laboratories); enforcement and compliance orders; citations; court action (if any). Note: Water quality monitoring is shared with Water Resources Control Board (S695).

S333   *Shellfish Growing Area, Shellfish Bed Permits.* For planting and harvesting of commercial shellfish. Contents: applicant's name, address, phone, location of beds, Fish and Game allotment no. (if applicable), and map.

S334   *Shellfish Plant Certification.* For processing shellfish for human consumption. Contents: business name, address, and phone; contact person; type of shellfish handled; type of operation (packer, shipper, or shucker); owner or corporate officer's name and addresse. Note: permits or certifications are also needed from the following state agencies: Regional Water Quality Control Board, Fish and Game Department, and Public Water Supply Branch, Health Services Department. The state Interagency Committee for Aquaculture Development sells a guide to licenses, laws, and regulations for aquaculture.

S335   *Shellfish Shipping Records.* Contents: date, kind of shellfish, origin, destination, grower, shipper, consignee names, and designation of original beds.

S336   *Water Treatment Operators List.* For water systems with more than 200 connec-tions; those with fewer than 200 are regulated by the county health department. Contents: name, address, phone, certificate no., birth year, date of issuance and renewal, and grade of operator. Note: List includes both active and inactive operators.

Environmental and Occupational Disease Control, Division of (510) 450-2400

S337   *Congenital Malformation File.* Malformation records from live births, fetal death, death certificates, and new malformations reported on death certificates. Years avail-able, 1950 to present. Available from: California Birth Defects Monitoring Program.

S338   *Hazard Evaluation System and Information Service (HESIS).* Current information on possible occupational health hazards of toxic chemical and other substances. Copies of journal articles are maintained in binders arranged by chemicals, industry or occupation, and health aspect. Public access is limited to personal visits. The service is maintained jointly with the Department of Industrial Relations.

Food, Drug and Radiation Safety, Division of (916) 324-3266

S339   *Device Manufacturing License Application.* Same as S340 for medical or health instrument, apparatus, or machine.

S340   ***Drug Manufacturing License Application.*** Required for manufacture for sale in the state of any drug. Contents: name of firm and DBA, street and mailing addresses, phone, U.S. FDA registration no., names of corporate owners or officers, person locally responsible, product code, title, and date.

S341   ***Food and Drug Licenses.*** For bottled water and water vending machines, bottle washers, canneries, cold storage warehouses, frozen-food locker plants, olive oil manufacturing, and pet food. Many permits are confidential because they contain trade secrets.

S342   ***Radioactive Equipment Registration.*** Contents: registrant's name, address, and phone; type of machine; brand; registration no.

S343   ***Radioactive Materials License.*** For possession of radioactive material. Contents: name, address, phone, type of radiation, safety and emergency procedures, description of facility and equipment, engineering control, qualifications of each user, instrumentation, and transfer of waste.

S344   ***Radiological Operator Permit.*** Contents: name, address, phone, type of examination, and date.

S345   ***Radiological Licenses and Certifications.*** Certified Radiological Technologist, Certified X-ray Supervisor and Operator, Permit for Limited X-ray Technician, Certificate for X-ray Training Approval.

S346   ***X-Ray Machine Inspection Report.*** Contents: inspector's name, address, and phone; type; brand name; registration no.; date; inspector's name.

Laboratories, Division of (510) 540-2408

S347   ***Biologics License Application.*** To produce or distribute human whole blood and products made from human or animal tissues or microorganisms. No permit is needed if already licensed by the U.S. Public Health Service or Animal and Quarantine Branch of the U.S. Department of Agriculture. Contents: type of facility, name, address, and phone; type of ownership; owner's and other partners' or corporate board members' names and addresses; person in charge of biologics production; products; manual of technical operations procedures, labeling, advertising samples; description and floor plan of facilities; list of equipment used; blood bank personnel list (name, address, date work began, hours per week, and California license no.).

S348   ***Clinical Laboratory License.*** Contents: name of lab, address/phone, date when lab opened/changed name or address/owner or director changed, name of owner, lab director's name, state license no., hours per week to be spent in lab, medical specialty, signatures of owner and director, and date.

S349   ***Other Laboratory Services Licenses, Certificates, and Approvals.*** Issued for tissue banks, laboratory animals, public health laboratories and their personnel, cholinesterase testing, alcohol and drug testing, and sickle-cell screening.

S350   ## Licensing and Certification (916) 445-2070

Licenses and certifies public and private health-care facilities such as general acute and acute psychiatric hospitals, skilled nursing facilities, psychiatric health facilities, clinics, intermediate care, developmentally disabled and habilitative intermediate care, nursing homes, home health agencies, referral agencies, 24-hour inpatient medical care chemical dependence recovery hospitals, hospices, and state prison hospitals. Also conducts annual inspections and complaint investigations, issues citations, and certifies institutional Medi-Cal providers. The state is divided into three major regions and 11 districts. Note: Los Angeles County provides its own licensing and inspection under a contract with the state. Other counties may conduct their own inspections, but the state does an official annual inspection. Records may require written application for viewing. Content and titles of these records change often.

S351   **Administrative Organization.** A statement of organizational structure of a health facility. Contents: name of facility; administrator; date and place of incorporation; location of business office; identification and location of any other owned facilities, past and present; governing board size, terms of office, meetings, and selection methods; officers' names, addresses, and phones; partners' names and addresses (if needed).

S352   **Affidavit Regarding Patient Money.** A form ensuring that a facility has complied with bonding requirements. Contents: names, facility name, amount of money to be handled.

S353   **Analysis of Accommodations.** Contents: facility name and address, room-by-room list of room nos., dimensions, floor area, number of beds, service, and maximum bed capacity. May also include facility floor plans.

S354   **Applicant Information Form.** Contents: applicant's name, address, phone, social security no., driver's license no., spouse, military service, criminal or civil convictions, mental health record, business ownership history, and professional and technical association memberships, licenses, and certificates.

S355   **Application for Facility License.** Contents: institution's name, address, and phone; applicant's name, address, and phone; type of establishment; number of beds; age range of clients; if previously licensed; property ownership; construction dates (if any); license fee; other facilities owned by applicant; if Medicare or Medi-Cal participant; date.

S356   **Application for Hospital Service Plan Certificate.** Contents: facility name, address, and phone; type of facility; owner's name, address, and phone; if exempt from license or already licensed; if accredited and by whom.

S357   **Bed or Service Request.** Identification of types of beds or services the facility plans to install. Contents: number and types of beds (maternity, pediatric, psychiatric, alcoholism, etc.), and services (anesthesia, surgical, dental, emergency, etc.) existing and requested.

S358   **Date of Ownership Change.** Record of new ownership. Contents: facility name and address; date of change; signatures of previous and new owners.

S359   **Designation of Administrative Responsibility.** Names of persons who will assume responsibility when the licensed operator is not present. Contents: facility name and address, name and title of relief person.

S360   **Disclosure of Ownership and Control Interest Statement.** Required by the federal government to show ownership and evidence of criminal involvement. Contents: facility name, address, phone, and I.D. nos.; record of criminal offenses; names and addresses of persons having any ownership interest and extent of the interest; any change in ownership or control; affiliation with a chain (if any); any change in number of beds; authorized representative and title; signatures and date.

S361   **Inspection Notice.** A statement delivered to facility owner after a Survey Report (S366) has been made. Contents: citation no.; notice of violations; licensee name, address and no.; facility name, address, and phone; type; codes violated; class and nature of violation; penalty assessment; deadline for compliance; evaluation; signature of recipient, date.

S362   **License for Health Services.** Contents: number of beds, type of care, names of owner and administrator, license fee, and I.D. no. of facility. Renewed annually.

(HEALTH SERVICES, CONT.)

S363   ***Medi-Cal Provider Data Form.*** Statement to determine extent of ownership in other facilities. Contents: facility name, address, and phone; tax I.D. no.; type of organization and ownership; list of owners and professional license nos.; name and address of any other owned facilities; Medi-Cal provider nos.; name, address, and extent of any relative owning an interest in a facility; percentage or dollar amount of the interest; signature and date.

S364   ***Request for Certification in Medicare and/or Medicaid Program.*** Contents: facility name, address, and phone; provider no.; state vendor no.; type of facility; type (nonprofit, proprietary, or government); services provided; number of employees and status (registered nurses, aides, etc.); date.

S365   ***Statement of Deficiencies and Plan of Correction.*** Contents: facility's name and address; I.D. no.; a side-by-side listing of non-compliant items and action taken; signature of facility representative; date.

S366   ***Survey Report.*** Details of an inspection of conditions in a facility. Contents: facility name and address; vendor no.; surveyor's name; date; observations made about compliance with state and local laws (medications not recorded) concerning medical direction, nursing services, dietetic services, specialized rehabilitation, and sterilizations; pharmaceutical services, lab and radiological services, social services, etc.; number and condition of residents or patients; medical treatment; transfer/discharge; financial affairs; etc. A narrative description is given for each non-compliance.

S367   ***Other Licensing and Certification Records.*** Fire Clearance (from State Fire Marshal); Health Insurance Benefit Agreement; Intermediary Preference (if new facility plans to participate in Medicare); Possession of Property (grant deed, lease, or other); Statement of Financial Solvency (no bankruptcy proceedings); Surety Bond (verifies that a facility handling money is bonded); Zoning approval (if new construction).

S368   **Medical Care Services** (916) 657-5173

Responsible for health-care for low-income persons through the Medi-Cal system, a joint federal-state program (known nationally as Medicaid). Most records are monthly, quarterly, and annual statistical reports.

S369   ***California's Medical Assistance Program Annual Statistical Report.*** An annual report showing Medi-Cal's average monthly number of eligible users, and payments by aid category and county; average monthly number of users and payments by selected providers and county; age and sex characteristics of eligible persons by county; participating physicians and hospitals by county; prepaid health plan enrollees and payments by county; distribution of payments by type of provider; users and payments by type of physician service; fiscal year Medi-Cal program expenditure.

S370   ***Health Care Provider and Fee-For-Service List.*** A list of facilities providing medical care. Contents: name, address, and type of service. Note: Hospital contracts are confidential until one year after execution. Contracts with primary care doctors and health maintenance organizations are public.

S371   ***Medi-Cal County Program Monthly Average.*** A report on the percent of the population eligible for Medi-Cal, average fee-for service eligible, users and cost per user.

S372   ***Medi-Cal Quarterly Statistical Report.*** A report of the number of persons using Medi-Cal programs, frequency of use, and costs.

S373   ***Persons Certified Eligible for Medi-Cal.*** A monthly report arranged by aid category and county, with state totals.

S374   *Physicians/Practitioners, Providers, and Other Suppliers Excluded or Reinstated Report.* A monthly list of doctors and other medical personnel excluded or reinstated by U.S. Health-care Financing Administration. Contents: name, address, type of service, notice date, exclusion period and reason, and law being violated. Note: Only social security nos. are confidential.

S375   *Services and Expenditures Reporting System.* Month-of-payment data by type of provider, aid category, and county.

S376   *Statistical Report on Medical Care, Recipients, Payments, and Services.* An annual report on the numbers of recipients and amount of medical care payments, by eligibility and type of service, and by age, sex, and type of service. Also includes discharges of recipients from general hospitals by basis of eligibility, physician visits by place of visit, rural health clinic, home health visits, and prescriptions by eligibility. For recipients of inpatient mental health, skilled nursing, or intermediate care, includes data by eligibility and days of care.

S377   *Other Medi-Cal Statistics Reports.* Medi-Cal eligible persons enrolled in prepaid health plans; Medi-Cal fee-for-service eligibles and prepaid health plan enrollees by age group, sex, and county; Medi-Cal funded abortions by age and type of facility in each county; Medi-Cal funded deliveries by age and type in each county. Also, special Medi-Cal studies have been done on aging and long-term care, children and youth, ethnicity, patterns of hospital use, the medically indigent, Medi-Cal trends, mental health services, abortions, malpractice, and other areas.

Primary Care and Family Health Division (916) 654-0265

S378   *Birth Cohort Perinatal File.* Statistics linking birth records and deaths of infants less than one year of age, and all fetal deaths for one calendar year. Years available. 1960 and 1965 to present. Available from Maternal and Child Health Branch.

S379   *California Children Services Files.* Data on physically disabled or potentially disabled children served. These include identifying and demographic information for each child; all services, expenditures, and related information; provider information.

S380   *Indian Health Program Allocation Records.* Contents: name of contractor, total funds and amounts awarded for meeting parts of programs, funds awarded for specific purpose (fiscal/administration, medical, dental, and outreach), number of Native Americans served, and total estimated population.

Vital Records and Statistics, Office of (916) 445-1719

S381   *Vital Statistics.* Birth, death, marriage, and marriage dissolution (divorce) records back from 1905 to present (marriage and divorce records were not kept from 1983 through 1994). For records contents, see birth (C258), death (C259–C260), divorce or marriage dissolution (C170), or marriage certificates (C431). Note: Copies may be ordered over the phone with Visa or MasterCard. Otherwise, requests must be submitted in writing with payment. Commercial services are also available to research these records.

S382   ## HIGHWAY PATROL, DEPT. OF (916) 657-7202

Responsible for safety of people and goods on state highways; enforces laws for motor carriers on the highways. Three major programs are traffic management, regulation and inspection, and vehicle theft prevention. As of July 1, 1995, assumed the function of the Office of the State Police including providing police and security for state property and officials, and air and land patrol of the California Aqueduct.

(HIGHWAY PATROL, CONT.)

S383   **Arrest Reports.** Records of persons arrested. Requests must be made to the local area office and include name, date, and location. Contents: name, time and date of arrest and booking, occupation, date of birth, physical description, charges, and location where held. No information is available on juveniles. See Appendix A, 6254(f)(2).

S384   **Licenses, Certification, Registration, and Permits.** For privately owned ambulances, armored cars, authorized emergency vehicles, explosives and hazardous materials transport, farm labor vehicles and drivers, fleet inspection and maintenance station (firms with three or more vehicles), school buses and drivers, noise limit registration for motorcycles, automobiles, and commercial vehicles.

S385   **Management Information System of Terminal Evaluation Records (MISTER).** A computerized database of information about motor carriers operating in California for the current year plus three prior years. Note: Fees are charged; requests must be made by letter and for specific data. Contents:

Basic Data—name, address, phone; principal cargo; carrier classification.

Accident Involvement—date, time, CHP area where accident occurred, officer's I.D. no., number killed or injured, and degree of fault of truck driver.

Carrier Fleet Information—inventory of vehicles (trucks by type, trailers by type, buses, cargo tanks, hazardous waste vehicles and containers); number of drivers employed; fleet mileage per year.

Citation Information—name of carrier; name of driver; date, time, and CHP area where issued; officer's I.D. no., type of violation, violator's driver license no.

Emergency Contacts—name, phone (day and night) of two emergency contacts for each carrier and each terminal.

Hazardous Materials Licenses—license no., expiration date, type, status, issue date, suspension, probation, or revocation (if any).

Hazardous Material Spills—date, time, location, product I.D., and number killed or injured.

Licenses and Permits—name of operating authority (state or federal); International Registration Plan no. and base state (if out-of-state); hazardous material license and hazardous waste registration.

Terminal Information—location, ratings, inspection dates, compliance ratings by category of maintenance records, driver records, regulated equipment, hazardous materials, and overall rating.

S386   **Statewide Integrated Traffic Report System (SWITRS).** Fatal and injury accident reports are fed into this computerized system. Public information includes location, number of accidents, dates. Fees are charged. See also Transportation (S686).

S387   **Vehicle Theft.** An annual report. Contents: categories of vehicles stolen, recovered, and rate of recovery for previous two years, number stolen by county, number recovered by county, names of three most frequently stolen models in all categories, and 10 highest theft areas.

S388   # HOUSING AND COMMUNITY DEVELOPMENT, DEPARTMENT OF (916) 445-4782

Establishes minimum standards for housing design and construction; enforces health and safety codes through local government (see Planning, C311; Public Works, C368); implements federal and state housing programs; regulates mobile homes, floating homes, and factory-built housing; researches housing and community development needs.

S389   *California Indian Assistance Program Files.* The program helps obtain funding for housing, jobs, water, roads, etc.; helps prepare grant applications; does economic development studies and environmental assessments; helps with administration where needed; inspects construction work and materials; protects against fraud. Most public records relate to grant application and monitoring.

S390   *Community Development Block Grant Applications.* See Housing (C263–C264).

S391   *Community Redevelopment Agencies, Questionnaire (Schedule HCD) of Annual Report of Financial Transactions.* Prepared by local redevelopment agencies for the state Controller and forwarded to the state Housing and Community Development Department. Contents: agency name and county; preparer's name and phone; reporting period; information for each project area including name, financial details, income levels of tenants or owners, tax subsidies, units destroyed, constructed, rehabilitated, displaced households, and affordable units.

S392   *Employee Housing Permit.* For operators or owners of farm labor camps, resorts, railroads, lumber camps. Contents: date, I.D. no., location, operator's name and address, phone; property owner's name, address, and phone; dates of occupancy (seasonal, year-round, etc.); nos. and types of accommodation; no. of employees; fee; map (if needed). Note: This notice must be posted at the site. Activities Reports are records of violations and corrections.

S393   *Housing Units Authorized by Article 34 Referenda.* An annual report on the accumulation of units authorized by community vote but not used. The units are "banked" or saved for future use. Contents: county, city, election date, no. and type of units, type of authority (public agency, county housing authority, etc.), and "banked" units.

S394   *Mobile Home Park Permit to Operate.* Contents: permit no., I.D. no., park name, address, owner name, address, number of mobile home lots with drains, number of recreational vehicle lots with and without drains, and conditional uses (snow-removal program). Note: must be renewed annually.

S395   *Mobile Home Parks Permit Control Log.* A computerized list of some 6,000 permits issued to mobile home parks and special occupancy parks. Contents: I.D. no., park name, location, permittee's address, number of lots, if under state or local jurisdiction.

S396   *Registration and Titling.* A record of ownership and description of a manufactured home, mobile home, commercial coach, floating home or truck camper. Contents: trade name, model name, year of manufacture, year first sold, manufacturer serial number(s), original sale date, registration status, owners name and mailing address, unit location address, name and address of lenders, pending escrows and other data. Ownership data is not recorded for units installed on a permanent foundation. Note: available by address only.

S397   *Technical Assistance Databank.* Contents: name of the Council of Government representing the jurisdiction; if in a coastal zone; population; number of housing units, mobile homes, and households; housing unit vacancy rate; population per household; number of units needing rehabilitation; number of units needing replacement; median household income; percent of households in poverty; percent of owner-occupied housing units; ordinances, local, state, and federal programs in use.

S398   *Manufactured Housing Production and Insignia Records.* A record of production and insignia of approval issuance to manufactured homes, mobile homes, commercial coaches, special-purpose commercial coaches, recreational vehicles, and factory-built homes and component systems. Contents: manufacturer name and address, plan approval and inspection, information, insignia and unit identification numbers, and date of manufacture, inspection and insignia issuance.

(HOUSING AND COMMUNITY DEVELOPMENT, CONT.)

S399 *Manufactured Housing Occupational Licensing.* A record of licenses issued to manufacturers, dealers and salespersons for the manufacture and sale of new and used manufactured homes, mobile homes, and commercial coaches, and of transportation decals issued to same for the movement of units on the highways. Contents: personal and business names and addresses, employment and financial information, criminal and enforcement actions, consumer complaints, and investigative findings.

S400 *Other Housing and Community Development Records.* Acquisition and Displacement Activities (economic levels of housing units subsidized and acquired, households displaced and future displacement); Effect of Activities on Housing Supply (units destroyed or added and economic level); Status and Use of Low and Moderate Income Housing Funds (a financial report of housing fund and number of households assisted by the fund); Tax Increment Set-Asides for Housing (amount of money generated by a tax increase that is put back into housing).

S401 **INDUSTRIAL RELATIONS DEPARTMENT** (415) 972-8835

Enforces and administers laws related to labor-management relations, workplace health and safety, and working conditions through divisions of Apprenticeship Standards, Industrial Accidents, Labor Standards Enforcement, Labor Statistics and Research, Occupational Safety and Health (Cal/OSHA), and State Mediation and Conciliation Service. Records are usually kept in the nearest district or branch office. Phone ahead to locate specific records. Note: From July 1, 1987, to May 1, 1989, U.S. OSHA assumed responsibility for private workplace health and safety. On May 1, 1989, it was returned to Cal/OSHA. Between those dates, records for public-sector enforcement are at Cal/OSHA; private-sector enforcement records are at U.S. OSHA.

S402 *Apprenticeship Standards Files.* Contents: apprenticeship agreements and program standards, administrative hearings records (for complaint resolution).

S403 *Cal/OSHA Inspection Files.* For elevators, escalators, aerial passenger trams, ski lifts, amusement rides, construction hoists, pressure vessels (boilers, air tanks, and LPG tanks); mining and tunneling blasters, gas testers; crane and derrick operators; ethylene oxide users; carcinogens (including asbestos); excavation, trenching, construction, and demolition; radio-controlled cable logging. Contents: employer's name, address, and phone; date of inspection; contractor's license no. and/or equipment operator's name and address (if any); location; hazardous situations or materials involved; citations; accident reports; special orders (issued when there exists an unsafe or unhealthy condition not covered by existing standards). Note: Files are arranged by employer name.

S404 *Civil Files.* Of cases involving wage and working condition laws. Contents: complaints by employees; division's statement of complaint to employer; employer's response; disposition. Note: Employee identity may be confidential.

S405 *Worker Compensation Appeals Cases.* Records of cases heard before the Worker Compensation Appeals Board. Contents: case no.; petitioner's name; date; decisions on reconsideration; petitions or answers for writ of review filed by the Board. Cases are filed by case no. This can be found if the name and year are known. Files are kept at the district offices, unless they are under review by the Board.

S406 *Criminal Files.* Of employers and employees for enforcement of laws related to wages and working conditions. Contents: complaint; division's statement of complaint to employer; employer's response; disposition; case referral to district attorney.

S407   *Hazard Evaluation System and Information Service (HESIS).* The service is maintained jointly with the Department of Health Services. For contents, see S338.

S408   *Industrial Accident Case Files.* Adjudication record of complaints related to worker compensation laws. Contents: case no.; application for adjudication of claim (details of employee's claim); hearing record; disposition.

S409   *Industrial Relations Licensing, Permits, and Registrations.* Includes: Athlete Agent (license), Employment of Minors in the Entertainment Industry (permit), Employment of Minors in Door to Door Sales (license). Exemption Permits (from one or more working conditions and from record-keeping requirements), Farm Labor Contractors (license), Garment Manufacturers (registration), Industrial Homework for Employers (license) and Employees (permit), Sheltered Workshops (license), Talent Agent (license), and Third Party Administrator Certificate (benefits for self-insured employees). Contents: See Licenses and Permits (A021).

S410   *Injured Employee Case Information Control Cards.* An index to the Industrial Accident Case Files (S408). Contents: injured employee's name, address, phone, birth date, and social security no.; employer's name, address, and phone; case no.; history of actions related to case; attorneys; date of injury.

S411   *Labor Union Agreements/Contracts Files.* Contents: collective bargaining agreements and memoranda of understanding from private sector, cities, counties, and the state. Includes information on working conditions, wages and benefits, and grievance procedures. Note: Contracts are filed voluntarily. Some are confidential.

S412   *Labor Union Agreements/Contracts Index.* A computerized index for Labor Union Agreements (S411). Contents: union name and local involved, employer's name, effective dates, Standard Industrial Classification no., and geographical area code.

S413   *Occupational Safety and Health Appeals and Standard Board Records.* The Board hears appeals from OSHA division decisions on citations, special orders, penalties, and abatement dates. Contents: employer's name, docket no., correspondence with other parties, hearings, administrative law judge decision, board review of case, decision, and superior court action (if any).

S414   *Radiation Health Files.* For industrial users only. Contents: radiation materials license, radiation machine registration, and inspection and investigative reports.

S415   *Self-Insurance Plans List.* A statewide list of self-insured employers.

S416   **INSURANCE, DEPARTMENT OF** (916) 445-5544, (415) 904-5410, (213) 346-6400, (800) 927-4357

Certifies, licenses, and regulates insurance companies, insurance producers (agents), and insurance holding companies; handles conservation and liquidation of insurers subject to court supervision; monitors insurers for compliance with laws; investigates and resolves complaints regarding claims, premiums, and fraud. Four regional offices in Los Angeles, Sacramento, San Diego, and San Francisco. Note: Until November 1989 insurers set their own rates. Since passage of Proposition 103, the Department must approve all insurance rate changes (except health and worker's compensation insurance). Files are located in the divisions and bureaus responsible for them. Complaint files are confidential.

S417   *Annual Report of the Commissioner.* Summarizes activities and reports on insurance business conditions. Contents: statistical summary of activities (number and disposition of complaints investigated, number and type of licenses issued, etc.);

(INSURANCE, CONT.)

listings of certificates of authority issued and revoked, mergers, name changes, and permits to issue securities; court actions; worker compensation hearings; status of insurers placed in conservation or liquidation; summary by individual insurer of assets, liabilities, and premiums. Available from San Francisco office.

S418   ***Annual and Quarterly Financial Statements of Insurance Company.*** Reports of companies and holding companies. Contents: company name, home office address, and phone; state of incorporation; officers' and directors' names; contact person and phone; financial statement; reporting of premiums collected; transactions with affiliates; securities held; subsidiaries and controlled companies. Note: Statements are arranged alphabetically by company name in a bound booklet and grouped by type of insurance sold (life and disability, fire and casualty, etc.), and then by code no. Available from the San Francisco and Los Angeles offices.

S419   ***Application for Increase of Insurance Rates.*** Also known as: Revision to Prior Approval Rate Application. Filed by insurance companies with the department for approval to increase insurance rates for all but health and worker's compensation insurance. Application is mandatory. Rejected applications may be appealed by administrative hearing. Contents: company name, address, phone, contact person, property and liability filing submission data sheet, line of business, ratemaking data, reconciliation of financial data per program, review of losses, review of company expenses, distribution of premiums to policy holders, number of claims, application for forms filing, policy count, federal income tax rates, projected investment income ratio and additional exhibits. Available for review from the department's public viewing rooms in Los Angeles and San Francisco.

S420   ***Certificates of Authority and Amendment Files.*** Files on all insurance companies in the state. Contents: application for name approval; state of incorporation; articles of incorporation; application for securities permit; detailed "biographical material" on officers and directors; proposed operating plan; projected income and disbursements; actuarial studies; sample contracts; proposed sales force recruiting and training program; description of accounting methods; documentation of paid-in capital; application for withdrawal (if needed); another insurer's commitment to reinsure and take over the business; mergers, name changes, and other certificate amendments. Available from San Francisco office, (415) 904-5843.

S421   ***Conservator or Liquidator Files.*** Records of insurance companies in receivership. Contents: company name, location, dates of conservation and liquidation, assets, cash receipts, cash disbursements, changes in assets other than cash, and narrative of actions taken. Available from San Francisco office, (415) 676-5000.

S422   ***Disciplinary Files.*** For enforcement of insurance laws and regulations. Contents: accusation (respondent's name, charges, and location); stipulation, notice of defense or default; evidence; proposed decision; final decision. Note: most hearings are held through the Office of Administrative Hearings; records are kept at the Compliance Bureau of the nearest Department district office. Available from the San Francisco office, (415) 904-5382.

S423   ***Holding Company Files.*** Records of the acquisition of control of a California insurance company. Contents: offerer's (buyer's) name, and address; company to be acquired; copy of offer; chart of identity of and interrelationships between buyer and those known to control buyer; identity and background of individuals associated with buyer (present business activities, occupation, and employment during last five years, and any criminal record during last ten years); future plans; detailed description of past, present, and future plans affecting ownership of voting securities of insurer by buyers, affiliates, or other individuals associated with buyer; agreements with broker dealer; financial statements and exhibits; signature and title of buyer.

Note: This is Form A. Form B is detailed, but confidential. The department also has insider trading files and proxy solicitation materials for those few insurers who do not file with the U.S. Securities and Exchange Commission. Available from Los Angeles office.

S424   ***Insurance Companies List.*** A listing of all insurance companies operating in the state. Available for purchase from the consumer hotline at (800) 927-4357.

S425   ***Insurance Companies Examination Reports.*** Contents: cover letter; name, address, date, scope of examination, finding, company history, organization chart, names of board of directors and officers, business territory, plan of operation, reinsurance, accounts and records, statement of financial condition, comments on financial statement, market conduct, and claims; names and signatures of examining officers. Available from the Field Examination Division: (415) 904-5326, (213) 346-6448.

S426   ***Insurance Company Licensees' Files.*** For fire/casualty and life/disability agents, travel agents, insurance adjusters, third-party administrators (who collect premiums or settle claims on health and annuities contracts), and bail bondsmen. Contents: name and address of licensee and organization or authorizing insurer; type of license; date of issuance; licensee's employment and criminal history. Available from Sacramento office, (916) 322-3555.

S427   ***Master Document File.*** A master file of licensing and regulation of insurance company sales and securities sales. Contents: application forms and attachments (articles of incorporation and by-laws); latest examination report from home state; certificate of organization, capital, and assets; securities permit applications (type, no., value of securities, financial statement, and prospectus). Note: Applications are kept separate from Master Document Files until processed and approved. Ask about the existence of any applications not yet processed. See also Annual Statements (S418). Available from San Francisco office, (415) 904-5843.

S428   ***Producer Information.*** Requests for data on a specific broker, solicitor, agent, or agency are answered by phone in local offices. The information is stored on microfiche. For more up-to-date information one must call Sacramento, (916) 322-3555. Contents: producer name, address, and phone; DBA; type of license(s); name(s) of company the producer represents; expiration date of license; record of complaints and disciplinary action. Note: All county clerks have bail bond licensee names, license nos., and other information.

S429   ***Statistical Analysis Bureau.*** Computerized databases available to the public include: Automobile Damage (physical damage to cars); Automobile Insurance Profitability (aggregate data on claims paid, premiums collected, and business costs); Market Share of Business (percentage each company has of total auto insurance business); Private Passenger Auto Liability (loss and premium data). Available from Los Angeles office, (213) 346-6329.

S430   **INTEGRATED WASTE MANAGEMENT BOARD,** (916) 255-2200

Responsible for the storage and disposal of non-toxic solid waste. See Toxic Substances Control (S638) for toxic and hazardous waste. Also coordinates local plans and promotes research into new ways to handle waste. Reviews local plans every three years. If no local agency is designated as the enforcement authority, the Waste Management Board assumes the function. This function is expanding and is subject to frequent new legislation. The enforcement authority is usually the county health department (C236), where records are kept. Operates under the authority of the Secretary of the California Environmental Protection Agency.

(INTEGRATED WASTE MANAGEMENT, CONT.)

S431　**Landfill Facility Files.** Includes all records corresponding to a landfill. Contents: file no., permit, plan, name, address, phone of owner/operator, responsible contact person, copies of local inspection records, correspondence, and meeting notes. Includes active and closed facilities, and non-compliance records. Indexed by common name of facility and name of owner/operator. Note: The landfill file may be under a familiar name, location, code no., government entity, or the contractor's name. See also Health Services, Solid Waste (C245–C247).

S432　**Solid Waste Information System (SWIS).** Permit records for more than 600 operating waste disposal facilities and 400 closed or inactive facilities. Contents: enforcement agencies; county; facility name, and I.D. no.; category; location; operator's name, title, address, phone; land owner's name, title, address, and phone; permit status; if active or closed; type of ownership (federal, state, private, etc.); types and amount of waste received; permit date; closure year. Includes active and closed landfills, transfer processing, and material recovery facilities and transformation facilities.

S433　**JUSTICE, DEPARTMENT OF** (916) 445-9555

Operates under the state Attorney General, an elected official. Functions are divided into four areas: Law Enforcement, Civil Law, Criminal Law, and Public Rights. The Department enforces state laws, provides legal services to state and local agencies, and provides training and support to local and state law enforcement agencies. Also supervises local district attorneys and sheriffs. See Courts (C154–C176), for discussion of courts at city and county levels. See Courts (S151–S153) for a discussion of courts above the county level.

Many records are confidential. Conviction or acquittal records are public; arrest records are not, except in certain instances. Pending litigation information, investigatory information (audits, governmental impropriety), and information received in confidence (financial, proprietary, and trade secrets) are confidential. See *Reporter's Handbook on Media Law* and *Tapping Official Secrets* (Bibliography) for a more detailed discussion of criminal records.

S434　**Law Enforcement, Division of** (916) 227-3884

Assists local, state, and federal criminal justice agencies, supplies information on organized crime, identification of people and property, laboratory analyses, and statistics on crime and delinquency.

S435　**Automated Firearms System.** A computerized file of weapons information, laws, and regulations. Public information is limited to statistics and concealed weapons permits. Permit information only is given to the person holding the permit if the request is accompanied by a notarized copy of the driver's license and written request.

S436　**Criminal Justice Profile.** An annual statistical summary of criminal justice data. Section I contents (partial): types of crimes (adult, juvenile, and disposition of), expenditures, personnel tables for a ten year-by-year span. Section II contents (partial): current year's data from Section I arranged by county; rates for crimes; offenses by county and sex; other breakdowns by age and ethnicity; probation statistics; disposition of cases by type of offense, sex, age, race, and defense representation.

S437　**Criminal Statistical Data.** Summaries or customized reporting of data collected and compiled from city, county, and state criminal justice agencies on crimes, arrests, processing of adult and juvenile offenders, number of adult and juvenile offenders in local detention facilities, law-enforcement personnel, citizen complaints against peace officers, domestic violence, and deaths in custody.

S438   *Directory of Services.* A list of services provided by Division of Law Enforcement. Contents: organization list (name, location, phone); name of service (asset forfeiture, gaming registration, humane societies in California, tear gas training, terrorism analysis, etc.); description; contact address and phone; reporting forms and sources for; publications; training services; index.

S439   *Gaming Registration Application.* Used to apply for a gaming or gambling venture license (e.g. card room, bingo parlor, race track). Contents: name of applicant; status (owner, investor, trustee, manager); address; phone; amount invested; title or nature of interest; physical description; photograph; marital status and name, address, date and place of birth of spouse; name and date of birth of applicant's children; criminal history of applicant and immediate family; 15-year history of residences and employment; character references, professional license status and disciplinary action history under license; current and past history of financial interest in gambling ventures; name of club; address; phone; name of previous owner of club and previous name of club.

S440   *Organized Crime in California—Annual Report to the California Legislature.* A yearly summary of organized crime in California with descriptions of various crime groups and the response by law enforcement.

S441   *Roster of Selected California Criminal Justice Agencies.* An annual list. Contents: name, title, mailing address, and phone for chiefs of police, sheriffs, district attorneys, highway patrol offices, county probation departments, contract cities, and selected statewide criminal justice agencies in California.

S442   *Status Report-California Identification (CAL-ID) System and Remote Access Network (RAN) for Calendar Year.* An annual report to the Legislature on automation of state fingerprint card file by the Criminal Identification and Information Branch. Contents: narrative of operations, personnel, conversion details, equipment, county-by-county reports, expenses, and funding sources.

S443   **Public Rights Division** (916) 324-5433

Represents state agencies and the state in cases related to the environment, consumer protection, charitable trust, resources, and civil rights.

S444   *Escheat Records.* Litigation files of unclaimed property that will revert to the state. Records are on file at the state Controller, Division of Unclaimed Property (S116).

S445   *Justice Department Licenses, Permits, Certificates, or Registration.* Destructive Device (explosive projectiles, incendiaries, weapons other than shotguns, rockets and launchers), Machine Guns, Non-Lethal Weapons (stun guns, mace, taser), Police Body Armor (anyone making or selling to law enforcement officers), Sawed-off Shotgun (barrel less than 18 inches), Tear Gas (manufacture, possession, or transport of), Tear Gas Training, Telephone Sellers, Travel Agents. See also S439.

S446   *Missing Children Bulletin.* Quarterly report of missing children and dependent adults. Distributed to law-enforcement officials, district attorneys and public and private school officials. Contents: name, alias, sex, race, date of birth, physical destruction, possible reason missing (runaway, stranger, or parent abduction etc.), location last seen, date, and photo.

S447   **Registry of Charitable Trusts** (916) 445-2021

The Registry of Charitable Trusts under the office of the Attorney General has jurisdiction over the activities and financial records of all active charitable organizations (charitable trusts and nonprofit corporations) that hold assets or do business in Cali-

(JUSTICE, CONT.)

fornia and commercial fund-raisers for charitable organizations and purposes (CFR). The Department collects, reviews and audits the financial records of these organizations. CFRs must also file with the sheriff of each county in which they intend to solicit funds. Some schools, hospitals, religious organizations, and government agencies are not required to register or file with the department.

For charitable organizations, files may contain some or all of the following: names and addresses of organization; trustees, directors, or officers; statement of operation; financial statements; articles of incorporation or association by-laws; trust instruments, wills, and decrees of distribution; rents; salaries; grants received; budgets; statement of purpose; contracts; meeting schedules; location of operation; founders' names; activities; miscellaneous. expenses; audit information (if any); Franchise Tax Board tax-exempt status notification; court action (if any); accountant's name, address and phone; if property is jointly held by any other organization/person, personal financial relationship to other organizations; donations received and any tax penalties levied.

To see more than 20 files per day, make arrangements in writing 5 days in advance. Files are destroyed after 10 years. Indexes are arranged by name, purpose, revenue, assets, location, and grants/operations of the organization and are available for purchase on microfiche. Federal law also requires tax-exempt organizations to make their IRS 990 tax returns available for public inspection during normal business hours. These documents are also available from the IRS. See also Franchise Tax Board, Exempt Organizations (S270).

S448   ***Periodic Report to the Attorney General of California (Form CT-2).*** For charitable organizations. Contents: name and address of organization, state charity registration no., corporate organization no., filing date, private or non-profit status, gross receipts, total assets, sources of revenue, payroll tax and, summary of investments.

S449   ***Annual income tax form for tax exempt organizations (Form 990).*** Tax return filed with the U.S. Internal Revenue Service for organizations with revenue over $25,000. Contents: statement of revenue, expenses, changes in net assets or final balances, charitable contributions received, statement of functional expenses, statement of program services and accomplishes, balance sheets (assets, liabilities, fund balances or net assets), list of officers, directors, trustees or key employees, analysis of income, statement of relationship of activities to the accomplishment of exempt purposes. Attached schedules including Schedule A: Organization Exempt Under 501(c)(3). Note: this form is also publicly available from the IRS.

S450   ***California Exempt Organization Annual Information Statement or Return (Form 199).*** Tax return filed with the State Franchise Tax Board. Contents: Similar to Form 990.

S451   ***Annual Registration Form: Commercial Fundraiser for Charitable Purposes (Form CF-1).*** Contents: name of commercial fundraising, address, federal employer identification no., state organized in, date of organization, and types of fundraising activities.

S452   ***Annual Financial Report: Commercial Fundraiser for Charitable Purposes (Form CF-2T).*** Contents: same as (S451) plus, revenue, expenses, management fees, net distribution to charities, and officers' signatures.

S453   ***Other Justice Department Reports.*** Homicide in California (annual); Major Narcotic Vendors Prosecution Program (annual); California Firearms Laws—Annual Update of State Laws.

S454 **LANDS COMMISSION, STATE** (916) 574-1900

Controls policy and programs for federal lands given to the state, including beds of all navigable waterways, tidelands, submerged lands out to three-mile limit, swamp and overflow lands, school lands (given by the federal government for the support of education), and state lands granted by the legislature to local jurisdictions. Manages mineral rights, oil, gas, and geothermal exploration and development on certain state-owned lands. Maintains basic state land title records, some of which may not be maintained by County Recorder (C420). Familiarity with the township method of dividing land (section, township, range, and meridian) is helpful in researching property. See also General Services, Proprietary Land Index (S303).

S455 *Dredging Permit.* Required for activities related to flood control, reclamation, navigation, etc. of land under jurisdiction of the Lands Commission. For removal of material, see Extractive Lease (S460). Contents: permit no.; owner's name, address, and phone; business address and phone; contact person; location; zoning; planning designation; current land use; other required permits; location of disposal site, chemical analysis and amount of material to be removed, future use of all mined material, and how and where spoils will be handled.

S456 *Land Sales Files.* Information related to land sales. Indexed by S457 and S463. Contents: application from potential purchaser, surveyor's notes, and payment history.

S457 *Land Sales Microfilm Index.* An index to Patents (S464) and Land Sales Files (S456). First use the Log of Prints (S462). Contents: buyer's or grantee's name, certificate of purchase no., patent no., book and page no. (for patent), legal description of land.

S458 *Lease Listing—Active.* A list of current leases and permits of state-owned land. Serves as an index to S460 and S461. Contents: name of lessee or permit holder, agreement or file no., type of lease or permit, county where located, place name of land (commonly used name), estimated acreage, date of lease, expiration date. Note: The index is also arranged by county.

S459 *Lease Listing—Inactive.* An index of expired leases and permits involving state-owned land (S460-S461). Contents: same as for Active Lease Listing (S458).

S460 *Lease and Permit Files—Extractive.* Records for state-owned lands involving mining or drilling of minerals other than gas, oil, or geothermal resources. Contents: application for permit or lease (name, address, phone, location, and purpose); permit or lease, appraisal of land, environmental impact report or "negative declaration" (no impact), maps; photographs; file no.; if in navigable waters, must include location of disposal site and permission to use, chemical analysis and volume of material to be removed and method, intended use of materials; for mining projects, information on what and how minerals will be extracted, deposit for each acre within extraction site. Indexed by Active Lease Listing (S458) and Inactive Lease Listing (S459).

S461 *Lease and Permit Files—Non-extractive.* Records for state-owned land not related to mining or drilling. Contents: same as for Lease and Permit Files—Extractive (S460). See also General Services, By-State Lease Files (S301), and Property Management Files (S302).

S462 *Log of Prints.* A geographical index by meridian and township nos. to the Microfilm Index to Land Sales (S457). Contents: meridian name, township no., Microfilm Index Reel no. Note: This Log is the starting point for finding land sales records geographically. The Log is divided into meridians and subdivided into townships. This leads to the microfilm reel no. for the index to land sales (S456).

(LANDS COMMISSION, CONT.)

S463 **Master Alphabetical Index.** An index of Patents (sale of state land to private party, S464) and Land Sales Files (S456), if only the buyer's name is known. Contents: buyer or grantee's name; patent book and page no.; Land Sales File no.

S464 **Patents.** A record of the sale of state land to a private party, similar to a deed for private land. Contents: name of buyer or grantee, description of land.

S465 **Other Lands Commission Permits.** County Assessor Rolls (microfiche copies); Geothermal Exploration or Prospecting Permit; Land Use Lease (use of state-owned lands for other than dredging, mining, or oil, gas, or geothermal exploration); Prospecting Permit (for exploration of minerals other than oil, gas, or geothermal resources on state-owned lands).

S466 **LEGISLATURE, CALIFORNIA STATE** Senate: (916) 445-4251; Assembly: (916) 445-3614

The lawmaking branch of state government. Records are exempt from the state Public Records Act and Information Practices Act, but with the Legislative Open Records Act (Cal. Gov. Code Section 9070 *et seq.*) Legislators have set up their own policies closely resembling the state's. Records not public include: meetings for personnel, security, or party caucuses; records of investigations; names and phones of persons using telephone and telegraph; names and locations of persons using cars; any agency report specifically restricted; members' and staff correspondence; preliminary drafts; notes and memos; pending litigation; personnel, medical files, and other records restricted by federal and state law.

Various records are available in addition to hearing transcripts, votes, calendar, copies of bills, etc. These include department reports required or requested by law (see individual departments) to be filed with the legislature or the Governor, reports of the Auditor-General, and Assembly or Senate Office Research Reports. A *List of Reports Prepared by State and Local Agencies* is published by the Legislative Council (see Bibliography). To search for reports by subject, check the listings under "California Legislature" in the monthly *California State Publications* (Bibliography). For historical legislative material, check the State Archives (S616).

The Legislature has made many documents and public records available on-line through the Internet including: Daily Files; Legislative Calendars; Assembly Rules; full bill text, tracking, history, status, analysis, index and voting history; bill keyword search, and the complete California Codes. See page 208 (Appendix C) for access information.

S467 **Analysis of the Budget Bill—Report of the Legislative Analyst to the Joint Legislative Budget Committee.** An annual report of analysis, recommendations for state revenues and expenditures, and changes to the Governor's budget. The report covers all branches of government. Contents: name of department; requested, estimated, and actual funds; funding by item and source; summary of major issues and recommendations; general statement of department functions; analysis and recommendations for department subdivisions and their programs. Produced by the Legislative Analyst Office, (916) 445-4656, which provides analysis and nonpartisan advice to the Legislature on fiscal and policy issues.

S468 **California Legislature at Sacramento.** An annual handbook for the Legislature. Contents: list of members, officers, committees, and rules of both houses.

S469 **Committee Bill Analysis.** Contents: bill number and title, date last amended, date of hearing, digest, summary of contents from bill sponsor, and public support and opposition.

S470   ***Current Bill Status.*** A computerized database of all bills under consideration. Information is available from each legislator. Contents: bill no., title, main subject, sponsor, text, history, and status. A printout of the text is available. Note: Requests should include the bill no. when possible. Copies of bills may be ordered and their status checked through the Legislative Bill Room, (916) 445-2323. See Appendix C for Internet access.

S471   ***Joint Publications Catalog.*** An annual list of reports and hearing transcripts available for sale. Contents: committee names, titles listed by committee name, stock no., price, libraries that receive the listed items, and addresses. Note: The catalog is difficult to use, with no direct title or subject access. Use *California State Publications* (see Bibliography) to search for a legislative report, summary, etc. by subject.

S472   ***Legislative Index.*** Cumulative subject index of all bills introduced and amended in a legislative session. Published approximately every two weeks and available from the Legislative Bill Room. A Final Index and Table of Sections Affected is published at the end of every two-year session.

S473   ***State Appointments List, Vol. II.*** Lists appointments made by the Legislature. Available from the Assembly Speaker's Office and the Secretary of State. See S586 for contents.

S474   ***Other State Legislature Publications.*** Daily File (Senate, Assembly); Daily Journal (Senate, Assembly); Daily Histories (Senate, Assembly); Floor Analysis (Senate, Assembly); Legislative District Maps; Legislative Index: Vol. 1—subject, Vol. 2—government code; Senate Rules Confirmation Hearings Transcripts; Summary Digest of Statutes Enacted and Resolutions Adopted Including Proposed Constitutional Amendments and Statutory Record; Standing Committee Roll Call Votes; Weekly History (Senate, Assembly); Zip Code Directory (for zip codes within Congressional and Legislative districts).

S475   ## LIBRARY, CALIFORNIA STATE (916) 654-0174

Under the direction of the State Librarian, the California State Library serves as the central reference and research library for state government agencies and the Legislature. The State Library also collects and preserves statistics and other information pertaining to the libraries of the state; administers federal and state grant programs for public library construction, renovation, finance, and special programs; serves as a regional library for the blind, in cooperation with the Library of Congress; serves as a regional depository library for government documents; administers the California Library Services Act under the direction of the California Library Services Board; publishes *California State Publications*, a monthly listing of official California state documents (see Bibliography).

S476   ***California Library Directory.*** Provides a listing and index for public, academic, special, state agency, and county law libraries. Published annually.

S477   ***California Library Statistics.*** Provides statistical data from reports requested by the State Library of all public, academic, special, and county law libraries in the State. Although public libraries are required by statute to report the statistical data requested, participation by some libraries is less than complete. Libraries failing to return reports for two years in a row are dropped from the free publication distribution list. Published annually.

S478   ***Library Services and Construction Act Application (LSCA).*** An application submitted to the State Library by a library jurisdiction to qualify a project for federal

(LIBRARY, CONT.)

LSCA funding. Contents: fiscal year, amount, project title, type of program and populations served, budget summary. Related notice of grant award or rejection, quarterly reports, and final report on the award also available.

S479   *Library Construction and Renovation Bond Act Application.* An application submitted by a local library jurisdiction for Bond Act funding of a local project. Contents: fiscal year, amount, amount of local matching funds, project title, type of construction or renovation, building plans, and budget summary. Notice of grant award or rejection; periodic reports, and final report on the awards are also available.

S480   *Annual Reports by local libraries to State Library.* Contents: name, director's name, location, phone, and telecommunications address, jurisdiction, and library system membership. Also contains annual statistical summary of library services.

S481   *Public Library Fund; Certification and Waiver Requests.* The State Library administers distribution of state supplemental funds to support specified foundation services provided by public libraries. Eligibility for funds is based on local support for public libraries at specified levels. Library jurisdictions which fall below specified local support levels in a given year may apply to the state Librarian for a waiver of the level of support requirement.

S482   *Families for Literacy Program; Grant Applications.* Grants awarded on a competitive basis to eligible libraries for coordinated literacy and preliteracy services to families that include illiterate adults and young children.

S483   *California Library Services Board Agendas and Minutes.* The Board directs the state Librarian in the administration of the California Library Services Act; reviews and approves all annual proposals submitted under the Act; requires participating libraries and systems to prepare and submit any reports and information necessary to carry out the provisions of the Act, and prescribes the form and manner for providing such reports and information.

S484   ## LITTLE HOOVER COMMISSION (916) 445-2125

Formally known as the Milton Marks Commission on California State Government Organization and Economy, this independent, bipartisan watchdog agency has a statutory mandate to examine any state program and make recommendations to improve effectiveness and efficiency. The Commission also has the statutory duty to conduct a 60-day review of any proposed Governor's reorganization plan. Reports are delivered to the Governor, the Legislature, and the public. The Commission testifies in support of legislation that implements report recommendations.

S485   *Reports.* More than 125 reports issued since 1962 on topics covering the broad range of government activities. In addition, biennial reports provide summaries of reports and an assessment of activities every two years, and *A Decade of Reports* provides summaries of all reports grouped by topics for the past 10 years.

S486   *Public Hearing Material.* Each study includes one or more public hearings. Binders of written testimony for each hearing are available, as well as audio tapes of the hearing itself. Transcripts are available for hearings held before September 1992.

S487   *Subject Files.* Contents: documentation, research, and interviews conducted for Commission-produced reports.

S488   *Reorganization Plan Files.* Governors have proposed 25 executive branch reorganization plans from 1968 to present. Each reorganization plan is analyzed by the Commission, which holds public hearings. A report is adopted, either supporting or opposing the plan. Files include research material on the reorganization plan by subject heading.

S489   **Legislative files.** The Commission supports between 40 and 80 bills during each two-year legislative session based on recommendation in Commission reports. Files include support material, letters, and other information.

S490   **Chronology files.** Copies of all out-going correspondence are retained in chronological order. Includes letters of invitation for public hearings to witnesses, legislators, and interested parties to participate in studies, and support for legislation.

S491   ## LOTTERY COMMISSION, CALIFORNIA (916) 323-0400

Sets policy for and administers the California Lottery. Composed of five commissioners approved by the governor. For all legally mandated reporting requirements of the Lottery, consult the California State Lottery Act (Cal. Gov. Code, Title 2, Division 1, Chapter 12.5, Sec. 8880 et seq.).

S492   **Daily Transaction Records.** Contents: receipt of funds, prize claims, prize disbursements or prizes liable to be paid, and expenses of the lottery.

S493   **Demographic Study of Lottery Players.** Independent analysis of the demographic characteristics of Lottery game players. Contents: income, age, sex, education, and frequency of play. Studies are conducted periodically.

S494   **Independent Audit of Lottery Finances.** Annual independent audit of all accounts and transactions of the Lottery. Contents: assets, liabilities, sales, expenses, cash flows, and investments.

S495   **Independent Audit of Lottery Security.** Analysis of computer, facility and systems security control procedures used by the Lottery. Portions containing specific recommendations are exempt from public disclosure. Conducted every two years.

S496   **Lottery Contractors Disclosures.** Contractors submitting bids for work with the State Lottery must submit the following disclosures: name, address, principal owners of entity, officers, directors and stockholders of parent company. Before the award of a contract, the Commission may also require the following information: all jurisdictions in which the bidder conducts business and the nature of the business; business history in gaming services; criminal and traffic violation history; bankruptcy, insolvency or reorganization history if any; political contributions made.

S497   **Quarterly Report of Operation.** Contents: statement of lottery revenues, prize disbursements, expenses, net revenues, and other financial transactions involving Lottery funds. Includes balance sheets, statements of operation, and changes in financial position with all attached financial notes.

S498   **Monthly Financial Reports.** Contents: statement of lottery revenues, prize disbursements, expenses, net revenues, and other monthly financial transactions.

S499   ## MANAGED RISK MEDICAL INSURANCE BOARD
(916) 324-4695

Administers three programs for Californians who are unable to obtain affordable health insurance through traditional means. Programs include the Major Risk Medical Insurance Program (MRMIP) for high-risk, uninsurable individuals; the Access for Infants and Mothers Program (AIM), for lower-income pregnant women

(MANAGED RISK MEDICAL INSURANCE, CONT.)

and infants of low-income parents; and The Health Insurance Plan of California (HIPC), to provide a health insurance pool for small groups. Contracts with private health service plans and administrators for management of the programs. Contracts are confidential for one year from date of signing, financial and rate information is confidential for four years.

S500   *Monthly Enrollment Report: MRMIP.* Enrollment information, including total enrollment and individual health plan enrollment.

S501   *Monthly Enrollment Report: AIM.* Enrollment information, including total enrollment, enrollment by county, ethnicity and individual health plan enrollment.

S502   *Monthly Enrollment Report: The HIPC.* Enrollment information, including employer group size, total enrollment, employee age categories, and individual health plan enrollment.

S503   **MOTOR VEHICLES, DEPARTMENT OF (DMV)**
(916) 657-6940

Registers vehicle and vessel ownership, licenses drivers, licenses and regulates business related to the manufacture, transporting, new and used sales, and disposal of vehicles. Issues identification cards for state residents who do not drive.

Certain DMV record information is confidential including driver's or owner's residential address, DMV personnel matters, driver's physical or mental disability, investigations in progress, and information on accident reports. Driver licenses and vehicle registrations are public information, except for residential information. Requests must be prepaid and made in writing on the proper form and include reason for request (such as insurance claims, legal action, or financial information). They must also include the subject's name, date of birth, or license no. for driver's license requests, and name, date of birth, or plate designation for vehicle or vessel registration requests. Commercial accounts may be set up to access driver's licenses or vehicle registrations.

S504   *Automobile Sellers, Manufacturers, Dismantlers and Distributors Records.* Includes files for new and used car dealers. Contents: company name, address, phone, owner's name and titles, branch addresses, dealer license no., sales person's name and individual license number, dates of employment, bonding company, bond number, bonding companies address, principal named on bond, and number of dealer plates in use (by new and used care dealers).

S505   *California Identification Card.* Issued to non-drivers. For contents, see Driver License Information (S506).

S506   *Driver License Information.* Contents: name, physical description, residential address (confidential as of January 1, 1990), mailing address, birthdate, license no. and status (valid, expired, suspended, or revoked), driving while intoxicated conviction (DUI), failures to appear in court (FTA), failures to pay traffic fines (FTP), traffic conviction record (major violations seven years back, minor violations three years back). Note: Similar information exists for identification cards (S505), which are issued to non-drivers. The license holder is notified of the request.

S507   *Hearing Transcripts.* Records of hearings for revocation or suspension of license, and re-registration in another state when fines are owed to California.

S508   *Investigative Review Request Form (INV 18).* For filing a complaint against a new, used, or third-party motor vehicle seller. Contents: complainant name, address, and phone; seller's name, address and phone; vehicle year, make, model, license plate no. sale date, salesperson; explanation of complaint; attachments. Complaints are investigated by the Department's Division of Investigations and Occupational Licensing Investigative Review Unit. Information is made public only after a complaint has been substantiated.

S509   ***Vehicle Registration Information.*** For automobiles, trucks, trailers, motor homes, buses, motorcycles, and snowmobiles. Contents: name, residential address of registered vehicle owner (confidential as of January 1, 1990), mailing address, vehicle year, make and body style; vehicle history (date purchased by current owner, previous owners' names and addresses going back three years); license plate no.; vehicle identification no. Note: The owner is notified unless requester holds a registered commercial account or purchases a copy of the entire statewide file.

S510   ***Vessel Registration Information.*** For motorized boats and vessel owners. Contents: registered owner's full name, residential address (confidential as of January 1, 1990), mailing address, vessel I.D. no.; vessel description (manufacturer, hull no., year, length, hull material, and type of propulsion); ownership history. Note: The owner is notified of the request. Data are available by county.

S511   ***Other Motor Vehicle Licenses, Permits, and Records.*** Driving Instructor; Driving School Operator; Driving School Owner; Independent Driving Instructor; Traffic Violator School Instructor or School Operator; Vehicle Dealer, Dismantler, Distributor, Lessor, Manufacturer, Re-manufacturer, Salesperson, Transporter, Verifier (for vehicle I.D. no.); Financial Responsibility Files (insurance information).

S512   ## PERSONNEL BOARD, STATE (916) 653-1028

Handles the appointment and promotion processes of the state civil service system, and for any local government, if requested. Administers the Civil Service Act, including affirmative action, examinations, appointments, appeals, and disciplinary complaints. Most records are confidential. Composed of five members appointed by the Governor. The Board's Office of Information Practices, which helped people identify state records containing their personal information and gain access to them, was eliminated in 1992. Persons attempting to secure these records must now contact state agencies directly. See also A011.

S513   ## PESTICIDE REGULATION, DEPARTMENT OF
(916) 445-4300

Enforces all laws governing the use of pesticides in California, including agricultural, industry, business, and home use. Assesses risks of use and exposure to pesticide products; licenses and certifies pesticide dealers and applicators; monitors use of pesticides; evaluates toxicology information; works with other agencies to evaluate pesticides as toxic air contaminants, surface and ground water contaminants. The department operates under the authority of the Secretary of the California Environmental Protection Agency. Reports of injury and illness from pesticide exposure are referred to county agricultural commissioners for investigation. See also Agriculture (C008–C021), Air Resources Board (S021), and Fish and Game Department (S207).

Enforcement Branch (916) 445-3920

S514   ***Pest Control Recommendation.*** Contents: grower/applicator name, address; location; commodity, area size; reasons for recommendation; pest(s); material and method of application; time and conditions; days before harvest or slaughter; worker re-entry date; if notice posted, warnings; advisor's name, address, date, and employer.

(PESTICIDE REGULATION, CONT.)

S515   *Produce Residue Sample.* A record of tests for pesticide residue. Contents: county or district; reference no.; testing program; type of sample site (processing plant, point of origin, etc.); sample no.; commodity; size of lot; container type; quantity sampled; identification; where grown; names of grower, packer/shipper, dealer/distributor, and processor; laboratory records of time of receipt, analyses performed, and results; lab no.; chemist's signature; date.

Environmental Monitoring Branch (916) 324-4100

S516   *California Pest Management Survey Database.* A survey of UC Cooperative Extension Farm Advisors (C555) listing California-produced crops and commodities, pests of those crops/commodities, and their respective chemical controls. Data is reported from seven different climatic regions of the state. Contents: crop/commodity, California region, common and scientific names of pests, chemical controls including active ingredients, and numerical rating of importance of controls for specific crop-pest-region combinations.

S517   *Crop Disposition Report.* A record of illegal amounts of pesticide found on a product. Contents: file no.; commodity; pesticide; residue data sheet; county where grown; county where sampled; packer; type sampling done; regulation violated; amount and disposition of crop.

S518   *Index to Environmental Monitoring and Pest Management Reports.* An index to reports concerning environmental monitoring of pesticides and integrated pest management evaluations. Includes a chronological index to reports produced by this branch and a chronological index to reprints of articles published in scientific journals available from the branch.

S519   *Sampling for Pesticide Residues in California Well Water—Annual Well Monitoring Report (Well Inventory Report).* A well inventory database. Contents: state well nos.; location; dates of sample and analysis; chemicals analyzed; individual sample concentration; minimum detectable limit; sampling agency; analyzing laboratory; well type; sample type. May also include: method of analysis; depth of well; depths of sources of incoming water; depth to standing water in well; year well was drilled; whether a driller's log was located; known or suspected source of contamination.

Information Systems Branch (916) 445-4110

S520   *Pesticide Use Report.* An annual report based on computerized records filed by county Agricultural Commissioners (C009), issued in two formats. Contents: chemicals, pounds used, acreage treated, number of applications, and purpose of use. One format shows use by chemical, then commodity or purpose; the other shows use by commodity or purpose, then chemical. Note: Data on locations and dates of applications are available by purchase of the tapes. For an individual farm or name of applicator, apply to the appropriate county Agricultural Commissioner. Fees are charged.

S521   *Pesticide Safety and Efficacy Data.* A service of the department's public records library. Contains over 100,000 volumes on pesticide data. Available information includes product and environmental chemistry; fish and wildlife toxicology; acute and chronic toxicology; residue, metabolism, efficacy and phytotoxicity data. Some information is considered proprietary under federal law. Expect a two-month wait for request to be filled. Fees are charged.

Medical Toxicology Branch (916) 445-4233

S522   *Prioritization and Status of Active Ingredients for Risk Characterization Report.* Lists what priority has been placed on the need to conduct a risk assessment of the active ingredients in pesticide products. Active ingredients are placed in one of three categories (high, moderate, or low priority) based on their possible adverse health effects. Risk assessments gauge the toxicity of a chemical based on expected human exposure to the product. Generated during the Department's initial phase in establishing a risk assessment for an active ingredient.

S523   ***Study Review Worksheets.*** A Department review of a toxicology study conducted on the active ingredient in a pesticide product as submitted to the Department by an outside entity such as a pesticide manufacturer or an independent laboratory. Contains a department characterization on the adequacy of the submitted study.

S524   ***Summary of Toxicology Data.*** A review and analysis of pesticide toxicology studies. Summaries are drawn from a compilation of all Study Review Worksheets (S523) completed on a specific pesticide chemical agent.

S525   ***Risk Characterization Document.*** A completed risk characterization evaluation of an active ingredient in a pesticide product. Contents: summaries of risk assessments; compilation and review of studies used in risk assessment; estimates of human exposure to active ingredients through industrial or home application and residue on food substances.

Pesticide Registration Branch (916) 445-4400

S526   ***Directory of Mailing List Databases.*** Lists include persons interested in specific departmental issues. For example: affirmative action recruitment, air-toxic contamination, pesticide regulatory affairs, pesticide related licensees and registrants; agricultural pest control businesses, agricultural commissioners, task forces, pest control air craft pilots, and pesticide dealer businesses and designated agents.

S527   ***Economic Poison (Pesticide) Registration Application.*** Required for sale of a pesticide in the state. Contents: firm name, mailing address; officer responsible for registration and phone; head office address, phone; type of registration; brand name; chemical name of active ingredients and percent by weight; inert ingredient name and percent by weight; type of pesticide; type of formulation; type of containers; signature of authorized representative; labels; copy of U.S. EPA data; data on toxicology, chemistry, efficacy, fish, and wildlife, phytotoxicity. Note: Registration must be renewed annually. Chemical and inert ingredients are considered trade secrets and may be confidential.

S528   ***Pesticide Label Database.*** Contents (if used once on a product): California product registration no., product name, registration type (regular, special local need, or experimental), original registration date, type of formulation, level of danger (warning, poison, etc.), general pesticide category (chemical, microbial). Note: For pesticides used more than once on a product, contents also include active chemical ingredient, site where used (box car, grain elevator), type (insecticide, fungicide, etc.), human health hazards, environmental hazards, application methods and instructions, and targeted pests.

S529   ***Pesticide Registration Number Book.*** Contents: name of producer, I.D. no., name of pesticide, and registration no.

S530   ***Pesticide Research Authorization.*** Required for all experimental uses of an unregistered pesticide. Contents: authorization no.; company name, address, and phone; brand or common name or I.D. no.; U.S. EPA registration no.; type of pesticide; amount to be applied, when, where, and why; expected result; disposition of treated product; signature of trial supervisor; signature of state official and date.

(PESTICIDE REGULATION, CONT.)

Worker Health and Safety Branch (916) 445-4222

S531   *Guide to the California Pesticide Illness Surveillance Program.* Background information and a brief, nontechnical synopsis of findings reported in "Pesticide Illness Surveillance Program, Summary Report" (see S534).

S532   *Index of Worker Health and Safety Branch Reports.* Index to more than 1,000 reports by a numerical and chronological index, an alphabetical index by specific pesticide, an occupational exposure index, and an index of other health and safety issues.

S533   *Worker Health and Safety Database.* A computerized, subject-based index of over 1,000 reports generated by this branch on pesticides as they relate to health and safety issues.

S534   *Pesticide Illness Surveillance Program, Summary Report.* Summarizes reported incidents of illness or injuries related to pesticide exposure. Contents: tables showing type of illness or injury; relationship to occupation; work activity (applicator, flagger, mixer/loader, etc.); hospitalization, disability, and pesticides related to type of illness or injury; county reports of agricultural and non-agricultural use and type of exposure. An annual report. (See S531 and S535)

S535   *Summary of Episodes Assigned Priority Investigation Status.* Describes cases of illness or injury from pesticide exposure resulting in a priority investigation. Describes the criteria for conducting a priority investigation. Contains case studies of such investigations with details of circumstances resulting in exposure, extent of injury or exposure, medical care necessitated by exposure, issuance of violation or action taken as a result of incident, and environmental effects of and property loss resulting from incident. An annual report (see S534)

S536   *Other Pesticide Licenses, Permits, Registrations, or Certifications.* Agricultural Pest Control Adviser; Aircraft Pilot Pest Control Certificate; Business Licenses (pesticide dealers, pest control business); Maintenance Gardener Pest Control Business License; Qualified Applicator License (for agricultural or gardener pest control business). Contents: see Licenses and Permits (A021).

S537   ## PRISON TERMS, BOARD OF (916) 445-4071

Sets terms for persons sentenced to life imprisonment with possibility of parole, and for those who have violated parole, reviews felony sentences for fairness and conformity; advises governor on clemency applications. Note: Board parole hearing transcripts should be requested in writing.

S538   *Life Parole Consideration Hearings Transcripts.* Contains verbatim record of parole hearing, including the board's decision to grant, deny, postpone, or rescind parole. Confidential information may be removed.

S539   *Parole Recission Hearing Decision.* Persons who have permission to attend a hearing may get a copy of the decision. Confidential information may be removed. Note: A recission hearing discusses change of parole date due to new information.

S540   *Summary of Revocation Hearing and Decision.* Persons who have permission to attend a hearing may get a copy of the decision. Confidential information may be removed.

S541 **PUBLIC EMPLOYEES RETIREMENT SYSTEM, CALIFORNIA (CALPERS)** (916) 326-3000

Administers retirement, health, and related benefit programs for state constitutional officers, legislators, judges, state employees, school employees, city and county employees, and other public agency employees if their employers choose to participate. Teachers retirement is handled by the State Teachers' Retirement System. (See also C307).

S542 *Retirement Benefit Records.* Contents: name, and gross amount of individual benefit payments. Note: Requests must include retiree's name, social security no., and written authorization from the retiree.

S543 **PUBLIC UTILITIES COMMISSION, CALIFORNIA (CPUC)** (415) 703-2782

Regulates intrastate rates of privately-owned energy, telecommunications, water utilities, and transportation companies; supervises their services; sets public liability requirements for public transporters; approves issuance of stocks and bonds, and sale or transfer of utility property; establishes safety rules for railroads, overhead power lines, and gas transmission and storage operations; grants operating rights; authorizes construction of major facilities. The CPUC does not regulate publicly owned utility and transportation systems.

CPUC records are voluminous; the Public Advisors Office can offer guidance in finding information. For information on licensing of electric power plants, see Energy Resources, Conservation and Development Commission.

S544 *Advice Letters.* Applications for changes in rates or service usually not involving a rate increase. Contents: description of proposed change in service or rates, tariff sheet no. Note: Advice letters are filed with the individual CPUC divisions and branches.

S545 *Annual Reports.* Summaries of operations for privately owned. Contents: balance sheet, income statement, depreciation, operations report, list of investments; reports on affiliates and subsidiaries; officers' and directors' addresses, shares owned, compensation; changes in ownership, control, and organization; names of largest stockholders; stock structure; campaign contributions. Note: These are often copies of reports filed with federal regulatory agencies.

S546 *Application.* For permission to revise utility rates, construct or relocate facilities, form a holding company or transfer ownership of a utility, implement non-standard energy contracts, issue stocks and bonds, insure debt, and offer new service. Filed by proceeding no. and applicant company name. Indexed in Docket Office Card Index (S548). Contents: application, testimony, exhibits, third-party comments and petitions, hearing transcripts, environmental impact reports, briefs, and CPUC decision. Note: Applications for certificates of public convenience and necessity (to begin operations or make additions to the plant) contain details on finances, proposed operations, ownership and control, and potential competitors. See also Advice Letters (S544).

S547 *Complaint ("C").* A formal complaint of violation of tariff, Public Utilities Code, CPUC order or regulations, or other requirement. Indexed in Docket Office Card Index (S548). Contents: complaint, utility answer, third-party filings, testimony, exhibits, hearing transcripts, briefs, and CPUC decision. Note: Informal complaints, which precede formal ones, are confidential.

(PUBLIC UTILITIES, CONT.)

S548   **Docket Office Card Index.** An index of public utility rate and service applications ("A"), complaints ("C"), CPUC-initiated investigations ("I"), and rulemakings ("R"). Contents: utility or complainant name and address, proceeding no., filing dates, names of assigned commissioner and administrative law judge, summary of disposition of case, and decision no.

S549   **General Order No. 77-K Report.** For monitoring certain expenditures of large public utilities. Contents: names, titles, duties, compensation, expense accounts, other direct and indirect payments to all executive officers and policymakers, and to all other employees paid a threshold annual salary; dues, donations, subscriptions, and contributions; payments to in-house and outside attorneys and law firms.

S550   **General Order No. 65-A Report.** Files of all financial statements prepared in the normal course of business for utilities with gross annual operating revenues of $200,000 or more, showing operating results and financial conditions; annual reports and other financial statements issued to stockholders.

S551   **Investigation ("I").** Files of a CPUC-initiated investigation of regulated utility or transport company, or of broad industry policy or rate design. Indexed in the Docket Office Card Index (S548). Contents: order instituting investigation of respondent companies, utility and third-party comments and petitions, testimony, exhibits, hearing transcripts, briefs, and CPUC decision.

S552   **Rulemaking ("R").** Files of a CPUC-initiated proceeding to revise or create new rules affecting more than one utility. Indexed in the Docket Office Card Index (S548). Contents: order instituting rulemaking, utility and third-party comments and proposals, and CPUC decision.

S553   **Tariff Schedule.** Published utility rates, charges, service and billing classifications and rules. Contents: table of contents; description of service provided; service area maps; customer eligibility; detail of rates or charges; conditions of service; service and billing rules; sample forms; list of special customer contracts. Current and canceled tariffs are filed in the appropriate branch (energy, telecommunications, and water). Note: All tariff schedules are open for public inspection.

S554   **Transportation Company Files.** Contents (railroads): applications for construction/upgrades; monthly lists of facilities improvements; monthly accident reports; proof of insurance. Contents (trucking companies and charter transportation services): operating permit applications; proof of insurance; compliance investigations and regulations; suspension, reinstatement, or revocation of operating rights (if any); documents filed by carriers that are "on probation." Note: Common carriers with fixed routes apply for certificates of public convenience and necessity. See application (S546).

S555   **Other Public Utility Commission Records.** Service Territory Maps; Lists of Carriers and Utilities; Public Utilities Code.

S556   **REAL ESTATE, DEPARTMENT OF** (916) 227-0931 (licensing), (916) 227-0864 (enforcement)

Licenses and regulates persons in the real estate business, salespersons, real estate brokers, mineral, oil, and gas brokers; issues public reports of subdivided lands; issues permits and endorsements for real property securities dealers. Make advance arrangements to view files.

S557   **Final Subdivision Public Report.** Contains certain information a developer must provide prospective purchasers about the subdivision. Contents: file no.; tract name, location, and size; easements; restrictions; uses and zoning; fire protection; sewage disposal; soil condition (geologic); water; telephone; natural gas; electricity; taxes; streets and roads; mortgage and sale conditions; purchaser signature and address; date.

S558   **Formal Action Files.** Records of official proceedings related to violations of real estate law by real estate licensees and subdivision developers. These are located at district offices. Contents: accusation (formal charge by department), statement to respondent, evidence, proposed decision of hearing officer, and orders and decisions of Real Estate Commissioner. Note: Proceedings become public after a formal accusation has been filed.

S559   **Order Directing Payment Out of the Real Estate Recovery Fund Application.** An order directing payment to defrauded buyers unable to collect from real estate licensees. Information is filed under the names of licensee (defendant) and buyer (plaintiff). Contents: names of plaintiff and defendant, total claim awarded by court, and description of plaintiff's efforts to recover award from defendant.

S560   **Permit to Sell Real Property Securities.** A permit for sale of guaranteed notes, promotional notes, and "advancing" (an arrangement for salesperson to advance own money for investment). Contents: real property securities dealer name and license no.; aggregate value of securities; whether applicant is a partnership or corporation, names and addresses of general partners or principal officers; applicant's audited financial statement; proposed plan of operations; copies of agreements, notes, and trust deeds; description of security for permit; prospectus; advertising copy; resume of default and foreclosure experience for past two years. Note: For real estate corporations and other entities, see Corporations.

S561   **Subdivision Files.** Records of California subdivisions, out-of-state subdivisions for sale in the state, common-interest developments and timeshare developments maintained for regulation of subdivided land sales. Records are located in Sacramento and Los Angeles. Contents: application (description of project, tract no., promotional name, names and addresses of promoters, developers, and others with substantial financial interest), map, title report, environmental impact report or negative declaration, restrictions on use or occupancy, escrow arrangements, bond statements, description of land conditions and services, sales program and advertising, and a public report issued by the Department on the subdivision. Make advance arrangement to view files. Indexed by subdivider or developer name, promotional name, or tract no.

S562   **Other Real Estate Licenses and Permits.** Prepaid rental listing service (companies that charge an advance fee to prospective tenants), real estate brokers and salespersons, and real estate corporations. Contents: see Licenses and Permits (A021).

S563   # REHABILITATION, DEPARTMENT OF (916) 445-3971

Assisting consumers with physical and mental disabilities achieve social and economic independence through employment and independent living opportunities. Assist with vocational rehabilitation of disabled persons. Advocates for the rights and opportunities of the disabled (blind, deaf and hard of hearing, mobility impared) Advises state agencies on compliance with the federal Americans with Disabilities Act.

S564   **California State Plan for Rehabilitation Programs.** Contents: department and division mission and goal statements; section, district, and division program and personnel directories; Consumer Service needs assessment by district; reference material; definitions and planning material; inventory of community rehabilitation programs in California; staff use resource documents; directory of department supported independent rehabilitation service.

(REHABILITATION, CONT.)

S565   *California State Plan for Vocational Rehabilitation Services.* Contents: program descriptions and analysis of vocational rehabilitation services provided by the Department.

S566   *Client Activities by Major Disabling Condition.* Statistical tables listing case loads of all major disabling conditions. Contents: new applications, new case plans nos., total active cases, and case closures. Available from the Statistical Services Bureau.

S567   *County Agency Report Forms.* Statistical reports submitted monthly, quarterly and annually by public and private agencies. Provides summary data on cash and non-cash assistance and social service programs. Filed in county folders. Cumulative totals are posted by the Department's Statistical Services Bureau.

S568   *Rehabilitation Pocket Reference Book.* Contents: demographic and statistical information on disabled population utilization of departmental services. Includes consumer information by sex, race, primary and any secondary disabilities, marital status, source of referral, SSDI and SSI beneficiaries, occupation, income, departmental service utilized, and how used.

S569   *Vocational Rehabilitation District Performance Report.* Contents: fiscal year, new activities, closures, open caseload of severely and non-severely disabled clients for previous and current fiscal year, rehabilitation success ratio by region and district, amount of non-block case service funds, percent cumulative case service encumbrances, annual encumbrances per new plan by region and district, cumulative allotted and filled case-carrier months, and percent distribution of filled case carrier months.

S570   **RESOURCES AGENCY** (916) 653-5656

A cabinet level agency that assists the Governor with supervision of the following departments, boards, and commissions responsible for the state's natural resources: Bay Conservation and Development Commission, Dept. of Boating and Waterways, Colorado River Board of Calif., Calif. Coastal Commission, Calif. Coastal Conservancy, Calif. Tahoe Conservancy, Santa Monica Mountains Conservancy, Dept. of Conservation, Calif. Conservation Corps, Calif. Energy Commission, Dept. of Fish and Game, Dept. of Forestry and Fire Protection, Dept. of Parks and Recreation, Dept. of Water Resources, State Land Commission, and San Francisco Bay Conservation and Development Commission.

Issues Resource Agency directives, and reviews budgets and legislative and administrative policies for these bodies. Issues guidelines for preparing environmental impact reports under the California Environmental Quality Act (CEQA). Forms and oversees periodic task forces on natural resources issues, such as hazardous substances, regulatory reform, law enforcement, Sacramento –San Joaquin Delta, Environmental License Plates, and the Salton Sea.

S571   **SAVINGS AND LOAN, DEPARTMENT OF** (213) 897-8202

Licenses, oversees and regulates state-chartered savings and loan associations, holding companies, and service corporations; approves acquisitions, mergers, conversions, and name changes; dissolves and liquidates associations; authorizes issuances of association stock; processes consumer complaints. The Department does not document association loan statistics (number of loan applications and loans made, loans by census tract or county and dollar amount, etc.); however, each association is required to maintain a public file containing such information. Complaint files are confidential.

S572   **Agency Application.** For establishing an association agency. Contents: description of office space, lease/purchase arrangements, statement of agency functions, operations and personnel, and estimated budget.

S573   **Application Files.** Files include license to establish new association; permission to open new branch or agency office, acquire existing association, merge, or sell additional stock; name change; acquisition of control; investment in service corporations; acquisition of assets or liabilities of another financial institution; conversion. Each application has a separate file, so requests should include "all files" for a specific savings & loan. Note: See also Legal Files (S579).

S574   **Applications.** For permitting, certifying or registering new savings & loan associations, new branches of existing associations, holding companies, and "agencies" (entities established on premises separate from home and branch offices to perform non-banking support services such as data processing). All applications submitted by a single association are consolidated into one file. Files also include Federal Home Loan Bank applications for approval of acquisitions, mergers, and name changes.

S575   **Association Financial Report Files.** For monitoring each association's financial condition. Contents: annual audited financial reports.

S576   **Association Organizational Files.** Contents: articles of incorporation, bylaws, and any amendments.

S577   **Certificate of Authority.** Permission for an applicant to issue stock and raise funds for a new savings & loan, after first obtaining an organizing permit (S580). Contents: proposed articles of incorporation and bylaws; names and addresses of proposed directors, officers, and holders of five percent or more of association stock; names, addresses, salaries, and (sometimes) "biographical sketches" of association officers and employees; proposed capital structure; names, addresses and projected percentage stock holdings of prospective stockholders; description of affirmative action plans and equal employment opportunities; economic report including arrangements for office space, description of primary service area, estimated first-year income and expenses, proposed loan marketing practices and policies, and community's credit needs. Note: The two-year business plan filed by applicant is confidential. Individuals' personal biographies and financial statements are confidential.

S578   **Financial Report Files.** Contents: annual audited financial report for each association; statement of condition, report on branches, branch address, number of accounts, total savings, and total loans for the association. Note: Parts of audits may be withheld under certain circumstances.

S579   **Legal Files.** For the licensing of savings & loan associations. Contents: articles of incorporation, and by-laws. Note: This file is kept separate from the Application Files (S573).

S580   **Organizing Permit.** The first step in creating a new savings & loan association. After the Department issues this permit, the applicant must file a petition for a Certificate of Authority (S577) to issue stock and raise funds for the association. Contents: names, addresses of proposed incorporators; name of proposed association; office location; copy of contract and advertising used for soliciting stock subscriptions; organizing agreement regarding collection and reimbursement of initial funding and names of proposed contributors of initial funding; statement of total funds to be solicited and collected before issuance of certificate of authority.

S581   **Permission to Establish a New Branch of an Existing Association.** Contents: description of proposed new branch office space including lease/ownership arrangements and estimated operating expenses; number of branch office employees; total assets;

(SAVINGS AND LOAN, CONT.)

number and map of operating offices; progress in achieving affirmative action goals; loan marketing practices and policies; record of meeting community's credit needs.

S582   ***Savings and Loan Holding Company Registration.*** Before an entity acquires owner-ship of at least 10% (if association has more than 500 shareholders) or 25% (if fewer than 500 shareholders) of an association's stock, control of the election of a majority of association's directors, or other means of control of an association, it must be approved as a savings & loan holding company, and, after it is approved, it must register with the state. Contents: name, address of registrant and all subsidiaries; ownership and control relationship between holding company and subsidiaries; date of incorporation (or formation of partnership); name and occupation of directors (or partners); number of stock shares and stockholders; primary shareholders' names, and addresses; list of recent contracts, service payments, or other transactions with association subsidiaries. For holding company and its non-association subsidiaries, see financial statements and annual reports to shareholders.

S583   # SECRETARY OF STATE (916) 653-7244

Responsible for examining and filing various financial statements and corporate documents, administering election and campaign reform laws, filing campaign disclosure statements, appointing notaries public, and managing state archives. Documents on file at the Secretary of State's office in Sacramento are among the most heavily used public records in the state. Commercial services are available to research many of these records.

S584   ***Governor's Proclamations.*** Contents: date, subject, and text of Governor's proclamations.

S585   ***Roster—California. State, County, City and Township Officials, State Officials of the United States, and Directory of State Services of the State of California.*** A list of most state agencies. Contents: legislative department national and state legislators; districts, address, Sacramento office phone, and district maps; list of state agencies, officials, and agency functions; agricultural associations, name, and officials; counties, government officials, judges, county seat address and phone, date of Board of Supervisors meeting; election days; incorporated city names, officials, city hall address and phone, date of council meeting, and county; unincorporated areas town name, and county; U.S., and state officers; members of California Congressional delegation and legal holidays (cost: $14.00). Annual.

S586   ***State Appointments List.*** (formerly known as the Registry of Appointments, the Central Appointment Registry, and the Maddy Register). A record of appointive offices. Vol. I lists appointments made by the Governor. Vol. II lists appointments made by the Legislature and other appointing authorities. Contents: entity title; code authority; number of appointments; qualifications; term; bond (if any); oath and code no.; compensation; purpose; names of persons appointed; date of terms. Indexed by title and name of board or commission. Available at county depository libraries.

Political Reform Division (916) 653-6224

S587   ***Campaign Bank Account*** (Form 502). Persons intending to raise funds must also open a campaign account and file Form 502 within 24 hours. Contents: filer's name, address, and phone; office sought; election date; bank, address, phone, account no., and date opened.

S588   ***Campaign Disclosure Statements, Campaign Finance Statements.*** Records of money raised and spent by candidates, ballot measure proponents and opponents, and committees involved in statewide elections. The statements must be filed with the Secretary of State, the registrars of voters in San Francisco and Los Angeles counties, and the county clerk where they reside. Those who must file include candidates and officeholders of state constitutional offices, the Insurance Commissioner, and judges of the Supreme Court. Candidates for the Legislature, Board of Equalization, and Appellate and Superior courts file with the Secretary of State and Clerk of the county of residence. Campaign statements filed before the most recent election are maintained at the State Archives. For campaign disclosure statement filings, see also Fair Political Practices Commission, County Clerk, and City Clerk. Microfiche is available of statements from the earliest to the most recent weekly update. Note: Candidates for city or county office who file with the city or county affected may need to make additional disclosure requirements. Contact the specific city or county. For contents, see S587, S589–S593, S598–S605, and S611.

S589   *Campaign Disclosure Statements Amendments (Form 405).* For changes in any campaign disclosure statement. Contents: filer and treasurer name, address, and phone; form being amended; date; reason. Note: not used to amend Form 410, statement of organization.

S590   *Campaign Disclosure Statements Audits.* Audits of campaign statements (S588) done by the Franchise Tax Board. For contents, see Fair Political Practices Commission.

S591   *Campaign Registration Records (Forms 401, 410, and 415).* For all state, county, and local political campaign committees. Contents: committee name, I.D. no., address, phone, treasurer, other affiliated committees or organizations, and purpose of activity.

S592   *Candidate and Officeholder Campaign Statement—Long Form/Consolidated Campaign Statement (Form 490).* Used by candidates who have raised or spent $1,000 or more. Contents: similar to Form 420 (S599).

S593   *Candidate and Officeholder Campaign Statement—Short Form (Form 470).* For candidates who do not have a controlled committee and who will not receive or spend more than $1,000 in a calendar year. Contents: name, office, mailing address, phone, election, committee name(s) and I.D. nos., address(es), and treasurer's name.

S594   *Lobbying Firm Files.* Contents: firm registration (name, address, phone, responsible officer, individual lobbyists, and lobbyist employers); lobbyist employer authorization (name, address, phone, and responsible officer); certification statements of individual lobbyists (name, address, and phone); firm's quarterly reports (partners and owners, itemization of payments received in connection with legislative or state agency administrative actions lobbied, payments for lobbying to other lobbying firms, who made the payments, and campaign contributions made); lobbyist quarterly reports (activity of expenses paid, incurred, and arranged).

S595   *Lobbying Firms, Lobbyist Employers, Lobbyist Audits.* Audits are done by the Franchise Tax Board and filed by the Secretary of State. Contents (varies if a routine audit or an investigation): names, address, phone, type of audit, whether record-keeping and reporting are adequate, and judgment or statement.

S596   *Lobbyists, Lobbying Firms, Lobbyist Employers Directory.* Contents: name, address, phone, clients, and lobbyist employers by subject category.

S597   *Lobbyist Employer Files.* Quarterly reports of legislative or state administrative actions lobbied and of payments made in connection with lobbying activities.

S598   *Independent Expenditure and Major Donor Committee Campaign Statement (Form 461).* Statements filed by persons who independently spend $1,000 or more in a calendar year for a candidate or campaign, or persons who spend and/or contribute

$10,000 or more directly to or at the behest of a candidate. Contents: donor name; address (residential, business, mailing), and phone; name and address of payee; candidate or ballot measure name(s); office of candidate or committee; ballot no. or letter; amount; cumulative totals donated; loan amount and by whom repaid.

S599   *Recipient Committee Campaign Statement—Long Form (Form 420).* A 34-page report of cumulative contributions of $100 or more from a single source and for use by more than one candidate or ballot measure. Contents: committee name, address, and phone; treasurer's name; contributions (monetary, loans and repayment information, non-monetary, and enforceable promises); name, address, employer, dates, and amounts for each contribution; payments and accrued expenses; miscellaneous adjustments.

S600   *Recipient Committee Campaign Statements—Short Form (Form 450).* Used by committees collecting less than $100 from one source. Contents: name and address of payee, amount and description of expenditure, date, and amount received. Note: Donor or contributor names are not included.

S601   *Recipient Committee Semi-Annual Statement of No Activity (Form 425).* Used by non-controlled recipient committees that have not received contributions or made expenditures during the preceding six-month period. Contents: committee name, address, and phone; treasurer's name, address, and phone; dates.

S602   *Recipient Committee Statement of Organization (Form 410).* Used by recipient committees that receive contributions of $1,000 or more. Contents: committee name, treasurer's mailing address, and phone; description of type of committee and purpose, and disposition of surplus funds.

S603   *Statement of Termination (Form 415).* Used by candidates and recipient committees that are no longer active. Contents: name(s), address, phone, treasurer's name and address, and termination date.

S604   *Supplemental Independent Expenditure Report (Form 465).* Used by a person or committee making independent expenditures for or against a candidate or measure. Contents: name, address of filer, treasurer, name of payee, description and amount of expenditure, filing location of other campaign statements, and date. Note: filed in addition to any other required campaign statements.

S605   *Supplemental Pre-Election Campaign Statement (Form 495).* Used as an attachment to Form 420, 450, or 490 for contributions of $5,000 or more during the six months prior to election by a contributor not otherwise required to file pre-election statements. Contents: filer and treasurer name, address, and phone; election; amount contributed.

Corporate Filing Division (916) 657-5448

S606   *Corporate Information.* Contents: corporate status; date of incorporation; and corporate no.; president and acting agent; any name changes; mailing address. Note: Caller must have the proper corporate name; no cross references are available. Names and addresses of other officers and directors are available in person or by mail for a fee. Information for up to two corporations is available by phone. Listings by classification are available for a fee on computer printout or magnetic tape. Information is available via telephone with a pre-paid account.

S607   *Corporation Files (California).* Registration of companies incorporated in California, renewed annually. Contents: articles of incorporation (name, purpose, directors' names and addresses, and number of shares of stock, and may include class and par value); certificates of amendment to articles (changes of name, purpose, stock structure, and mergers); certificates of dissolution, and merger; agent for service of process; corporate name reservation (claim to a specific name is checked for duplication or confusion with a similar name). Non-profits do not list directors' names. See also C127.

S608   *Corporation Files (foreign or out-of-state).* Registration of foreign or out-of-state corporations doing business in California, renewed annually. Contents: statement and designation (name, state of incorporation, address of head office, address of main office in state, if any, agent for service of process, signature and title of officer signing form, DBA, if any); amendments to statement; statement of good standing from state of incorporation.

S609   ***Domestic Corporation Statements, Corporate Officer Statements.*** Records of corporate officers and directors. Contents: statement by domestic corporation (address of head office, mailing address, names and addresses of top officers); statement by domestic stock corporation (address of head office, mailing address, name and address of chief executive officer, secretary, chief financial officer, and directors for stock corporations); statement by domestic non-profit corporation (address of principal office, if any, name and address of CEO, secretary, CFO, and agent for service of process); agent for service of process; type of business for stock and foreign corporations. Note: All California corporations must file a statement within 90 days of filing articles of incorporation and annually thereafter, if for-profit. Foreign corporations file annually.

S610   ***Statement by Foreign Corporations.*** Contents: name of foreign corporation doing business in California, signatures of two officers, and name of company's California agent. Annual statements of foreign corporations and foreign parent corporations doing business in state.

Elections Division (916) 657-2166

S611   ***Declaration of Candidacy.*** Records of all candidates for judicial, legislative, Congressional, and constitutional offices (including Board of Equalization). Contents: See Registrar of Voters (C477). Note: The Secretary of State receives original declarations forwarded by local registrars of voters. After each election, the declarations are forwarded to the State Archives.

S612   ***Election Results.*** Results are available for state certified races by total, and by city and county. Precinct results are available from the local jurisdiction. For results before November 1962, see State Archives (S616).

Limited Partnership Unit (916) 653-3365

S613   ***Limited Partnership Files.*** Registration of California and foreign limited partnerships doing business in the state. Contents: certificate of limited partnership (partnership name, and address; original recording date if before 1984; general partners' names and addresses; agent for service of process name and address; signatures and titles, date); amendments to certificate (change of name, address, etc.); certificates of continuation, dissolution and cancellation, and name reservation. Foreign limited partnerships application for registration (name, state of formation, executive office address, California address, agent for service of process, and general partners' names and addresses); amendment to application; cancellation of; name reservation. Note: information available by phone for two partnerships (status, date of filing, file no., general partners, agent for service of process, any name changes, mailing address, and name availability check). Prepayment required to receive information via telephone (see also S623).

(SECRETARY OF STATE, CONT.)

Notary Public Division (916) 653-3595

S614   *Notaries Public Information.* For all public notaries in California. Contents: name, current business address, county where current oath and bond are filed, and dates of commission. Note: See also notary records at County Clerk (C143–C145).

Human Resources Office (916) 653-6974

S615   *Oaths of Office Log Book.* Records of the administration of official oaths. Contents: appointment date, name, date of oath, date when logged, term of office, and whether new or name of predecessor.

State Archives (916) 653-7715

S616   *State Archives.* A repository of historic documents of state government, including state election records, State Supreme and Appellate court cases, executive records, legislative records, prison papers, state land deeds, oaths of office, and records retention schedules.

Uniform Commercial Code Division (916) 653-3516

S617   *Tax Liens and Attachments.* Notices of federal tax liens against partnerships and corporations, state tax liens against personal property, and attachment liens against equipment. Contents: taxpayer name, DBA, address, lien type, date of assessment; release of lien (when filed), and attachments.

S618   *Uniform Commercial Code (UCC) Filings.* For debts secured by business and farm equipment, assignment by creditors of accounts payable, inventory, and trust receipts. These offer protection against debtor bankruptcy, insolvency, and default. Contents UCC1—Financing Statement: debtor and lender (name; mailing, residential, and business addresses, social security or federal tax no.); trade name or style; description of assigned property or collateral; signatures. UCC2—Financing Statement of Amendments, Assignment, Continuation, Release, and Termination: same as for UCC1 plus type of change being recorded; UCC3—Request for Information: debtor name, address, and social security or federal tax no. The Secretary of State has financing statements for debts secured by business and farm equipment, accounts payable, inventory, and trust receipts. The County Recorder has statements for debts secured by household goods and furnishings, farm crops, and timber (C446). UCC Filing inquiries should be made in writing using Form UCC-3 and paid in advance.

Special Filings Unit (916) 653-3984

S619   *Bond Filings.* For services required to be bonded including: auctioneer/auction companies, credit service organizations, dance studios, discount buying organizations, employment agencies, employment counselors, immigration consultants, invention developers, job listing services, and nurses' registries. Contents: name and address of bonding company.

S620   *Change of Legal Name Information.* Statewide registration of legal name changes by individuals. Contents: current and, former name. Note: Individuals may also record a legal name change with the County Recorder (C420).

S621   *Corporate Director Candidates Registry (for women and minorities).* Registry of women and minority persons seeking appointments to corporate boards of directors. Contents: candidate's name, address, phone, field of specialization, occupation, education, career history, civic activities and professional affiliations, awards and honors, past and present service on profit and non-profit boards, race/ethnicity, disabilities, sex, and language skills.

S622   ***Durable Power of Attorney for Health Care Registration (DPAHC).*** Non-compulsory filing of an authorization to allow an individual to make health-care decisions for a principal. Contents: registrant's name, address, social security and driver's license no., date and place of birth, attorney in fact, persons authorized to receive registry information, and location of deposit or storage of the DPAHC.

S623   ***Other Secretary of State Records.*** The Limited Partnership Division's Trade Marks Unit has filings for service marks, trademarks (used in intrastate commerce) and claims to names and insignia of organizations. The Special Filings Unit has filings for certificates of incumbency, certification of public officials, city and county charters and amendments, registration of international wills, joint powers agreement or amendment between public agencies, oaths of office, registration of redevelopment agencies, seals of counties, registration for special districts, and successor-in-interest (celebrity filings).

S624   ## SOCIAL SERVICES, DEPARTMENT OF (916) 657-3661

Supervises county administration of income maintenance and social service programs coordinated with federal programs. These include welfare and other financial assistance, job training and employment, abuse prevention for children and adults, child support enforcement, licensing and monitoring of non-medical day and residential care facilities, and eligibility for benefits.

Welfare programs are carried out and monitored at the county level. Records are maintained there and forwarded to the state. See Social Services (C508-C520). The county may choose to have the state administer a program directly. Records for individuals are rarely public. Summary statistics are available for most programs with various breakdowns, such as for county, employment status, number of persons no longer on programs, average payments, number of cases and hours, expenditures, etc.

S625   ***Public Welfare in California.*** A monthly statistical report by county. Contents: county data for nos. and payments; case loads; averages for Aid to Families with Dependent Children, Family Group, Food Stamps, General Relief, and Special Circumstances.

S626   ## STATE BAR OF CALIFORNIA (415) 561-8200

Examines and admits attorneys to practice law in California. Regulates ethical and professional practices of attorneys, investigates complaints, and imposes disciplinary actions. The State Bar Court holds open hearings, and recommends and takes disciplinary action against attorneys. The Bar's Client Security Fund reimburses clients who lose money due to dishonest conduct from a member attorney. Seven areas of specialization exist in which the Bar may certify attorneys: criminal; bankruptcy; family; immigration and nationality; probate, estate planning and trust law; workers compensation and taxation. The State Bar exists under statute as a public corporation and arm of the California Supreme Court. Attorneys must belong and pay dues to the Bar in order to practice law in California. The State Bar is funded primarily by fees paid to it by member attorneys and receives no public financing. Local bar associations exist, but these are unofficial, nongovernmental organizations to which membership is not required.

S627   ***Annual Report.*** Contents: statistics tables and analysis of State Bar membership and admissions; attorney specialty certifications; attorney disciplinary actions including number of complaints made, disbarments, investigations conducted, and settlements.

(STATE BAR, CONT.)

S628   *California Bar Journal.* Contains news articles on major legal and ethical issues and a listing of recently disciplined attorneys (published monthly).

S629   *Disciplinary Records.* Records are made public at the time formal charges are brought by the Bar. Contents: attorney's name; name of complainant; complaint; hearing transcripts; stipulations; exhibits; motions filed and final disposition and rulings of case including whether the case was dismissed without cause or merit, public reproval, probation, suspension, disbarment or appeal.

S630   *Membership Handbook.* Contents: An explanation of what the State Bar is and how it operates; explanation of member benefits; listing of the Bar's 23-member Board of Governors and its executive officers; Rules of Professional Conduct for attorneys; ethics alerts for attorneys; status reporting requirements.

S631   *Membership Records.* Contains information on attorneys admitted to the State Bar, including name, membership no., date of birth, date admitted to Bar, mailing address, phone, history of name changes, history of address changes, undergraduate schools attended, law school attended, participation in any sections or on any committees of State Bar, record and any summaries of discipline activity proceedings, active or inactive status, eligibility to practice, continuing education courses taken, and any notification of arrears on child support payments.

S632   **TEALE DATA CENTER, STEPHEN P.** (916) 263-1816

The state's largest computer facility, provides data processing, storage and retrieval services for state, local, and federal government organizations. (See also S316).

S633   *Annual Report.* Contents: agency directives; revenue and expenses, listings of new technology, current service offerings, typical client applications, and current client list.

S634   *Interagency Agreement.* Agreement between the Data Center and a government agency (customer) for services to be performed. Contents: description of service to be performed, terms of performance, date of commencement, date of completion, terms of payment, invoice number, name of agency receiving services, fund number payment to be drawn from, amount encumbered, program category (code and title), fund title, total amount encumbered to date, and object of expenditure.

S635   *Service Request.* Details data processing services requested from the Data Center by a government agency. Contents: requester's and agency name, billing prefix, department authorization, request title, summary of request, installation address if applicable, contact name, executive decision, security checklist, and cost associated with request.

S636   *Feasibility Study Report.* Summarizes the results of a feasibility study. Studies are conducted to establish the financial basis for the investment of state resources in a project by setting out the reasons for undertaking the project and analyzing its cost and benefits. Contents: description of problem or opportunity the project is intended to address; project objectives; description of selected alternatives considered; discussion and economic analysis of each alternative considered; reason for rejecting alternatives; description of information technology capabilities and conditions that must exist to meet objectives; economic analysis of project life cycle costs; benefits of the project and the costs and benefits of the current method of operation; source for funding the project; detailed project schedule showing key milestones and accomplishments during the project life cycle.

S637   **Resource Utilization Report.** Weekly system utilization report. Provides a primary source of information to ensure adequate availability of central data processing unit resource capacity to meet customers' service level needs. Uses Center's Systems Measurement Unit. Contains 27 individual charts showing average computer mainframe or central processing unit utilization figures for each production project; ratios of workloads; resources required for completion of workloads; usage by technology; usage by customer within each technology for largest use customers.

S638   ## TOXIC SUBSTANCES CONTROL, DEPT. OF (916) 322-0476

Regulates the handling, cleanup, treatment, storage, and disposal of hazardous waste. Issues ID numbers to facilities that generate hazardous waste. Investigates contaminated sites. Maintains database of contaminated sites. Emergency assistance to local agencies during hazardous-materials incidents. The Department maintains most records at regional or field offices in Sacramento, Clovis, Berkeley, Glendale and Long Beach. Other records are kept mostly at the Department's Sacramento headquarters. Operates under the authority of the Secretary of the California Environmental Protection Agency.

S639   **Treatment, Storage and Disposal Permits.** Records related to permits issued to facilities for treatment, storage (longer than 90 days), and/or disposal of hazardous waste. Contents: permit applications; detailed specifications of waste-management units; permits and facility operations plans; California Environmental Quality Act (CEQA) documents; corrective actions; facility closure plans; transcripts of public hearings; responses to public comments.

S640   **Surveillance and Enforcement Files.** Enforcement and surveillance actions taken against hazardous waste facilities, generators, and transporters involving violations of hazardous waste requirements. Contents: field orders, reports of violations, enforcement orders, inspection reports, settlements, and citations.

S641   **Site Mitigation Files.** Records related to the investigation and remediation of specific contaminated sites. Contents: preliminary assessments; remedial action orders; consent orders; voluntary cleanup agreements; remedial investigation workplans and reports; feasibility studies; health risk assessments; remedial action plans; California Environmental Quality Act (CEQA) documents; transcripts of public hearings; responses to public comments; certification documents; emergency response actions.

S642   **CalSites Database.** Listing by zip code of approximately 10,000 California sites with known or suspected contamination. Contents: name, address, zip code, status and I.D. no. of individual sites; summary of site history.

S643   **Pollution Prevention and Technology Development Files.** Contents: certifications of new environmental technologies; technology-demonstration reports; hazardous waste-reduction plans developed by specific companies/facilities.

S644   **Extremely Hazardous Waste Disposal Permit.** Contents: permit no.; waste producer's name, address, and phone; business address and U.S. EPA I.D. no.; proposed hauler name, address, and U.S. EPA I.D. no.; proposed disposal facility name and address; description of waste and quantity; method of disposal.

S645   **Hazardous Waste Complaint.** Contents: if an emergency; log no.; date; time; received by; officials notified; informant's name, address, phone, and whether anonymous; alleged responsible party address, and phone; description of incident; amount and condition of material; response time and comments; investigator.

(TOXIC SUBSTANCE CONTROL, CONT.)

S646   ***Hazardous Waste Facility Permit.*** Part A contents: owner's name, address, and phone; latitude and longitude; business description; if facility is new or pre-existing, if application is new or revised; description of treatment, storage and disposal of waste, and design capacity; specification of wastes and processes to be used; topographic map extending one mile beyond property boundaries; scale drawing and photographs of facility; which activities necessitate a permit; facility name, mailing address and location; principal Standard Industrial Classification; operator's name, address, and phone; if facility is on Native American land. Part B contents: voluminous and detailed data including engineering and environmental plans, location of water in surrounding areas, emergency procedures, approved closure plans, financial documents, listing of equipment used, etc.

S647   ***Hazardous Waste Hauler Registration.*** Contents: business name, address, and phone; U.S. EPA I.D. no.; certificate of insurance; ownership (partners, corporate officers) address/title; name and signature of authorized agent; date.

S648   ***Hazardous Waste Information System (HWIS).*** Computerized data on where hazardous wastes (except infectious and household) are generated and disposed. Contents: waste category descriptions; handling methods; dates; location by county; specific facility; facility type; U.S. EPA I.D. no.; tonnages; where disposed of; facility name, address, mailing address and operator name, and phone; manifest no. Note: Includes data from Hazardous Waste Manifest (S649). Contents can be sorted and displayed in many combinations. Example: total tons of hazardous waste handled by a specific facility.

S649   ***Hazardous Waste Manifest.*** A record of transportation of hazardous waste. Contents: state I.D. no.; manifest document and U.S. EPA I.D. nos.; generator name, mailing address, and phone; transporter, vehicle, or container no. and EPA I.D. no.; disposal facility name and phone; U.S. Department of Transportation data (name, hazard class, identifying characteristics, amount, components, and handling instructions); transporter's receipt and date; indication of discrepancy noted by disposal site owner; certification of receipt by site owner; date; signature. Data are entered into Hazardous Waste Information System (S648).

S650   ***Hazardous Waste Notification Statement.*** Not required if the business has a U.S. EPA I.D. no. Contents: business name, and address; county; Standard Industrial Classification; tax no.; type of business; emergency contact and phone; owner and operator's name, address; type of waste and average annual amounts; date; signature and title.

S651   ***Notification to Counties of Hazardous Waste Discharge—Safe Drinking Water and Toxic Enforcement Act of 1986.*** A notice to counties of possible drinking water contamination. Contents: filer's name, address, and phone; discharge type, location, volume, form, and chemical I.D.; probable discharger; date of filing and probable date of discharge, how discovered. Note: This record is commonly known as "Prop 65 Notification."

S652   ***Vehicle/Container Inspection.*** Contents: business name, address, and phone; contact person; U.S. EPA I.D. no.; hauler registration no.; vehicle make, license or container no., body type; State Highway Patrol certificate no., date, and specification; signature/title; date.

S653   ***Other Toxic Substances Control Records.*** Assessment of Abandoned Sites and Hazardous Substances; Hazardous Waste Facility Monitoring (24-hour data are gathered only from specific sites).

S654   **TRADE AND COMMERCE AGENCY** (916) 322-1394

Promotes and coordinates international and domestic efforts for economic development, job creation, and job retention in the state. Publishes annually the *California Permit Assistance Handbook* (see Bibliography).

Divisions and examples of functions and services include Economic Development (assists businesses locating or expanding their operation in the state), Major Corporate Projects (promotes tax incentives, investment tax credits, and the removal of fees and disclosure requirements), Permit Assistance (counsels the private sector on the permit process in the state), California Office of Small Business (assistance to small business owners), Office of Business Development (enterprise zone programs, start-up and working capital loans and infrastructure development loans to local government in rural areas), Defense Industry Conversion (assistance for converting military facilities to civilian economic enterprises), Enterprise Zone Program (promotes business activity in 34 designated areas), Main Street (revitalization of downtown areas), California Film Commission (assists film production), Office of Strategic Technology (grants to high technology companies), International Trade and Investment, (promotes international trade), Division of Tourism (promotes tourism).

S655   **TRANSPORTATION, DEPARTMENT OF** (916) 654-2852

Popularly known as CalTrans, the department is divided into 18 divisions. Responsibilities include development and operation of state transportation system. CalTrans records are voluminous, with 1,344 types (not all public) using more than 15,000 forms. Only a few examples are covered here. Records of local projects are typically found in the district offices, which manage most of the Department's planning, contracting, construction, and maintenance.

Aeronautics Division (916) 322-9944

S656   *Airport and Heliport Inventory.* For each known airport or heliport in the state. Contents: physical data (location, size of runways, etc.) and operational data (number of planes landing/taking off, etc.).

S657   *Permits.* For airport, heliport, transportation, and any use or activity encroaching on such land. Contents: developer-applicant name, address, and phone; approval permit application; layout plans; topographic map; U.S. Federal Aviation Administration clearance; county Board of Supervisors and planning approval; ownership documents or landowner's approval; California Environmental Quality Act compliance document; other pertinent documents. Note: Personal airports and seaplane airports do not need a permit.

S658   *Statewide Airport System Plan.* A continuously updated document of current status and future needs for all state airports.

S659   *Other Aeronautics Division Publications.* Aid and Loan Programs for Airports; Airport and Heliport Regulations; Airport Pavement Management System Reports; Noise Standards; aeronautical charts; Airport Land Use Commission handbook (see Airports, C025).

S660   **District Records**

These records are kept at each of the department's 12 district offices. Inventory of park and ride lots, bicycle route maps, alternative transportation studies, highway travel forecast projections, alternative route and corridor projections.

(TRANSPORTATION, CONT.)

S661   **Equipment Division** (916) 227-9626

Records include purchases; repairs; projects (by location); inspections; mileage monitoring; motor vehicle mileage; property records; stock inventory; vehicle accidents; vendor files.

S662   **Environmental Division** (916) 653-7136

Responsible for administering the Department's environmental program statewide. Develops and maintains environmental standards, policies, procedures and practices to meet federal and state environmental laws applicable to transportation project development. Records of project files are maintained primarily at district offices and include meteorological data, noise element contour maps, archeological and historical preservation, ambient air sampling, biological studies and assessments.

S663   **Highway Maintenance Division** (916) 654-2224

Responsible for repair and maintenance of pavement, landscaping, and roadside management, rest and vista point areas; snow, ice, and litter; storm damage; signals, pavement marking, lighting, and structures; hazardous-materials response; emergency planning; telecommunications; outdoor advertising; adopt-a-highway; toll bridges; flexible and rigid pavement.

S664   *Highway Maintenance Statistics.* Includes data on slopes, drainage, vegetation, litter and debris, landscaping, public facilities, roadside and rest vista areas, bridges, other structures (pumping plants, tubes, tunnels, ferries, and docks); traffic signals and other facilities; traffic guidance (pavement marking, guardrails, median barriers, etc.); storm, snow, and ice control. Note: Inquiries should be made to Division of Highway Maintenance in Sacramento.

S665   *Other Highway Maintenance Records.* Radio logs; maintenance photos.

S666   **Mass Transportation Division** (916) 654-8811

Allocates and administers grants for transit systems. Records include: local agency plans and bus branch surveys.

S667   **Rail Program** (916) 327-6200

Records include State Rail Program report and abandoned railroad right-of-way acquisition plans.

New Technology and Research Division (916) 654-8899

S668   *New Technology and Research Reports.* Asphalt recycling, alternative fuels, collision avoidance systems, electronic vehicle registration at toll bridges, transportation kiosks, and wheelchair lifts. Research is largely contracted out to the University of California at Berkeley, where the research records are kept.

S669   **Project Development Division** (916) 654-3858

Responsible for project planning, management, and control; design standards; landscaping; sound walls; scenic highways; safety roadside rest areas and vista points; roadside management; review of environmental impact reports; engineering technology development. Records of project files are maintained primarily in district offices and may include topographic maps, meteorological data, noise element contour maps, archaeological and historical preservation (in some cases not publicly available), final environmental documents, ambient air sampling from highway reports, and local assistant records.

Public Affairs Division (916) 654-4020

S670   *Directory of Small Minority and Women-Owned Businesses.* A computerized list of certified businesses, updated every three months. Contents: work category code; county; company name and address; contact person and phone; certification expiration date; if disadvantaged, female, or both; ethnicity. Note: Available on subscription and 24 hours a day on the CalTrans DB/WBE Electronic Information System. See also Department of General Services, Small Business Directory (S298).

S671   *Disadvantaged Business, Minority Business, and Woman Business Enterprise Certification Application.* Contents: business name, address, and phone; federal and/or state I.D. no.; contact person; ownership type; controlling interest ethnicity, sex, and citizenship; if registered with the U.S. Small Business Administration; copies of appropriate permits and licenses; name, title, ethnicity, and sex of management, proprietor, shareholders (if any), company officers, and board of directors; employee information; gross receipts; loans; bonding data; affidavit. Contact district Civil Rights Office.

S672   ### Right of Way Division (916) 654-5413

Responsible for right-of-way engineering, appraisal, vending, and outdoor advertising acquisition, relocation assistance, utility relocation, property management, airspace leasing, and excess land sales. Records related to land and the structures on them are maintained in the district offices.

S673   *Excess Land Files (Director's Deed Files).* Records of state-owned lands sold by the Department. Contents: property appraisal, description maps, photographs, and Director's Deed.

S674   *Land Acquisition Files.* Records of state-owned land acquired for highway purposes. Contents: property appraisal, comparable sales used in appraisal, description, maps, photographs, memoranda of settlement, contracts of sale, and deed.

S675   *Other Right-of-Way Division Records.* Airspace reports; demolition and removal contracts (improvements, barricades, weeds, and hazards); leases; parcel summaries; project files; record maps and index; rehabilitation contracts for state-owned housing relinquishment (property transferred to another state agency); rentals; utilities locations; vacation (property returned to original owner).

Engineering Service Center (916) 227-8704

S676   *Transportation Laboratory, Organization and Services Guide.* Contents: organization chart; guide to sources of information for various stages of construction; expert's name and phone for specific activity or product (epoxy, noise studies); description of lab units (structural testing).

S677   *Transportation Laboratory Records.* Files include results of research and materials testing on a wide range of equipment, materials, and techniques, including adhesives, asphalt, cement, electronic traffic monitoring equipment, metals, paints, plastic, rope, sealants, soil stability, and effects on waterlife of road runoff; research on metal failure, corrosion, soil mechanics, erosion, noise barriers, and vibration effects on private and commercial structures; effects of road design, construction, and maintenance on air quality. Requests for test results and survey reports can be made by letter or phone to the laboratory or the Technical Library.

(TRANSPORTATION, CONT.)

S678 **Construction Division** (916) 654-3081

Part of the Department's Engineering Service Center. Awards and manages billions of dollars worth of contracts (each contract has a specific file no.) for new and ongoing work. Files for construction projects are kept at the district office while active, then sent to State Archives (S616). Records include: bid summary; construction data sheets; historical records; history cards of highway construction (composite record of each contract with index job nos.); index of agreements (work done for other state agencies); map files (cross-sections, blueprints, highway specifications, freeway agreement, aerials, etc.); plant and seal files (chemical make-up, properties of pavement); preliminary and completion reports; project histories (notice to contractors, special provisions, proposal and contract, preliminary and completion reports, expenditures, final letters, photos, and contract change orders); statement of ongoing contracts (unadvertised); unsuccessful bidders books; other construction-related files. Note: Public access to some files may require written permission of the public affairs office. Some highway maps are also filed at the County Recorder's office (C420).

S679 *Highway Log.* Detailed engineering information, by district, for each mile of state highway. Contents: county name and route no.; mile post; federal aid; roadbed construction; average daily traffic; date; significant changes. Maintained at state and district offices by the Division of Highway Maintenance.

S680 **Structures Division** (916) 227-8800

A subdivision of the Engineering Service Center

S681 *As-Built Plans.* Technical construction data (maps, specifications, engineering drawings, etc.) for each structure.

S682 *Bridge Reports.* Results of biennial inspections filed by engineers on all state and local bridges, excluding federal agency bridges (national parks, Native American lands) and the Golden Gate Bridge (special district). Each bridge has a unique code that identifies location and bridge. Files include all correspondence related to the bridge.

S683 *Log of Bridges on State Highways.* An inventory that includes data on tunnels, retaining walls, dams, and ferry boats. Contents: bridge no., name or description, route no. and post mile, city (if within), structure type, length, and width, travel width under bridge, vertical clearance, and type of surface; year built and year of structural changes, capacity, types of transport permits required.

S684 *Structure Maintenance System (SMS).* A computerized database for structures on state highways (bridges, tunnels, tubes, pumping stations, ferries, slips, docks, overhead signs, etc.). Data, derived from the Bridge Reports (S682), include 92 elements required by federal law. Contents: location, structure type, foundation type, custodian, maintenance, owner, proposed improvements, budget, maintenance reports, and cost.

Traffic Operations Division (916) 654-5147

S685 *Encroachment Permit.* Needed for repairing, changing, constructing a state highway, planting beside a highway, tire chain installation business, movie or television filming or any other activity affecting highway use. Contents: location of work; complete description and detailed plans; applicant's name, address, and phone; estimated starting and ending dates; exact extent and scope of work; map; graphic outline of all work with explanations; surety bond (if required).

S686 **Traffic Accident Surveillance and Analysis System (TASAS).** A computerized system based on accident statistics from Statewide Integrated Traffic Reporting System at the state Highway Patrol (S386). Contents: location, number of accidents, time frame. Note: Requests should be submitted in writing to the department.

S687 **Transportation Permit.** Issued and maintained locally for transporting overweight or oversize loads. Contents: name, address, phone; load or equipment; type of vehicle; maximum height, width, length, and overhang; number of axles, tires, etc.; origin, destination, and no. of trips; authorized state highways; if pilot car required; fees; authorized signature; date.

Transportation Planning Division (916) 653-1637

S688 **Transportation Planning Support Information System (TPSIS).** Computerized data from various sources. Contents: accidents (fatal and injury by county and statewide); air passengers (commercial air travel for 14 major airports by airport); California road mileage (number of miles of all except private roads, by county and by jurisdiction); fuel costs (service station survey); fuel sales (includes diesel, gasohol, and aviation); highway gas consumption; licensed drivers (by county and statewide); population (by county and statewide); rail passengers (state Amtrak routes by tickets sold per route); transit passengers (ridership by 11 major transit operators); vehicle miles of travel (number of miles traveled by trucks and all vehicles by county and statewide); vehicle registrations (of all vehicles registered and paid by vehicle type); vehicle speeds (data on percentage of drivers exceeding 55, 60, and 65 mph). Other areas with reported data are aircraft registration, auto costs, ferry passengers, general aviation, intercity bus passengers, ride-sharing, and vessel registrations.

S689 **Other Transportation Licenses and Permits.** Outdoor advertising (as a business); outdoor advertising signs; outdoor advertising structures; viability improvement request; right of way and permits.

S690 **Other Transportation Department Records.** Aerial photography (star and post routes), motion pictures, negatives, photo files and logs (for legal and historical purposes), project files (interstate, primary, and urban), right-of-way strip, slide shows, traffic surveys, urban area boundaries and designations, urban area mapping, video tapes, and work safety statistics.

S691 **TREASURER, STATE** (916) 653-2995

The official state banking agency, responsible for investing temporarily idle public funds, supervising state bond and note sales, safekeeping all securities and personal property owned or pledged to the state, and managing checks and warrants. The Treasurer sits on more than 40 boards and commissions, most of which are involved in bond sales. These include California Educational Facilities Authority, California Pollution Control Financing Authority, California Alternative Energy Source Financing Authority, California Health Facilities Financing Authority, and California Industrial Development Financing Advisory Commission.

S692 **Bond Sales Official Statement.** Contents: bond title; amount offered; purpose; maturity date; detail background information for agency and officials benefiting from the sale; background discussion of the finances of the agency or state (if a general obligation bond); economic and demographic data; legal opinion; tax status; litigation pending (if any); balance sheets; conditions and terms of sale.

S693 **Local Agency Investment Fund Resolution.** An agreement to deposit money with the state for investment. Contents: local agency name and address; agency agreement to

(TREASURER, CONT.)

participate in the fund; names and titles of authorized officials; resolution no. and date when passed by governing body; signature authorized to sign resolutions; agency seal (if used).

S694   ***Pooled Money Investment Board Report.*** A monthly report on investment of funds shows average daily activity, dollar values, number of security transactions, number of time deposits, total daily balances, outstanding warrants, bank names, locations, and amount on deposit. Annual Report gives statistics for year for all funds, average balances, types of securities and their performance, distribution of money into various investments, and names of banks, brokers, dealers and corporations where money is invested.

S695   **WATER RESOURCES CONTROL BOARD, STATE** (916) 657-2390

Shares with Department of Health Services responsibility for the quality of state water. The board allocates surface water (water above ground) rights and administers state and federal funds for improving waste-treatment plants and developing alternative systems. Nine Regional Water Quality Control Boards develop water pollution control programs and establish waste water discharge requirements. Appeals are heard and decided by the state Board. Office of Water Recycling provides information on uses of reclaimed water. Operates under the authority of the Secretary of the California Environmental Protection Agency.

S696   ***Complaint Files.*** Regional Boards compile complaint reports for Toxic Pits Cleanup Act files. Complaints that reach the investigation stage are computerized by the state Board. Contents: investigation report; fines imposed; results of cleanup.

S697   ***Hydrogeological Assessment Report (HAR).*** A report required by Toxic Pit Cleanup Act for discharge or storage of hazardous waste into a pit or pond. Contents: facility name; U.S. EPA I.D. no.; owner's name, and address; operator; location; identification of materials impounded; name and address of person preparing report; chemical makeup of waste; physical plant; climatology; evaporation rates; surface water; hydrology; water quality; ground water, vadose (strata above water table) zone; existing monitoring systems; maps, boring logs; sampling procedures. Note: Reports are kept with the name of company operating the facility and are maintained at the local Regional Water Quality Control Board. The Water Quality Division can direct a caller to the proper regional board.

S698   ***Notification to Counties of Hazardous Waste Discharge ("Prop 65 Notification").*** See Department of Toxic Substances Control (S638).

S699   ***Report of Waste Discharge and Application for National Pollutant Discharge Elimination System Permits (NPDES).*** Required of companies discharging pollutants into any water except a community sewer system. Water Discharge Reports filed with the Regional Water Quality Control Board. Contents: owner's name, address, and phone; owner's agent or lessee; description of facility or activity; location (with map) of facility; description of discharge; source of contributing or transporting water; location of all discharge points; waste discharge requirement permit (permissible discharge levels); monthly self-monitoring reports; staff inspection reports; violation notices; disciplinary orders; environmental document (if needed); how and when changes will be made. Note: The regional board must hold a public hearing near the site of the discharge. The application may be made wholly or partly confidential at the applicant's request. Other permits may be required from city and county planning commissions, city or county health departments, Air Pollution Control District, Coastal Commission, Fish and Game, Forestry, Health Services, and Parks and Recreation; Water Resources, Division of Safety of Dams, Reclamation Board, State Lands Commission, and Tahoe Regional Planning Agency.

S700   **Waste Discharger System.** A computerized summary of monthly data maintained at Regional Water Quality Boards. Contents: physical characteristics of facility; location and type of discharge; date of permit expiration; date of last site inspection; enforcement action (if any).

S701   **Water Appropriation Permits.** Required of anyone diverting water from streams, rivers, and lakes. Exemptions are given to those claiming riparian or pre-1914 rights. Contents: applicant's name, address, and phone; source of water being diverted; location by section, environmental assessment, township, range, base and meridian, and county; landowner name; if rights to access are obtained; purpose, amount; season (beginning and ending dates); description of diversion to storage (acre-feet, dates, intended use, and diversion facilities); project start and end dates; connection to any subdivision registered with Real Estate Department; Fish and Game Department opinion; names of other involved public agencies; proposed use of reclaimed water; description of applicant's existing water rights. Other documents, such as maps, may be required according to the intended purpose of the diversion (crop protection, industrial, mining, power, storage reservoir, etc.).

S702   **Water Diversion and Use Statement.** A statement filed to divert water under a riparian claim or pre-1914 claim. Contents: similar to those for Water Appropriation Permits (S701).

S703   **Other Water Resources Control Board Licenses, Permits, and Certificates.** Certification for weather modifier (rainmaker), liquid-waste hauler, water quality laboratory certification (for water-quality analysis), underground tank-testers, marine vessel pump-out, waste water treatment plant operators, and oil spill clean-up agent license. (Other permits must be obtained from Departments of Fish and Game and Health Services).

S704   # WATER RESOURCES, DEPARTMENT OF (916) 653-5791

Responsible for protecting, developing, and managing the state's water, coordinating master plan for state water (including the State Water Project), and ensuring safety through flood control, supervision of dams, and safe drinking water projects: works with local, state, and federal agencies to develop and manage state water resources.

S705   **California Data Exchange Center (CDEC).** Contents: "real-time" data (via radio at 15-minute intervals) on river flow, rain, snow, water quality, and weather; reservoir conditions, runoff, historical precipitation, and climate from individual stations; river forecasts, flood warnings, road conditions, water supply forecasts, and weather forecasts; drought conditions. Note: available to the public by computer link-up for a subscription fee.

S706   **Dam or Reservoir Construction Certificate Approval Application.** Needed for construction or enlargement of non-federal dams of more than a certain size. Contents: applicant and owner names, and addresses; location by section, township, and range; creek or river being impounded; complete description of dam (type, length, height, thickness at top, elevation, area, capacity, etc.); precipitation, flood, and inflow data; plans and specifications; engineering data; environmental documents; estimated costs; evidence of water rights; other general information. Note: Each project may be required to keep records and make reports on maintenance, operation, engineering, and geologic investigations.

(WATER RESOURCES DEPT., CONT.)

S707   **Dam or Reservoir Removal Approval.** Contents: similar to those of S708.

S708   **Dam or Reservoir Repair or Alteration Approval.** Contents: developer-applicant names and addresses; owners; engineers; location by section, township, and range; creek or river being impounded; description of proposed work; plans and specifications; engineering data; environmental documents.

S709   **Energy Records.** The State Water Project uses electricity to pump water to areas that have contracted for it, especially the Los Angeles area. Surplus electricity is sold. Records include energy sources, purchases, use sales, projections for all the above, costs, and contracts.

S710   **Flood Control Center Files.** Records of river flow on major rivers and tributaries. Contents: river discharge, velocities, and time-weighted predictions.

S711   **Floodway Encroachment Permit.** Needed for any activity (gravel removal, pipes, utility lines, oil or gas drilling, etc.) along or near the banks of the Sacramento and San Joaquin rivers or tributaries and any other area within a flood-control plan. Issued by the Reclamation Board. Contents: applicant's name, address, phone, and signature; description of activity; location by county, section, township, and range; estimated starting and ending dates; names and documents from any other affected agency; adjacent landowner's name and address; signatures of agency trustees responsible for levee maintenance; statement of water rights (if public water is to be diverted); map and topographic features; plans and specifications; profiles of existing elements; environmental assessment and impact reports (if necessary).

S712   **Land and Right-of-Way Records.** Land ownership, lease, and easement records are maintained by geographical location. Each project has a separate file. Contents: project name, title reports, deeds, appraisals, correspondence, legal documents, and all papers relating to that project. Confidential until bid is made or agreement reached.

S713   **Reclamation Board Records.** Plans for flood-control construction projects for Sacramento and San Joaquin Drainage District in cooperation with the U.S. Army Corps of Engineers. See S711.

S714   **State Water Project Management—Bulletin 132.** An annual summary of operations and management of the California State Water Project, including the California Aqueduct, flood control, recreation, fish and wildlife habitat. Contents: contracts, data on water purchasers, water delivered, water stored, construction and maintenance of dams, reservoirs, aqueducts, power plants, pumping plants, costing factors, entitlements to water, etc.

S715   **Water Data Information System (WDIS).** Water quality/quantity data from local monitoring stations for ground and surface water, especially in the Delta and for the State Water Project. Information can vary depending on locality. Data are divided into surface/ground water measurements and water-quality sampling. Contents: surface—cubic feet per second, acre feet, and daily highs and lows in Delta; ground—depth below ground surface to water; quality—chemicals, minerals, bacteria, acidity, and oxygen content; climatological—rainfall. The Department of Water Resources contracts to provide these data to the Water Resources Control Board and other state agencies. Data are available for a fee on magnetic tape, microfiche, and paper.

S716   **Water Resources Photographs.** A large collection of aerial photographs covering much of the state (all coastline and state parks). Arranged geographically. Land and right-of-way photographs are arranged geographically and by subject.

S717   **Watermaster Service.** Records of water rights and supply in areas covered by legal agreements, and of closed or capped wells. Each participant submits monthly data that are summarized in an annual report for a specific water basin. Daily stream flow measurement are made to determine distribution allotments. Contents: monthly amount of water extracted for each well.

S718   *Well Logs.* Each well log is filed according to township, range, and section. Some wells are field located and assigned state well numbers.

S719   *Other Water Resources Records.* Safety of Dams Annual Report; flood control maintenance and repair files.

S720   ## OTHER STATE AGENCIES, AUTHORITIES, BOARDS, COMMISSIONS, AND DEPARTMENTS

Listed below are major departments, offices, boards, and commissions at the state level not covered in this guide. For a complete list of boards and commissions, consult the most recent *State of California Telephone Directory* and *California Roster* (see Bibliography).

Aging, California Commission on
Alcoholic Beverage Control Appeals Board
Alternative Energy Source Financing Authority, California
Arts Council, California
Auctioneer Commission, California
Building Standards Commission
Child Development Programs Advisory Committee
Chiropractic Examiners, Board of
Coastal Conservancy, State
Conservation Corps, California
Control, Board of
Debt Advisory Commission, California
Debt Limit Allocation Committee, California
Developmental Disabilities, Area Boards on
Developmental Disabilities, Council on
Economic Development, Commission for
Economic Opportunity, Department of
Educational Facilities Authority, California
Exposition and State Fair, California
Finance, Commission on State
Fire Marshal, Office of State
Fish and Game Commission
Hazardous Substance Cleanup Arbitration Panel
Health Facilities Financing Authority, California
Health Policy and Data Advisory Commission, California
Heritage Preservation Commission, California
Horse Racing Board, California
Housing Finance Agency, California
Industrial Development Financing Advisory Commission, California
Judicial Performance, Commission on

(OTHER STATE AGENCIES, CONT.)

Law Revision Commission, California
Legislative Audit Committee, Joint
Legislative Counsel, Office of
Lieutenant Governor, Office of the
Mandates, Commission on State
Medical Assistance Commission, California
Military Department
Museum of Science and Industry, California
Native American Heritage Commission
New Motor Vehicle Board
Occupation Information Coordinating Committee, California
Osteopathic Medical Board of California
Parks and Recreation, Department of
Peace Officer Standards and Training, Commission on
Personnel Administration, Department of
Pilot Commissioners, Board of
Planning and Research, Office of
Pollution Control Financing Authority, California
Prison Industry Authority
Public Defender, State
Public Employment Relations Board
Rapid Transit District, Southern California
San Francisco Bay Conservation and Development Commission
Seismic Safety Commission
Sir Francis Drake Commission
Status of Women, Commission on
Student Aid Commission, California
Teachers' Retirement System, State
Traffic Safety, Office of
Transportation Commission, California
Uniform State Laws, California Commission on
Urban Waterfront Area Restoration Financing Authority, California
Veterans Affairs, Department of
Vocational Education, California State Council on
Wildlife Conservation Board
World Trade Commission, California State
Youth and Adult Correctional Agency
Youth Authority, Department of the
Youth Offender Parole Board

Appendix A:
Text of the California Public Records Act

[For an overview of public records law, see A010–A012 in this guide].

Section 6250. Intent

In enacting this chapter, the Legislature, mindful of the right of individuals to privacy, finds and declares that access to information concerning the conduct of the people's business is a fundamental and necessary right of every person in this state.

Sec. 6251. Title

This chapter shall be known and may be cited as the California Public Records Act.

Sec. 6252. Definitions

As used in this chapter:

(a) "State agency" means every state office, officer, department, division, bureau, board, and commission or other state body or agency, except those agencies provided for in Article IV [Legislative branch] (except Section 20 thereof) or Article VI [Judicial branch] of the California Constitution.

(b) "Local agency" includes a county; city, whether general law or chartered; city and county; school district; municipal corporation; district; political subdivision; or any board, commission or agency thereof; other local public agency; or nonprofit organizations of local governmental agencies and officials which are supported solely by public funds.

(c) "Person" includes any natural person, corporation, partnership, limited liability company, firm, or association.

(d) "Public records" includes any writing containing information relating to the conduct of the public's business prepared, owned, used, or retained by any state or local agency regardless of physical form or characteristics. "Public records" in the custody of, or maintained by, the Governor's office means any writing prepared on or after January 6, 1975.

(e) "Writing" means handwriting, typewriting, printing, photostating, photographing, and every other means of recording upon any form of communication or representation, including letters, words, pictures, sounds, or symbols, or combination thereof, and all papers, maps, magnetic or paper tapes, photographic films and prints, magnetic or punched cards, discs, drums, and other documents.

(f) "Member of the public" means any person, except a member, agent, officer, or employee of a federal, state, or local agency acting within the scope of his or her membership, agency, office, or employment.

Sec. 6253. Records inspection guidelines

(a) Public records are open to inspection at all times during the office hours of the state or local agency and every person has a right to inspect any public record, except as hereafter provided. Every agency may adopt regulations stating the procedures to be followed when making its records available in accordance with this section.

The following state and local bodies shall establish written guidelines for accessibility of records. A copy of these guidelines shall be posted in a conspicuous public place at the offices of these bodies, and a copy of the guidelines shall be available upon request free of charge to any person requesting that body's records:

> Department of Motor Vehicles, Department of Consumer Affairs, Department of Transportation, Department of Real Estate, Department of Corrections, Department of the Youth Authority, Department of Justice, Department of Insurance, Department of Corporations, Secretary of State, State Air Resources Board, Department of Water Resources, Department of Parks and Recreation, San Francisco Bay Conservation and Development Commission, State Board of Equalization, State Department of Health

Services, Employment Development Department, State Department of Social Services, State Department of Mental Health, State Department of Developmental Services, State Department of Alcohol and Drug Abuse, Office of Statewide Health Planning and Development, Public Employees' Retirement System, Teachers' Retirement Board, Department of Industrial Relations, Department of General Services, Department of Veterans Affairs, Public Utilities Commission, California Coastal Commission, State Water Quality Control Board, San Francisco Bay Area Rapid Transit District, all regional water quality control boards, Los Angeles County Air Pollution Control District, Bay Area Air Quality Management District, Golden Gate Bridge, Highway and Transportation District, Department of Toxic Substances Control, Office of Environmental Health Hazard Assessment

(b) Guidelines and regulations adopted pursuant to this section shall be consistent with all other sections of this chapter and shall reflect the intention of the Legislature to make the records accessible to the public. The guidelines and regulations adopted pursuant to this section shall not operate to limit the hours public records are open for inspection as prescribed in subdivision (a).

Sec. 6253.1. Adoption of rules for increased access

Except as otherwise prohibited by law, a state or local agency may adopt requirements for itself which allow greater access to records than prescribed by the minimum standards set forth in this chapter.

Sec. 6253.5. Inspection of election petitions

Notwithstanding Sections 6252 and 6253, statewide, county, city, and district initiative, referendum, and recall petitions, petitions circulated pursuant to Section 5091 of the Education Code, petitions for the reorganization of school districts submitted pursuant to Article 1 (commencing with Section 35700) of Chapter 4 of Part 21 of the Education Code, petitions for the reorganization of community college districts submitted pursuant to Part 46 (commencing with Section 74000) of the Education Code and all memoranda prepared by the county elections officials in the examination of the petitions indicating which registered voters have signed particular petitions shall not be deemed to be public records and shall not be open to inspection except by the public officer or public employees who have the duty of receiving, examining or preserving the petitions or who are responsible for the preparation of that memoranda and, if the petition is found to be insufficient, by the proponents of the petition and the representatives of the proponents as may be designated by the proponents in writing in order to determine which signatures were disqualified and the reasons therefor. However, the Attorney General, the Secretary of State, the Fair Political Practices Commission, a district attorney, a school district or a community college district attorney, and a city attorney shall be permitted to examine the material upon approval of the appropriate superior court.

If the proponents of a petition are permitted to examine the petition and memoranda, the examination shall commence not later than 21 days after certification of insufficiency.

(a) As used in this section, "petition" shall mean any petition to which a registered voter has affixed his or her signature.

(b) As used in this section, "proponents of the petition" means the following:

(1) For statewide initiative and referendum measures, the person or persons who submit a draft of a petition proposing the measure to the Attorney General with a request that he or she prepare a title and summary of the chief purpose and points of the proposed measure.

(2) For other initiative and referenda on measures, the person or persons who publish a notice of intention to circulate petitions, or, where publication is not required, who file petitions with the elections official.

(3) For recall measures, the person or persons defined in Section 343 of the Elections Code.

(4) For petitions circulated pursuant to Section 5091 of the Education Code, the person or persons having charge of the petition who submit the petition to the county superintendent of schools.

(5) For petitions circulated pursuant to Article 1 (commencing with Section 35700) of Chapter 4 of Part 21 of the Education Code, the person or persons designated as chief petitioners under Section 35701 of the Education Code.

(6) For petitions circulated pursuant to Part 46 (commencing with Section 74000) of the Education Code, the person or persons designated as chief petitioners under Sections 74102, 74133, and 74152 of the Education Code.

Sec. 6253.6. Ballots

(a) Notwithstanding the provisions of Sections 6252 and 6253, information compiled by public officers or public employees revealing the identity of persons who have requested bilingual ballots or ballot pamphlets, made in accordance with any federal or state law, or other data that would reveal the identity of the requester, shall not be deemed to be public records and shall not be provided to any person other than public officers or public employees who are responsible for receiving those requests and processing the same.

(b) Nothing contained in subdivision (a) shall be construed as prohibiting any person who is otherwise authorized by law from examining election materials, including, but not limited to, affidavits of registration, provided that requests for bilingual ballots or ballot pamphlets shall be subject to the restrictions contained in subdivision (a).

Sec. 6254. Exempted records

Except as provided in Section 6254.7, nothing in this chapter shall be construed to require disclosure of records that are any of the following:

(a) Preliminary drafts, notes, or interagency or intra-agency memoranda which are not retained by the public agency in the ordinary course of business, provided that the public interest in withholding those records clearly outweighs the public interest in disclosure.

(b) Records pertaining to pending litigation to which the public agency is a party, or to claims made pursuant to Division 3.6 (commencing with Section 810), until the pending litigation or claim has been finally adjudicated or otherwise settled.

(c) Personnel, medical, or similar files, the disclosure of which would constitute an unwarranted invasion of personal privacy.

(d) Contained in or related to:

(1) Applications filed with any state agency responsible for the regulation or supervision of the issuance of securities or of financial institutions, including, but not limited to, banks, savings and loan associations, industrial loan companies, credit unions, and insurance companies.

(2) Examination, operating, or condition reports prepared by, on behalf of, or for the use of, any state agency referred to in paragraph (1).

(3) Preliminary drafts, notes, or interagency or intra-agency communication prepared by, on behalf of, or for the use of, any state agency referred to in paragraph (1).

(4) Information received in confidence by any state agency referred to in paragraph (1).

(e) Geological and geophysical data, plant production data, and similar information relating to utility systems development, or market or crop reports, which are obtained in confidence from any person.

(f) Records of complaints to, or investigations conducted by, or records of intelligence information or security procedures of, the office of the Attorney General and the Department of Justice, and any state or local police agency, or any investigatory or security files compiled by any other state or local police agency, or any investigatory or security files compiled by any other state or local agency for correctional, law enforcement, or licensing purposes, except that state and local law enforcement agencies shall disclose the names and addresses of persons involved in, or witnesses other than confidential informants to, the incident, the description of any property involved, the date, time, and location of the incident, all diagrams, statements of the parties involved in the incident, the statements of all witnesses, other than confidential informants, to the victims of an incident, or an authorized representative thereof, an insurance carrier against which a claim has been or might be made, and any person suffering bodily injury or property damage or loss, as the result of the incident caused by arson, burglary, fire, explosion, larceny, robbery, car-jacking, vandalism, vehicle theft, or a crime as defined by subdivision (c) of Section 13960, unless the disclosure would endanger the safety of a witness or other person involved in the investigation, or unless disclosure would endanger the successful completion of the investigation or a related investigation. However, nothing in this division shall require the disclosure of that portion of those investigative files which reflect the analysis or conclusions of the investigating officer.

Other provisions of this subdivision notwithstanding, state and local law enforcement agencies shall make public the following information, except to the extent that disclosure of a particular item of information would endanger the safety of a person involved in an investigation or would endanger the successful completion of the investigation or a related investigation:

(1) The full name, current address, and occupation of every individual arrested by the agency, the individual's physical description including date of birth, color of eyes and hair, sex, height and weight, the time and date of arrest, the time and date of booking, the location of the arrest, the factual circumstances surrounding the arrest, the amount of bail set, the time and manner of release or the location where the individual is currently being held, and all charges the individual is being held upon, including any outstanding warrants from other jurisdictions and parole or probation holds.

(2) Subject to the restrictions imposed by Section 841.5 of the Penal Code, the time, substance, and location of all complaints or requests for assistance received by the agency and the time and nature of the response thereto, including, to the extent the information regarding crimes alleged or committed or any other incident investigated is recorded, the time, date, and location of occurrence, the time and date of the report, the name, age, and current address of the victim, except that the address of the victim of any crime defined by Section 261, 264, 264.1, 273a, 273d, 273.5, 286, 288, 288a, 289, 422.6, 422.7, or 422.75 of the Penal Code shall not be disclosed, the factual circumstances surrounding the crime or incident, and a general description of any injuries, property, or weapons involved. The name of a victim of any crime defined by Section 261, 264, 264.1, 273a, 273d, 273.5, 286, 288, 288a, 289, 422.6, 422.7, or 422.75 of the Penal Code may be withheld at the victim's request, or at the request of the victim's parent or guardian if the victim is a minor. When a person is the victim of more than one crime, information disclosing that the person is a victim of a crime defined by Section 261, 264, 264.1, 273a, 273d, 286, 288, 288a, 289, 422.6, 422.7, or 422.75 of the Penal Code may be deleted at the request of the victim, or the victim's parent or guardian if the victim is a minor, in making the report of the crime, or of any crime or incident accompanying the crime, available to the public in compliance with the requirements of this paragraph.

(g) Test questions, scoring keys, and other examination data used to administer a licensing examination, examination for employment, or academic examination, except as provided for in Chapter 3 (commencing with Section 99150) of Part 65 of the Education Code.

(h) The contents of real estate appraisals or engineering or feasibility estimates and evaluations made for or by the state or local agency relative to the acquisition of property, or to prospective public supply and construction contracts, until all of the property has been acquired or all of the contract agreement obtained. However, the law of eminent domain shall not be affected by this provision.

(i) Information required from any taxpayer in connection with the collection of local taxes which is received in confidence and the disclosure of the information to other persons would result in unfair competitive disadvantage to the person supplying the information.

(j) Library circulation records kept for the purpose of identifying the borrower of items available in libraries, and library and museum materials made or acquired and presented solely for reference or exhibition purposes. The exemption in this subdivision shall not apply to records of fines imposed on the borrowers.

(k) Records the disclosure of which is exempted or prohibited pursuant to federal or state law, including, but not limited to, provisions of the Evidence Code relating to privilege.

(l) Correspondence of and to the Governor or employees of the Governor's office or in the custody of or maintained by the Governor's legal affairs secretary, provided that public records shall not be transferred to the custody of the Governor's legal affairs secretary to evade the disclosure provisions of this chapter.

(m) In the custody of or maintained by the Legislative Counsel, except those records in the public data base maintained by the Legislative Counsel that are described in Section 10248.

(n) Statements of personal worth or personal financial data required by a licensing agency and filed by an applicant with the licensing agency to establish his or her personal qualification for the license, certificate, or permit applied for.

(o) Financial data contained in applications for financing under Division 27 (commencing with Section 44500) of the Health and Safety Code, where an authorized officer of the California Pollution Control Financing Authority determines that disclosure of the financial data would be competitively injurious to the applicant and the data is required in order to obtain guarantees from the United States Small Business Administration. The California Pollution Control Financing Authority shall adopt rules for review of individual requests for confidentiality under this section and for making available to the public those portions of an application which are subject to disclosure under this chapter.

(p) Records of state agencies related to activities governed by Chapter 10.3 (commencing with Section 3512) of Division 4 of Title 1, Chapter 10.5 (commencing with Section 3525) of Division 4 of Title 1, and Chapter 12 (commencing with Section 3560) of Division 4 of Title 1, which reveal a state agency's deliberative processes, impressions, evaluations, opinions, recommendations, meeting minutes, research, work products, theories, or strategy, or which provide instruction, advice, or training to employees who do not have full collective bargaining and representation rights under the above chapters. Nothing in this subdivision shall be construed to limit the disclosure duties of a state agency with respect to any other records relating to the activities governed by the employee relations acts referred to in this subdivision.

(q) Records of state agencies related to activities governed by Articles 2.6 (commencing with Section 14081), 2.8 (commencing with Section 14087.5), and 2.91 (commencing with Section 14089) of Chapter 7 of Part 3 of Division 9 of the Welfare and Institutions Code, which reveal the special negotiator's deliberative processes, discussions, communications, or any other portion of the negotiations with providers of health care services, impressions, opinions, recommendations, meeting minutes, research, work product, theories, or strategy, or which provide instruction, advice, or training to employees.

Except for the portion of a contract containing the rates of payment, contracts for inpatient services entered into pursuant to these articles, on or after April 1, 1984, shall be open to inspection one year after they are fully executed. In the event that a contract for inpatient services which is entered into prior to April 1, 1984, is amended on or after April 1, 1984, the amendment, except for any portion containing the rates of payment, shall be open to inspection one year after it is fully executed. If the California Medical Assistance Commission enters into contracts with health care providers for other than inpatient hospital services, those contracts shall be open to inspection one year after they are fully executed.

Three years after a contract or amendment is open to inspection under this subdivision, the portion of the contract or amendment containing the rates of payment shall be open to inspection.

Notwithstanding any other provision of law, the entire contract or amendment shall be open to inspection by the Joint Legislative Audit Committee. The Joint Legislative Audit Committee shall maintain the confidentiality of the contracts and amendments until such time as a contract or amendment is fully open to inspection by the public.

(r) Records of Native American graves, cemeteries, and sacred places maintained by the Native American Heritage Commission.

(s) A final accreditation report of the Joint Commission on Accreditation of Hospitals which has been transmitted to the State Department of Health Services pursuant to subdivision (b) of Section 1282 of the Health and Safety Code.

(t) Records of a local hospital district, formed pursuant to Division 23 (commencing with Section 32000) of the Health and Safety Code, or the records of a municipal hospital, formed pursuant to Article 7 (commencing with Section 37600) or Article 8 (commencing with Section 37650) of Chapter 5 of Division 3 of Title 4 of this code, which relate to any contract with an insurer or nonprofit hospital service plan for inpatient or outpatient services for alternative rates pursuant to Section 10133 or 11512 of the Insurance Code. However, the record shall be open to inspection within one year after the contract is fully executed.

(u) Information contained in applications for licenses to carry firearms issued pursuant to Section 12050 of the Penal Code by the sheriff of a county or the chief or other head of a municipal police department which indicates when or where the applicant is vulnerable to attack or which concerns the applicant's medical or psychological history or that of members of his or her family.

(v)(1) Records of the Major Risk Medical Insurance Program related to activities governed by Part 6.3 (commencing with Section 12695), and Part 6.5 (commencing with Section 12700), of Division 2 of the Insurance Code, and which reveal the deliberative processes, discussions, communications, or any other portion of the negotiations with health plans, or the impressions, opinions, recommendations, meeting minutes, research, work product, theories, or strategy of the board or its staff, or records that provide instructions, advice, or training to employees.

(2)(A) Except for the portion of a contract that contains the rates of payment, contractor health coverage entered into pursuant to Part 6.3 (commencing with Section 12695), or Part 6.5 (commencing with Section 12700), of Division 2 of the Insurance Code, on or after July 1, 1991, shall be open to inspection one year after they have been fully executed.

(B) In the event that a contract for health coverage that is entered into prior to July 1, 1991, is amended on or after July 1, 1991, the amendment, except for any portion containing the rates of payment shall be open to inspection one year after the amendment has been fully executed.

(3) Three years after a contract or amendment is open to inspection pursuant to this subdivision, the portion of the contract or amendment containing the rates of payment shall be open to inspection.

(4) Notwithstanding any other provision of law, the entire contract or amendments to a contract shall be open to inspection by the Joint Legislative Audit Committee. The Joint Legislative Audit Committee shall maintain the confidentiality of the contracts and amendments thereto, until the contract or amendments to a contract is open to inspection pursuant to paragraph (3).

(w)(1) Records of the Major Risk Medical Insurance Program related to activities governed by Chapter 14 (commencing with Section 10700) of Part 2 of Division 2 of the Insurance Code, and that reveal the deliberative processes, discussions, communications, or any other portion of the negotiations with health plans, or the impressions, opinions, recommendations, meeting minutes, research, work product, theories, or strategy of the board or its staff, or records that provide instructions, advice, or training to employees.

(2) Except for the portion of a contract that contains the rates of payment, contracts for health coverage entered into pursuant to Chapter 14 (commencing with Section 10700) of Part 2 of Division 2 of the Insurance Code, on or after January 1, 1993, shall be open to inspection one year after they have been fully executed.

(3) Notwithstanding any other provision of law, the entire contract or amendments to a contract shall be open to inspection by the Joint Legislative Audit Committee. The Joint Legislative Audit Committee shall maintain the confidentiality of the contracts and amendments thereto, until the contract or amendments to a contract is open to inspection pursuant to paragraph (2).

(x) Financial data contained in applications for registration, or registration renewal, as a service contractor filed with the Director of the Department of Consumer Affairs pursuant to Chapter 20 (commencing with Section 9800) of Division 3 of the Business and Professions Code, for the purpose of establishing the service contractor's net worth, or, financial data regarding the funded accounts held in escrow for service contracts held in force in this state by a service contractor.

Nothing in this section prevents any agency from opening its records concerning the administration of the agency to public inspection, unless disclosure is otherwise prohibited by law.

Nothing in this section prevents any health facility from disclosing to a certified bargaining agent relevant financing information pursuant to Section 8 of the National Labor Relations Act.

Disclosure of residence, mailing address or results of test for competency to safely operate motor vehicle

Sec. 6254.1. Exemption of residence or mailing address

(a) Except as provided in section 6254.7, nothing in this chapter requires disclosure of records that are the residence address of any person contained in the records of the Department of Housing and Community Development, if the person has requested confidentiality of that information, in accordance with Section 18081 of the Health and Safety Code.

(b) Nothing in this chapter requires the disclosure of the residence or mailing address of any person in any record of the Department of Motor Vehicles, except in accordance with Section 1808.21 of the Vehicle Code.

(c) Nothing in this chapter requires the disclosure of the results of a test undertaken pursuant to Section 12804.8 of the Vehicle Code.

Sec. 6254.2. Pesticide safety and efficacy records

(a) Nothing in this chapter exempts from public disclosure the same categories of pesticide safety and efficacy information that are disclosable under paragraph (1) of subsection (d) of Section 10 of the Federal Insecticide, Fungicide, and Rodenticide Act (7 U.S.C. Sec. 136h(d)(1)), if the individual requesting the information is not an employee or agent specified in subdivision (h) and signs the affirmation specified in subdivision (h).

(b) The Director of Food and Agriculture, upon his or her initiative, or upon receipt of a request pursuant to the California Public Records Act (Chapter 3.5 (commencing with Section 6250) of Division 7 of Title 1) for the release of data submitted and designated as a trade secret by a registrant or applicant, shall determine whether any or all of the data so submitted is a properly designated trade secret. In order to assure that the interested public has an opportunity to obtain and review pesticide safety and efficacy data and to comment prior to the expiration of the public comment period on a proposed pesticide registration, the director shall provide notice to interested persons when an application for registration enters the registration evaluation process.

(c) If the director determines that the data is not a trade secret, the director shall notify the registrant or applicant by certified mail.

(d) The registrant or applicant shall have 30 days after receipt of this notification to provide the director with a complete justification and statement of the grounds on which the trade secret privilege is claimed. This justification and statement shall be submitted by certified mail.

(e) The director shall determine whether the data is protected as a trade secret within 15 days after receipt of the justification and statement or, if no justification and statement is filed, within 45 days of the original notice. The director shall notify the registrant or applicant and any party who has requested the data pursuant to the California Public Records Act of that determination by certified mail. If the director determines that the data is not protected as a trade secret, the final notice shall also specify a date, not sooner than 15 days after the date of mailing of the final notice, when the data shall be available to any person requesting information pursuant to subdivision (a).

(f) "Trade secret" means data that is nondisclosable under paragraph (1) of subsection (d) of Section 10 of the Federal Insecticide, Fungicide, and Rodenticide Act.

(g) This section shall be operative only so long as, and to the extent that, enforcement of paragraph (1) of subsection (d) of Section 10 of the Federal Insecticide, Fungicide, and Rodenticide Act has not been enjoined by federal court order, and shall become inoperative if an unappealable federal court judgment or decision becomes final that holds that paragraph invalid, to the extent of the invalidity.

(h) The Director of Food and Agriculture shall not knowingly disclose information submitted by an applicant or registrant pursuant to Article 4 (commencing with Section 12811) of Chapter 2 of Division 7 of the Food and Agricultural Code to any employee or agent of any business or other entity engaged in the production, sale, or distribution of pesticides in countries other than the United States or in other countries in addition to the United States, or to any other person who intends to deliver this information to any foreign or multi-national business or entity, unless the applicant or registrant consents to this disclosure. To implement this subdivision, the director shall require the following affirmation to be signed by the person who requests information pursuant to this section:

Affirmation of Status:

This affirmation is required by Section 6254.2 of the Government Code.

I have requested access to information submitted by an applicant or registrant under the California Food and Agricultural Code. I hereby affirm all of the following:

(1) I do not seek access to the information for purposes of delivering it or offering it for sale to any business or other entity engaged in the production, sale, or distribution of pesticides in countries other than the United States or in other countries in addition to the United States, or to the agents or employees of such a business or entity.

(2) I will not purposefully deliver or negligently cause the data to be delivered to such a business or entity or its agents or employees.

I am aware that I may be subject to criminal penalties under Section 118 of the Penal Code if I make any statement of material facts knowing that the statement is false or if I willfully conceal any material fact.

[Include at the bottom of the request for space for, name, signature, organization, address, date, request no, and client, if you are requesting access on behalf of someone other than the organization or affiliation listed above.]

(i) Notwithstanding any other provision of this section, the Director of Food and Agriculture may disclose information submitted by an applicant or registrant to any person in connection with a public proceeding conducted under law or regulation, if the director determines that the information is needed to determine whether a pesticide, or any ingredient of any pesticide, causes unreasonable adverse effects on health or the environment.

(j) The director shall maintain records of the names of persons to whom data is disclosed pursuant to this section and the persons or organizations they represent and shall inform the applicant or registrant of the names and the affiliation of these persons.

(k) Section 118 of the Penal Code applies to any affirmation made pursuant to this section.

(l) Any officer or employee of the state or former officer or employee of the state who, because of this employment or official position, obtains possession of, or has access to, material which is prohibited from disclosure by this section, and who, knowing that disclosure of this material is prohibited by this section, willfully discloses the material in any manner to any person not entitled to receive it, shall, upon conviction, be punished by a fine of not more than ten thousand dollars ($10,000), or by imprisonment in the county jail for not more than one year, or by both fine and imprisonment.

For purposes of this subdivision, any contractor with the state who is furnished information pursuant to this section, or any employee of any contractor, shall be considered an employee of the state.

(m) This section does not prohibit any person from maintaining a civil action for wrongful disclosure of trade secrets.

(n) The director may limit an individual to one request per month pursuant to this section if the director determines that a person has made a frivolous request within the past 12-month period.

Sec. 6254.3. Confidentiality of state and school district employee home address and phone number

(a) The home addresses and home telephone numbers of state employees and employees of a school district or county office of education shall not be deemed to be public records and shall not be open to public inspection, except that disclosure of that information may be made as follows:

(1) To an agent, or a family member of the individual to whom the information pertains.

(2) To an officer or employee of another state agency, school district, or county office of education when necessary for the performance of its official duties.

(3) To an employee organization pursuant to regulations and decisions of the Public Employment Relations Board, except that the home addresses and home telephone

numbers of employees performing law enforcement-related functions shall not be disclosed.

(4) To an agent or employee of a health benefit plan providing health services or administering claims for health services to state, school districts, and county office of education employees and their enrolled dependents, for the purpose of providing the health services or administering claims for employees and their enrolled dependents.

(b) Upon written request of any employee, a state agency, school district, or county office of education shall not disclose the employee's home address or home telephone number pursuant to paragraph (3) of subdivision (a) and an agency shall remove the employee's home address and home telephone number from any mailing list maintained by the agency, except if the list is used exclusively by the agency to contact the employee.

Sec. 6254.4. Voter registration records

(a) The home address, telephone number, occupation, precinct number, and prior registration information shown on the voter registration card for all registered voters is confidential, and shall not be disclosed to any person, except pursuant to Section 615 of the Elections Code.

(b) For purposes of this section, "home address" means street address only, and does not include an individual's city or post office address.

Sec. 6254.5. Agency waivers of exemptions

Notwithstanding any other provisions of the law, whenever a state or local agency discloses a public record which is otherwise exempt from this chapter, to any member of the public, this disclosure shall constitute a waiver of the exemptions specified in Sections 6254, 6254.7, or other similar provisions of law. For purposes of this section, "agency" includes a member, agent, officer, or employee of the agency acting within the scope of his or her membership, agency, office, or employment.

This section, however, shall not apply to disclosures:

(a) Made pursuant to the Information Practices Act (commencing with Section 1798 of the Civil Code) or discovery proceedings.

(b) Made through other legal proceedings.

(c) Within the scope of disclosure of a statute which limits disclosure of specified writings to certain purposes.

(d) Not required by law, and prohibited by formal action of an elected legislative body of the local agency which retains the writings.

(e) Made to any governmental agency which agrees to treat the disclosed material as confidential. Only persons authorized in writing by the person in charge of the agency shall be permitted to obtain the information. Any information obtained by the agency shall only be used for purposes which are consistent with existing law.

(f) Of records relating to a financial institution or an affiliate thereof, if the disclosures are made to the financial institution or affiliate by a state agency responsible for the regulation or supervision of the financial institution or affiliate.

(g) Of records relating to any person that is subject to the jurisdiction of the Department of Corporations, if the disclosures are made to the person that is the subject of the records for the purpose of corrective action by that person, or if a corporation, to an officer, director, or other key personnel of the corporation for the purpose of corrective action, or to any other person to the extent necessary to obtain information from that person for the purpose of an investigation by the Department of Corporations.

Sec. 6254.6. Private industry wage data

Whenever a city and county or a joint powers agency, pursuant to a mandatory statute or charter provision to collect private industry wage data for salary setting purposes, or a contract entered to implement that mandate, is provided this data by the federal Bureau of Labor Statistics on the basis that the identity of private industry employers shall remain confidential, the identity of the employers shall not be open to the public or be admitted as evidence in any action or special proceeding.

Sec. 6254.7. Air pollution data

(a) All information, analyses, plans, or specifications that disclose the nature, extent, quantity, or degree of air contaminants or other pollution which any article, machine, equipment, or other contrivance will produce, which any air pollution control district or air quality management district, or any other state or local agency or district, requires any applicant to provide before the applicant builds, erects, alters, replaces, operates, sells, rents, or uses the article, machine, equipment, or other contrivance, are public records.

(b) All air or other pollution monitoring data, including data compiled from stationary sources, are public records.

(c) All records of notices and orders directed to the owner of any building of violations of housing or building codes, ordinances, statutes, or regulations which constitute violations of standards provided in Section 1941.1 of the Civil Code, and records of subsequent action with respect to those notices and orders, are public records.

(d) Except as otherwise provided in subdivision (e) and Chapter 3 (commencing with Section 99150) of Part 65 of the Education Code, trade secrets are not public records under this section. "Trade secrets," as used in this section, may include, but are not limited to, any formula, plan, pattern, process, tool, mechanism, compound, procedure, production data, or compilation of information which is not patented, which is known only to certain individuals within a commercial concern who are using it to fabricate, produce, or compound an article of trade or a service having commercial value and which gives its user an opportunity to obtain a business advantage over competitors who do not know or use it.

(e) Notwithstanding any other provision of law, all air pollution emission data, including those emission data which constitute trade secrets as defined in subdivision (d), are public records. Data used to calculate emission data are not emission data for the purposes of this subdivision and data which constitute trade secrets and which are used to calculate emission data are not public records.

(f) Data used to calculate the costs of obtaining emissions offsets are not public records. At the time that an air pollution control district or air quality management district issues a permit to construct to an applicant who is required to obtain offsets pursuant to district rules and regulations, data obtained from the applicant consisting of the year the offset transaction occurred, the amount of offsets purchased, by pollutant, and the total cost, by pollutant, of the offsets purchased is a public record. If an application is denied, the data shall not be a public record.

Sec. 6254.8. Public employment contracts

Every employment contract between a state or local agency and any public official or public employee is a public record which is not subject to the provisions of Sections 6254 and 6255.

Sec. 6254.9. Computer software

(a) Computer software developed by a state or local agency is not itself a public record under this chapter. The agency may sell, lease, or license the software for commercial or noncommercial use.

(b) As used in this section, "computer software" includes computer mapping systems, computer programs, and computer graphics systems.

(c) This section shall not be construed to create an implied warranty on the part of the State of California or any local agency for errors, omissions, or other defects in any computer software as provided pursuant to this section.

(d) Nothing in this section is intended to affect the public record status of information merely because it is stored in a computer. Public records stored in a computer shall be disclosed as required by this chapter.

(e) Nothing in this section is intended to limit any copyright protections.

Sec. 6254.10. Archeological site information

Nothing in this chapter requires disclosure of records that relate to archeological site information maintained by the Department of Parks and Recreation, the State Historical Resources Commission, or the State Lands Commission.

Sec. 6254.11. Volatile organic compounds or chemical substances information

Nothing in this chapter requires the disclosure of records that relate to volatile organic compounds or chemical substances information received or compiled by an air pollution control officer pursuant to Section 42303.2 of the Health and Safety Code.

Sec. 6254.12. Broker-dealer license information

Any information reported to the North American Securities Administrators Association/National Association of Securities Dealers' Central Registration Depository and compiled as disciplinary records which are made available to the Department of Corporations through a computer system, shall constitute a public record. Notwithstanding any other provision of law, the Department of Corporations may disclose that information and the current license status and the year of issuance of the license of a broker-dealer upon written or oral request pursuant to Section 25247 of the Corporations Code.

Sec. 6254.25. Legal memorandum to government agency

Nothing in this chapter or any other provision of law shall require the disclosure of a memorandum submitted to a state body or to the legislative body of a local agency by its legal counsel pursuant to subdivision (q) of Section 11126 or Section 54956.9 until the pending litigation has been finally adjudicated or otherwise settled. The memorandum shall be protected by the attorney work-product privilege until the pending litigation has been finally adjudicated or otherwise settled.

Sec. 6255. Justification for withholding of records

The agency shall justify withholding any record by demonstrating that the record in question is exempt under express provisions of this chapter or that on the facts of the particular case the public interest served by not making the record public clearly outweighs the public interest served by disclosure of the record.

Sec. 6256. Copies of records; rights; time limits

Any person may receive a copy of any identifiable public record or copy thereof. Upon request, an exact copy shall be provided unless impracticable to do so. Computer data shall be provided in a form determined by the agency.

Each agency, upon any request for a copy of records shall determine within 10 days after the receipt of such request whether to comply with the request and shall immediately notify the person making the request of such determination and the reasons therefor.

Sec. 6256.1. Time extension for unusual circumstances

In unusual circumstances, as specified in this section, the time limit prescribed in Section 6256 may be extended by written notice by the head of the agency to the person making the request setting forth the reasons for the extension and the date on which a determination is expected to be dispatched. No such notice shall specify a date that would result in an extension for more than 10 working days.

As used in this section "unusual circumstances" means, but only to the extent reasonably necessary to the proper processing of the particular request:

(a) The need to search for and collect the requested records from field facilities or other establishments that are separate from the office processing the request.

(b) The need to search for, collect, and appropriately examine a voluminous amount of separate and distinct records which are demanded in a single request.

(c) The need for consultation, which shall be conducted with all practicable speed, with another agency having a substantial interest in the determination of the request or among two or more components of the agency having substantial subject matter interest therein.

Sec. 6256.2. Delays and notification of denial

Nothing in this chapter shall be construed to permit an agency to delay access for purposes of inspecting public records. Any notification of denial of any request for records shall set forth the names and titles or positions of each person responsible for the denial.

Sec. 6257. Fees; exempt portions

Except with respect to public records exempt by express provisions of law from disclosure, each state or local agency, upon any request for a copy of records, which reasonably describes an identifiable record, or information produced therefrom, shall make the records promptly available to any person, upon payment of fees covering direct costs of duplication, or a statutory fee, if applicable. Any reasonably segregable portion of a record shall be provided to any person requesting such record after deletion of the portions which are exempt by law.

Sec. 6258. Enforcement of rights

Any person may institute proceedings for injunctive or declarative relief or writ of mandate in any court of competent jurisdiction to enforce his or her right to inspect or to receive a copy of any public record or class of public records under this chapter. The times for responsive pleadings and for hearings in these proceedings shall be set by the judge of the court with the object of securing a decision as to these matters at the earliest possible time.

Sec. 6259. Court costs and attorney fees

(a) Whenever it is made to appear by verified petition to the superior court of the county where the records or some part thereof are situated that certain public records are being improperly withheld from a member of the public, the court shall order the officer or person charged with withholding the records to disclose the public record or show cause why he or she should not do so. The court shall decide the case after examining the record in camera, if permitted by subdivision (b) of Section 915 of the Evidence Code, papers filed by the parties and any oral argument and additional evidence as the court may allow.

(b) If the court finds that the public official's decision to refuse disclosure is not justified under Section 6254 or 6255, he or she shall order the public official to make the record public. If the judge determines that the public official was justified in refusing to make the record public, he or she shall return the item to the public official without disclosing its content with an order supporting the decision refusing disclosure.

(c) In an action filed on or after January 1, 1991, an order of the court, either directing disclosure by a public official or supporting the decision of the public official refusing disclosure, is not a final judgment or order within the meaning of Section 904.1 of the Code of Civil Procedure from which an appeal may be taken, but shall be immediately reviewable by petition to the appellate court for the issuance of an extraordinary writ. Upon entry of any order pursuant to this section, a party shall, in order to obtain review of the order, file a petition within 20 days after service upon him or her of a written notice of entry of the order, or within such further time not exceeding an additional 20 days as the trial court may for good cause allow. If the notice is served by mail, the period within which to file the petition shall be increased by five days. A stay of an order or judgment shall not be granted unless the petitioning party demonstrates it will otherwise sustain irreparable damage and probable success on the merits. Any person who fails to obey the order of the court shall be cited to show cause why he or she is not in contempt of court.

(d) The court shall award court costs and reasonable attorney fees to the plaintiff should the plaintiff prevail in litigation filed pursuant to this section. The costs and fees shall be paid by the public agency of which the public official is a member or employee and shall not become a personal liability of the public official. If the court finds that the plaintiff's case is clearly frivolous, it shall award court costs and reasonable attorney fees to the public agency.

Sec. 6260. Prior rights and proceedings

The provisions of this chapter shall not be deemed in any manner to affect the status of judicial records as it existed immediately prior to the effective date of this section, nor to affect the rights of litigants, including parties to administrative proceedings, under the laws of discovery of this state, nor to limit or impair any rights of discovery in a criminal case.

Sec. 6261. Inspection of expenditures and disbursements

Notwithstanding Section 6252, an itemized statement of the total expenditures and disbursement of any agency provided for in Article VI of the California Constitution shall be open for inspection.

Sec. 6262. Licensing complaints and district attorney investigation records exemptions

The exemption of records of complaints to, or investigations conducted by, any state or local agency for licensing purposes under subdivision (f) of Section 6254 shall not apply when a request for inspection of such records is made by a district attorney.

Sec. 6263. Inspection or copying of public records on request of District Attorney

A state or local agency shall allow an inspection or copying of any public record or class of public records not exempted by this chapter when requested by a district attorney.

Sec. 6264. Order to allow district attorney to inspect or copy records

The district attorney may petition a court of competent jurisdiction to require a state or local agency to allow him to inspect or receive a copy of any public record or class of public records not exempted by this chapter when the agency fails or refuses to allow inspection or copying within 10 working days of a request. The court may require a public agency to permit inspection or copying by the district attorney unless the public interest or good cause in withholding such records clearly outweighs the public interest in disclosure.

Sec. 6265. Disclosure of records to district attorney

Disclosure of records to a district attorney under the provisions of this chapter shall effect no change in the status of the records under any other provision of law.

Sec. 6267. Registration and circulation records of publicly funded libraries

All registration and circulation records of any library which is in whole or in part supported by public funds shall remain confidential and shall not be disclosed to any person, local agency, or state agency except as follows:

(a) By a person acting within the scope of his or her duties within the administration of the library.

(b) By a person authorized, in writing, by the individual to whom the records pertain, to inspect the records.

(c) By order of the appropriate superior court.

As used in this section, the term "registration records" includes any information which a library requires a patron to provide in order to become eligible to borrow books and other materials, and the term "circulation records" includes any information which identifies the patrons borrowing particular books and other material.

This section shall not apply to statistical reports of registration and circulation nor to records of fines collected by the library.

Sec. 6268. Records in custody or control of governor leaving office

Public records, as defined in Section 6252, in the custody or control of the Governor when he or she leaves office, either voluntarily or involuntarily, shall, as soon as is practical, be transferred to the State Archives. Notwithstanding any other provision of law, the Governor, by written instrument, the terms of which shall be made public, may restrict public access to any of the transferred public records, or any other writings he or she may transfer, which have not already been made accessible to the public. With respect to public records, public access, as otherwise provided for by this chapter, shall not be restricted for a period greater than 50 years or the death of the Governor, whichever is later, nor shall there be any restriction whatsoever with respect to enrolled bill files, press releases, speech files, or writings relating to applications for clemency or extradition in cases which have been closed for a period of at least 25 years. Subject to any restrictions permitted by this section, the Secretary of State, as custodian of the State Archives, shall make all such public records and other writings available to the public as otherwise provided for in this chapter.

Except as to enrolled bill files, press releases, speech files, or writings relating to applications for clemency or extradition, this section shall not apply to public records or other writings in the direct custody or control of any Governor who held office between 1974 and 1988 at the time of leaving office, except to the extent that that Governor may voluntarily transfer those records or other writings to the State Archives.

Notwithstanding any other provision of law, the public records and other writings of any Governor who held office between 1974 and 1988 may be transferred to any educational or research institution in California provided that with respect to public records, public access, as otherwise provided for by this chapter, shall not be restricted for a period greater than 50 years or the death of the Governor, whichever is later. No records or writings may be transferred pursuant to this paragraph unless the institution receiving them agrees to maintain, and does maintain, the materials according to commonly accepted archival standards. No public records transferred shall be destroyed by that institution without first receiving the written approval of the Secretary of State, as custodian of the State Archives, who may require that the records be placed in the State Archives rather than being destroyed. An institution receiving those records or writings shall allow the Secretary of State, as custodian of the State Archives, to copy, at state expense, and to make available to the public, any and all public records, and inventories, indices, or finding aids relating to those records, which the institution makes available to the public generally. Copies of those records in the custody of the State Archives shall be given the same legal effect as is given to the originals.

Appendix B:
Sample Public Records Act Request Letter

Chief Executive
Name of Agency
Subject: Request to Inspect and Copy Public Records

Dear _____ :

This letter is to request access to records in the possession of [name of agency and/or department, division, etc.] for the purpose of inspection and copying pursuant to the California Public Records Act (Government Code Section 6250 *et seq.*).

The information that I ask to inspect is as follows: [Describe the record as specifically as possible, including, if known, the form in which it is recorded—writings, maps, computer storage, photographs, audio or video tapes, etc.—and, if known, the designation of the file or register where it is to be found. You need not state any reason for your request.]

This request reasonably describes (an) identifiable record(s) or information produced therefrom, and I believe that there exists no express provision of law exempting the record(s) from disclosure. Pursuant to Government Code Section 6257, I ask that you make the record(s) "promptly available," for inspection and copying, based on my payment of "fees covering direct costs of duplication, or statutory fee, if applicable."

If a portion of the information I have requested is exempt from disclosure by express provision of law, Government Code Section 6257 additionally requires segregation and deletion of that material in order that the remainder of the information may be released.

If you determine that an express provision of law exists to exempt from disclosure all or a portion of the material I have requested, Government Code Section 6256 requires notification to me of the reasons for the determination not later than 10 days from your receipt of this request.

Government Code Section 6256.2 prohibits the use of the 10-day period, or any provisions of the Public Records Act "to delay access for purposes of inspecting public records."

To expedite compliance, I am sending a copy of this request to the office of your legal advisor.

Thank you for your timely attention to my request.

Sincerely,

_____ [*Signature*]

cc: Name and title of agency's legal adviser
Your legal counsel, if any

NOTES ON PUBLIC RECORDS ACT REQUEST LETTER:

The sample letter is to be used only as an example. It is written in rather formal language, and cites the law upon which your request is based. You may wish to send the letter, as written, depending on the need to educate the agency, or if you have already reached a point where your relationship with the agency might be characterized as "adversarial." However, depending on your relationship with the agency, you may wish to edit your letter to delete citations of statues or the courtesy copy to the agency's legal adviser, or to eliminate entirely the educational sections of the letter when it is clear that the agency knows the law. [Source: CNPA]

Appendix C:
California Public Records On-Line

Public access to government records is gradually being made available via on-line computer. On the Internet and computer bulletin boards (BBS), some significant records are already posted to search and download. Future legislative and technological developments are certain to increase the quantity of records provided in this manner. Most state agencies and many cities in California have already established World Wide Web sites. Unfortunately, the number of agencies including public records on their publicly available computer platforms is low. Most have chosen instead, at least for the time being, to limit content to items such as the agency mission statement, names of agency officials, and bulletins and reports. The net result is that, for the foreseeable future, most public records will continue to be filed, maintained and made accessible to the public on paper only.

Researchers should be aware, however, that conditions change almost daily and that records not available in electronic format today may be tomorrow. Provided below are some key Web addresses and on-line computer access points to search California state and local government computer sites. It should be noted that addresses change frequently, and this list is not exhaustive. The best way to determine what on-line services a particular agency may be providing is to tap one of the Internet's increasingly user-friendly on-line search engines, or to make direct contact with the agency by phone. Several guides to using the Internet and conducting on-line research are listed in the Bibliography.

General Internet Access Points for Government Agencies in California

The World Wide Web site addresses listed below act as keys to finding government Web sites. By using one of these keys, researchers can easily scroll through lists of agency sites and connect to them directly.

California State Government Network (California State Home Page)
http://www.ca.gov/gov/servers.html
A primary home page for Internet sites operated by the State of California.

California Electronic Government Information
http://cpsr.org/dox/cegi.html
A list of governmental and related Web sites and computer bulletin boards with descriptions of their contents. Maintained by Computer Professionals for Social Responsibility.

Health and Welfare Data Center Grid
http://www.cahwnet.gov/hwdc/state.htm
A list of Web sites for departments under the Health and Welfare Agency.

Resources Agency CERES System
http://www.ceres.ca.gov
Links to departments within the Agency, such as the Tahoe Conservancy and the California Conservation Corps.

Teale Data Center
http://ts1.teale.ca.gov
Links to state government home pages.

Library of Congress California Government Home Page
http://lcweb.loc.gov/global/state/ca-gov.html
Links to government agency and institution home pages.

California Virtual Tourist
http://www.research.digital.com/SRC/virtual-tourist/California.html
Privately operated with links to state, county and city government home pages.

City Net
http://www.city.net/countries/united_states/california/
Privately operated with links to city government home pages.

USA City Link
http://www.neosoft.com/citylink/ca.html
Privately operated with links to city government home pages.

Planet Earth Home Page — California
http://www.nosc.mil/planet_earth/california.html

Yahoo California
http://www.yahoo.com/regional/states/california

State Government On-Line Sites

The following list provides home page address for World Wide Web sites operated by state government agencies. Phone numbers are for electronic bulletin boards (BBS).

Air Resources Board
http://www..arb.ca.gov
Modem BBS access: (916) 322-2826

Alcoholic Beverage Control, Department of
http://www.abc.ca.gov/

Alcohol and Drug Programs, Dept. of
Modem BBS access: (916) 657-5364
Research abstracts, forums, discussion groups, file libraries, and surveys.
Pre-registration required.

Audits, Bureau of State
ftp://leginfo.public.ca.gov/pub/bureau_state_audits/
Bureau audit reports.

Banking Department, State
http://www.sbd.ca.gov/

Conservation, Dept. of
http://www.consrv.ca.gov/

   Division of Mines and Geology
   Modem BBS access: (916) 327-1208

   Division of Recycling (Info Cycle)
   Modem BBS access: (916) 445-0518

   Division of Resources and Land Use (CalSources)
   Modem access: (916) 327-1811

Consumer Affairs, Department of
   Contractors State License Board
   http://www.ca.gov/cslb/home.html

Controller, State
http://www.ca.gov/sco/ and *http://www.sco.ca.gov/*

Courts
http://www.courtinfo.ca.gov
Links to California Courts of Appeal, Superior Courts, Municipal Courts, the
Judicial Council, the Commission on Judicial Appointments, and the Commission
on Judicial Performance. Also contains Supreme Court and Appellate Court slip
opinions, court calendars and minutes.
Modem BBS access: (415) 904-9454

Emergency Services, Office of
http://www.oes.ca.gov:8001/

Employment Development, Dept. of
http://wwwedd.cahwnet.gov/
Modem BBS access: (916) 262-2227
Local and statewide census and labor market data, including employment projections, wages, and other pay information.

Energy Resources, Conservation and Development Commission
http://energy.ca.gov/energy/homepage.html
gopher://energy.ca.gov/11/CECIS
Modem BBS access: (916) 654-4069, (916) 654-4021

Environmental Health Hazard Assessment, Office of
http://www.cahwnet.gov/epa/oehha.htm

Environmental Protection Agency, California (CalEPA)
http://www.cahwnet.gov/epa/
Modem BBS access: (916) 322-5041

Equalization, State Board of
http://www.boe.ca.gov/BOE/

Fair Political Practices Commission
http://www.fppc.ca.gov/FPPC/

Finance, Department of
http://www.dof.ca.gov/

Fish and Game, Department of
http://spock.dfg.ca.gov/ and *http://www.dfg.ca.gov/*

Forestry and Fire Protection, Dept. of
http://spp-www.cdf.ca.gov/
http://www.fire.ca.gov/
http://cdf.fire.ca.gov/

Franchise Tax Board
http://www.ftb.ca.gov
Modem BBS access: (916) 858-0575
New tax laws.

General Services, Department of
http://www.dgs.ca.gov/

Governor's Office
http://www.ca.gov/gov/governor.html
Governor's State of the State Address, Inaugural Address, Governor's Budget
Summary, and Economic Report of the Governor.

Health and Welfare Data Center
http://www.cahwnet.gov/
Link to California State Information Kiosk.

Health Services, Department of
http://www.cahwnet.gov/dhs/

Industrial Relations, Department of
http://www.dir.ca.gov/

Integrated Waste Management Board, California
http://www.ciwmb.ca.gov

Lands Commission, State
http://diablo.slc.ca.gov/
http://www.slc.ca.gov/

Legislature, California State
See S466 for contents.
    Assembly *http://www.assembly.ca.gov/*
    Senate *http://www.sen.ca.gov/* and *gopher://gopher.sen.ca.gov/*
    Legislative Analyst's Office *http://www.lao.ca.gov/*
    Legislative Counsel Bureau *http://www.leginfo.ca.gov*

Library, State
http://library.ca.gov/california/State_Library/
http://library.ca.gov/california/

Motor Vehicles, Dept. of
http://www.ca.gov/dmv/dmv.html

Parks and Recreation, Department of
http://agency.resource.ca.gov/parks/dpr.html

Personnel Board, State
http://www.spb.ca.gov/

Pesticide Regulation, Dept. of
http://www.cdpr.ca.gov

Public Utilities Commission, California
http://www.cpuc.ca.gov/
gopher://gopher.cpuc.ca.gov/
Modem BBS access: (415) 703-1297

Public Defender, State
http://www.ospd.ca.gov/

Secretary of State
http://www.ss.ca.gov/
gopher://secstate.public.ca.gov/

Elections Division
http://www.elections.ca.gov/
gopher://gopher.elections.ca.gov/
Partial campaign finance data, election returns.

Teale Data Center, Stephen T.
http://www.ca.gov/teale/Index.html

Toxic Substances Control, Dept. of
http://www.cahwnet.gov/epa/dtsc.htm

Trade and Commerce Agency
http://www.ca.gov/commerce/home.html

Transportation, Department of (CalTrans)
http://www.dot.ca.gov

Treasurer, State
http://www.treasurer.ca.gov/

Water Resources Control Board
http:www.cahwnet.gov/epa/wrcb.htm
http://swrcb.ca.gov/
http://www.water.ca.gov/DWR.ISSO.Home.html
http://www.ca.gov/gov/servers.html
Modem access:
Los Angeles region BBS (213) 266-7663
San Diego region BBS (619) 467-2958
San Francisco Bay region BBS (510) 286-0404
Storm Water Unit BBS (916) 654-3692

Water Resources, Department of
http://www.water.ca.gov
http://snow.water.ca.gov/
http://www.water.ca.gov/DWR.ISSO.Home.html
Water supply updates and forecasts, hydrologic data such as river states, and precipitation totals.

County Government and Regional On-Line Sites
Use the Association of Bay Area Governments Web site to locate home pages for
California counties.
http://www.abag.ca.gov/

City Government On-Line Sites
Hundreds of California cities have established Internet sites on the World Wide Web
providing everything from e-mail addresses for city council members, council
committee agendas, and meeting notes, to court calendars, library catalogues, demographic information, links to school districts, crime statistics and more. To connect
to the computer site for the city you want, try the following:

Association of Bay Area Governments (ABAG)
http://www.abag.ca.gov/

California City Net
http://www.city.net/countries/united_states/california/

USA CityLink for California
http://www.NeoSoft.com/citylink/ca.html

Assembly Computer Services
http://www.assembly.ca.gov/PLACES.HTM#LocalWeb

California City Net
http://www.city.net/countries/united_states/california/

Education Agencies On-Line
For access to local school districts, check the district's city government home page by
using one of the keys for finding cities listed above.

Education, Department of
http://goldmine.cde.ca.gov/
gopher://goldmine.cde.ca.gov/
Modem BBS access: (916) 657-5371, (916) 657-4881
California Basic Education Data System, daily report cards, student demographics,
dropout rates and gopher links to local education districts.

Post-Secondary Education Commission, State of California
Statistical data on post-secondary education. Internet access by special request;
pre-approval for access required, fees charged. Contact the Commission for
further information.

University Of California (UC)
http://www.ucop.edu
Links to UC Campus Internet sites and the UC campus library card catalogs.

University of California News Service
http://www.ca.gov/gov/bbs.html#uc
Modem BBS access: (209) 244-6971

Public Records Discussion Groups

These e-mail conferences are a valuable way to stay current on developments in California concerning public records access, open government laws and legislation, and computerization of public records.

CAL-FOI

Discussion of freedom of information, public records, First Amendment legislation and issues, and court cases in California.

To subscribe, send e-mail to *Maiser@rosebud.berkeley.edu* and include the following message: *subscribe cal-foi [your name]*.

Send messages to the list at *CAL-FOI@rosebud.berkeley.edu*.

Sponsor: Northern California Chapter, Society of Professional Journalists, Freedom of Information Committee.

calgovinfo

Discussion of public records access and computerization of government records in California.

To subscribe, send e-mail to *listserve@cpsr.org* and include the following message: *subscribe calgovinfo [your name]*.

Send messages to the list at: *calgovinfo@cpsr.org*.

Sponsor: Computer Professionals for Social Responsibility.

CALDOC-L

Discussion of California state and local government documents and related issues of concern to California federal and state document depositories.

To subscribe send e-mail to *listproc@CSUS.edu* and include the following message: *subscribe CALDOC-L [your name]*.

Send messages to the list at *Caldoc-l@csus.edu*.

Sponsors: California State University at Sacramento and California State Library.

 **Bibliography**

ORGANIZATIONS AND ASSOCIATIONS

Professional associations are good sources of specialized information. See the *Encyclopedia of Associations*. Peggy Kneffel and Carol A. Schwartz, eds., Gale Research Co., Detroit, 1993.

California First Amendment Coalition, 926 J Street, Suite 1406, Sacramento, CA 95814. (916) 447-2322.

California Institute for Rural Studies, P.O. Box 2143, Davis, CA 95617. (916) 756-6555.

California Institute of Public Affairs, P.O. Box 189040, Sacramento, CA 95818. (916) 442-2472.

California Newspaper Publishers Association, 1225 Eighth St., Suite 260, Sacramento, CA 95814. (916) 443-5991.

California State Association of Counties, 1100 K St., Suite 101, Sacramento, CA 95814. (916) 327-7500. Lobbies on behalf of county governments.

Center for Public Interest Law, University of San Diego School of Law, 5998 Alcala Park, San Diego, CA 92110. (619) 260-4806. Monitors regulatory functions of state government agencies.

Institute of Governmental Studies, University of California at Berkeley, 109 Moses Hall, Berkeley, CA 94720. (510) 642-1472.

Institute of Governmental Affairs, Shields Library, University of California at Davis, Davis, CA 95616. (916) 752-2043.

League of California Cities, 1400 K St., Sacramento, CA 95814. (916) 658-8200.

League of Women Voters of California, 926 J St., Suite 1000, Sacramento, CA 95814. (916) 442-7215. Contact local League offices for excellent local government information.

PERIODICALS

California County, Journal of the California State Associations of Counties. Bi-monthly.

California in Print. Government Research, 815 N. Brea, Suite 197, Inglewood, CA. (213) 678-3851. Bi-weekly during legislative session, monthly when not in session. List of titles and sources for all legislative and executive publications.

California Journal. California Journal Press, Sacramento, CA. Monthly.

California Regulatory Law Reporter. Center for Public Interest Law (see above). Quarterly. (619) 260-4806.

California State Publications. California State Library. Sacramento, CA. (916) 654-0069. A monthly listing of official California state documents received by the Government Publications Section of the California State Library. Listings are entered by originating agency. The index has entries by title and subject.

Flash. California First Amendment Coalition. Bi-weekly newsletter covering open government and freedom of information issues in California (see above under Organizations and Associations).

HANDBOOKS, GUIDES, AND DIRECTORIES

The Brown Act: Open Meetings for Local Legislative Bodies. California Attorney General's Office. Summary and text of the state's Brown Act which covers public access to meetings held by legislative bodies.

The California Handbook. Thaddeus C. Trzyna, ed. California Institute of Public Affairs (see above), seventh edition, 1994. Best guide to sources of information about California in general. Organized by general subject area (general information, environment and natural resources, social problems, government and politics, economy, education and art, history, and anthropology). There are four indexes: organizations, periodicals, authors, and subjects.

California License Handbook. Annual. Department of Commerce, Office of Small Business, Sacramento, CA, (916) 324-1295. Four sections include legal requirements, list of state agencies, key-word list of business, vocation, or occupation, and a summary of taxes involved with setting up a business. Annual.

California Permit Handbook. California Trade and Commerce Agency, 1994. Local land use permit programs that real estate developers must satisfy. Includes agency, permit, summary of requirements, application process, rights, and obligations.

California Roster: California State, County, City and Township Officials, State Officials of the United States. Secretary of State, Sacramento, CA. Annual listing of legislators in Congress, district maps, state agencies with descriptions of functions, historical lists of certain officials, county and city elected officials with addresses and phones, agricultural association members with addresses, unincorporated areas in California with location, state and congressional officers for other states with data about capital, population, area, nickname, motto, and dates when legislature convenes.

California State Telephone Directory. Department of General Services. Purchase from Documents Section, P.O. Box 1015, North Highlands, CA 95660. (916) 574-2200. Annual.

California Statistical Abstract. Department of Finance, 915 L St., Sacramento, CA 95814. (916) 445-3878. Annual. Index.

City Hall Roster. League of California Cities. Address book of California city halls (see above under Organizations and Associations).

The Courts and the News Media. Albert G. Pickerell, ed. Details the structure and procedures of the court and legal system. Also provides information on court access issues, rules, and legal research. California Judges Association, 301 Howard St., Suite 1040, San Francisco, CA 94105. (415) 495-1999.

Fundamentals of Legal Research. J. Myron Jacobstein, *et al.*, Foundation Press Inc., Westbury, NY. A standard on legal research for first-year law students.

Get the Facts on Anyone. Dennis King, 2nd edition, Macmillan General Reference, 1995. Techniques and resources for locating, backgrounding, and investigating people. Includes investigative resources on the Internet and bibliography.

Guide to California Government. League of Women Voters of California. 14th edition, 1992 (see above under Organizations and Associations).

The Information Practices Act of 1977: Guidelines and Commentary. Published by the State Personnel Board. Contains full text and guidelines to using and complying with the Act.

Legal Research: How to Find and Understand the Law. Stephen Elias and Susan Levinkind. Nolo Press, Berkeley, CA. (800) 992-6656. How to locate and understand statutes, regulations, and case law.

List of Reports Prepared by State and Local Agencies. Legislative Counsel of California. Quarterly. Available from State Legislature, Joint Publications Office, (916) 445-4874.

Little Hoover Commission Report to the Governor and Legislature. Commission on California State Government Organization & Economy, 1303 J St., Suite 270, Sacramento, CA 95814. A 17-page survey of California boards and commissions. Two appendices. 1989.

Media Law. Rex S. Heinke, BNA Books, (202) 833-7496. Detailed legal guide to the First Amendment and right-of-access law. 1994.

Open & Public II: A User's guide to the Ralph M. Brown Act. Ted Fourkas. Available from the California First Amendment Coalition, (916) 447-2322. See also *The Brown Act* in this Bibliography.

A Public Records Primer & Investigator's Handbook. Don Ray, ENG Press, 5th ed., 1995, (818) 843-6397. An excellent companion to this guide. Explains the "how to" of using public records and conducting investigations. Sections include: investigative strategies, case studies and non-governmental resources.

Raising Hell: How the Center for Investigative Reporting Gets the Story. David Weir and Dan Noyes, Center for Investigative Reporting, 500 Howard St., Suite 206, San Francisco, CA 94105. (415) 543-1200. Annotated bibliography. Index. 1983.

Raising Hell: A Citizens Guide to the Fine Art of Investigation. Dan Noyes, Mother Jones magazine, rev. ed., 1983. Available from the Center for Investigative Reporting (see above). Annotated bibliography.

The Reporter's Handbook: An Investigator's Guide to Documents and Techniques. Steve Weinberg, 3rd edition, Investigative Reporters & Editors, Inc. (IRE), St. Martin's Press, New York, Index. 1996.

Reporter's Handbook on Media Law: A Practical Guide to the Public's Right of Access. Renee C. Allison and Thomas W. Newton. California Newspaper Publishers Association, 1225 Eighth St., Suite 260, Sacramento, CA 95814. (916) 443-5991.

Tapping Officials' Secrets: The Door to Open Government in California. The Reporters Committee for Freedom of the Press, 1993, 1101 Wilson Blvd., Suite 1910, Arlington, VA 22209. (800) 336-4243.

Telling It All: A Legal Guide to the Exercise of Free Speech. Harold Fuson, Jr., Andrews and McMeel, (800) 826-4216.

Vital Statistics of California. California Department of Health Services, Health Demographics Section. Annual. (916) 657-3057.

FEDERAL RECORDS

Information about U.S. government publications is available at most large public, college, and university libraries. See "Suggested Readings" in *Raising Hell* by Weir and Noyes, and various sections of *The Reporter's Handbook* by Weinberg. Contact the U.S. Government Printing Office, Washington, D.C., 20402, (202) 512-1800; GPO Bookstore, Arco Plaza, 505 S. Flower St., Los Angeles, CA 90071, (213) 239-9844; or GPO Bookstore, Marathon Plaza, 303 2nd St., Room 141S., San Francisco, CA 94107, (415) 512-2770 for the current prices and availability of:

> *Congressional Directory*
> *Monthly Catalog of U.S. Government Publications*
> *Selected List of U.S. Government Publications*
> *United State Government Manual*

GUIDES TO ON-LINE AND COMPUTER-ASSISTED RESEARCH

Computer Assisted Research: A Guide to Tapping On-line Information. Nora Paul, 3rd ed., 1996. Provides an overview on conducting on-line research projects. The Poynter Institute, St. Petersburg, FL, (813) 821-9494.

The Little On-line Book. Alfred Glossbrenner, 1995. Assumes you know absolutely nothing about on-line communications. Introduces modems, on-line services, electronic bulletin boards, and the Internet. Peachpit Press, Berkeley, CA.

The On-line Journalist: Using the Internet and Other Electronic Resources. Randy Reddick and Elliot King, 1995. Describes and demonstrates how reporters may use the Internet and other on-line resources. Brace College Publishers, Fort Worth, TX.

Secrets of the Super Searchers. Reva Basch, 1993. Hints, tips, shortcuts and insights from professional on-line researchers. Eight Bit Books. Wilton, CT.

Washington On-line: How to Access the Government's Electronic Bulletin Boards. Bruce Maxwell, 1995. Describes and provides access phone numbers for 200 federal electronic bulletin board systems. Congressional Quarterly Inc.

The Whole Internet: User's Guide & Catalog. Ed Krol, second edition, 1994. Known as the bible of the Internet, provides a comprehensive overview of the Internet. O'Reilly & Associates, Inc.

Index

Index entries in italics indicate a record title. Numbers preceded by an "A" indicate introductory material or routine records; by a "C" indicate city or county records; by an "E" indicate education records; by an "R" indicate special district or regional government records; by an "S" indicate state records. Information contained in appendices is not indexed.

A

abortions
  Medi-Cal, S377
  statistics, S318–S319
Abstract of Judgment, C159, C162, C421
Access for Infants and Mothers Program (health insurance), S501
accidents
  in business and industry, S403
  govt. employees, C487, C498
  injury reports, C493
  in parks, C297, C299
  prevention of, C492, C496
  safety audit, C498
  traffic, *see* traffic accidents
Accountancy, Board of, S100
accreditation of schools, E026, E096, E098
Achievement Test Files, E052
Acquired Immune Deficiency Syndrome, *see* AIDS
Acupuncture Committee, S100
ADA, *see* school attendance
add-on parts (of vehicles), S026
address and phone directories, C528, S001
addresses, *see* names and addresses (individuals); corporate information
Administrative Hearings Office (state), S273–S274
Administrative Law Office (state), S002–S008
adult education, E018
  See also California Community Colleges; vocational education
Advanced Placement Examination, E025
advertising
  highway, S672, S689
  by private schools, E094
  of real estate subdivisions, S560–S561
aeronautics, *see* aircraft; airports
AFDC, C509–C511, S625
aftermarket parts (of vehicles), S026
affirmative action, S298, S512, S621, S670, S671
age, *see* birth, dates

aged
  abuse of, S013–S014
  funding, C004
  health care of, S010–S012, S016
  non-English speaking, C006
  program compliance, C007
  statistics, C003, C006, S012–S014, S331
  taxation of, S188
  See also hospitals; long-term care; Senior Citizens Property Tax
Aging, Area Agency on the (city/county depts.), C002–C007
Aging, Dept. of (state), S009–S016
Agricultural Inspection Station Files, S257
Agricultural Labor Relations Board (state), S017–S020
agricultural marketing agreements, S239, S248, S250
agriculture
  inspection reports, C015, S238
  pests, C016–C017, S260, S514, S516, S518
  produce inspection, S237–S241
  producer licenses, S246
  research in, C555
  vocational education for, E040
  See also dairy products; farm; Food and Agriculture, Dept. of; pesticides
Agriculture, (county dept.), C008–C021
Aid to Families with Dependent Children, C509–C511, S625
AIDS
  in alcohol and drug abuse programs, S045
  county reports on, C234–C235
  in prisons, S141
  statistics, S327–S328
air ambulance, list, S164
air pollution
  by business and industry, S023, S029
  effects of highways, S662, S669, S677
  measurement of, S022
  Permit to Operate, S023
  regulations, S025, S027, S030
  smog control warranty complaints, S028
  statistics, S022, S029
  violation hearings, S025, S029

occupational safety and health
employee complaints, S404, S406
hazardous materials, S338, S407
industrial accidents, S408, S410
inspections, S403
legal action, S404–S406, S413
pesticides, C019–C020
statistics, S288
See also Cal/OSHA; risk management
Offender Information Services Branch Reports, S145
Official Bonds, C146
Official Records (Recorder), C439
oil and gas
maps, S095
permits, S074, S076–S077, S095
production data, S093
title leasing, S120
usage of, S176
well drilling records and data, S090–S093
oil spills, S229, S703
ombudsman, for aged, S013–S015
Opticians, Registered Dispensing, S100
Optometry, Board of, S100
Order (court), C468
Organized Crime in California, S440
outdoor advertising, S689
oversize loads (on highways), S687

P

paramedic testing, S162, S163, S165
paratransit, C534, C536
pardons (of criminals), S314
parking
garage construction, C291
meters, C293, C551
residential permits, C294
tickets, C292, C341, C550
Parking (city/county depts.), C290–C294
parks
equipment inspection, C302
real property, C298, C300
Parks and Recreation (city/county depts.), C295–C306
parole hearings, S537–S540
Parole and Inmate Information, S146
Partnership Agreement, C440
patents
inventions at Univ. of Calif., E064
land (state), S464
paternity cases, C177
Payee Index, S115
payroll, city/county employees, C052

PCBs, removal of, S275
Pending Action (Lis Pendens), Notice of, C438
pensions
govt. employees, C053, S118, S542
investments, C309
statistics, C308
Pensions and Retirement (city/county depts.), C307–C310
Performance Audit Report (state), S062
Performance Report for California Schools, E025
Permit to Operate (industrial pollutants), S023
PERS, S541-S542
personal information records, of govt. employees, S512
personal names and addresses, *see* names and addresses
personal property
of arrested person, C054, C344
of deceased, C120
of hospital patients, S352
of jailed persons, C503
ownership of, C529–C532
sale of, by sheriff, C501
taxes, C529–C532
unclaimed, S116, S444
See also Tax Collector; unsecured property
Personnel Board (city/county depts.), C109
Personnel Board, State, A012, S512
Pest Control Board, Structural, S100
Pest Management Library, S001
pesticide dealers, licenses and permits, C021
Pesticide Label Database, S528
Pesticide Regulation Dept.(state), S181, S513–536
pesticides
application of, S514, S520
databases and directories, S526, S528, S533
effect on fish, wildlife, S211, S527
experimental, S530
illegal use on crops, S517
illnesses, injuries due to, S531–S535
ingredients of, S527
inspections of use, C018–C020
labels, C009, S528
library on, S521
licenses and permits, C021, S536, medical toxicity of, S522–S525
registration of, S527, S529
residue, S515, S517, S519
use of, C009, C013–C014, C016, C018–C020, C304, S520
in well water, S519

About the Authors and Publishers

Stephen Levine is a staff writer at the Center for Investigative Reporting in San Francisco. He has worked as a reporter for *The Washington Post, California Lawyer,* and other publications. While at CIR he has worked on stories for *Frontline, POV, 60 Minutes, Hippocrates, Parenting* and *Mother Jones.* His reporting on the dangers of generic drug use won the National Press Club's first place award for consumer journalism in 1989.

Barbara T. Newcombe began news library work in the Washington, D.C., bureau of the *Chicago Tribune* during the Watergate scandal. She was promoted to Chief Librarian at the newspaper's main library in Chicago and continued there until her retirement in 1985. Ms. Newcombe has written articles for professional journals and helped organize workshops and regional conferences on news librarianship. In 1986 she received the Roll of Honor Award from the Special Libraries Association News Division and in 1992 the James Madison Freedom of Information Award from the Northern California Chapter of the Society of Professional Journalists.

The California Newspaper Publishers Association has represented the interests of the state's newspaper proprietors, executives, and journalists for more than a century. With a membership that includes the publishers of most California daily and weekly general interest newspapers, the association provides legislative advocacy as well as information services on legal, business, and professional matters. Among CNPA's services are seminars, hot-line assistance, weekly bulletins, a monthly association newspaper, and a variety of specialty publications. For more information, contact CNPA at 1225 8th Street, Suite 260, Sacramento, CA 95814, (916) 443-5991.

The Center for Investigative Reporting, founded in 1977, is the only independent, nonprofit organization in the country established as an institution to conduct investigative reporting. From Center offices in San Francisco and Washington, D.C., CIR reporters work with leading newspapers, magazines, and television news programs throughout the U.S. and abroad. The Center's award-winning stories have helped spark Congressional hearings and legislation, U.N. resolutions, public interest lawsuits, and changes in the activities of multinational corporations, government agencies, and public figures. For more information, contact CIR at 500 Howard St., Suite 206, San Francisco, CA 94105, (415) 543-1200.